D0718250

WORKING WITH STRUCTURALISM

'This is a sane, highly intelligent, lucidly written book, and one which everyone concerned with literature must read at least once.' – Christopher Stace, *Daily Telegraph*

David Lodge is actively involved in university teaching, academic criticism, literary journalism and novel writing; this book reflects his concern to preserve the connection and continuity between these different discourses.

His discussion ranges from Thomas Hardy to Tom Wolfe and from the poetics of fiction to the poetry of Psychobabble. His work applies directly to structuralist methods of analysis, and the book as a whole aims to demonstrate the possibility of working with structuralism in the sense of working alongside it, recognizing its existence as a fact of intellectual life without being totally dominated by it.

DAVID LODGE

David Lodge is Professor of Modern English Literature at the University of Birmingham. He is also a novelist, and his books include *Changing Places* (1975), *How Far Can You Go?* (1980) and *Small World* (1984). His numerous critical publications include *Language of Fiction* (1966) and *Novelist at the Crossroads* (1971).

DAVID LODGE

WORKING WITH STRUCTURALISM

ESSAYS AND REVIEWS ON NINETEENTH- AND TWENTIETH-CENTURY LITERATURE

London and New York

First published in 1981
ARK edition 1986
Reprinted in 1991 by
Routledge

11 New Fetter Lane, London EC4P 4EE

29 West 35th Street, New York, NY10001

Printed in Great Britain
by TJ Press (Padstow) Ltd, Padstow, Cornwall.

© David Lodge 1981, 1986

No part of this book may be reproduced in
any form without permission from the publisher,
except for the quotation of brief passages
in criticism

ISBN 0 415 06598 4

Contents

v

V   Contemporary Culture

Preface

Literary criticism is at present in a state of crisis which is partly a consequence of its own success. One might compare its situation to that of physics after Einstein and Heisenberg: the discipline has made huge intellectual advances, but in the process has become incomprehensible to the layman – and indeed to many professionals educated in an older, more humane tradition. This incomprehensibility is not simply a matter of jargon – though that is a real stumbling block; more fundamentally, the new criticism, like the new physics, often runs counter to empirical observation and common sense. It therefore tends to alienate and exclude the common reader.

By the 'new criticism' I do not of course, mean the New Criticism – that now venerable Anglo-American enterprise extending from Eliot, Richards and Empson to, say, Ransom, Brooks and Wimsatt, which tried, with considerable success, to refine and systematise the common reader's intuitive reading of literary texts – but the European tradition of literary theory and critical practice that is loosely called 'structuralist'. Originating in the linguistics of Saussure and the work of the Russian Formalists in the revolutionary period, developed by the Prague School of linguistics and poetics in the 1930s, and nurtured through the 1940s and 1950s by *émigré* scholars in the USA, this tradition of thought about language, art and sign systems in general has provided the methodological impetus for an exciting new wave of research in the humanities in the last two decades. Emanating principally from Paris in the 1960s, this wave spread out in all directions; in the East, opening up long neglected riches in the Russian Formalists and their modern successors, the Soviet semiologists; in the West, being welcomed enthusiastically by those for whom the wells of the New Criticism had run dry.

Nobody professionally involved in the world of literary scholarship and academic criticism in England or America can deny that the most striking development of the last twenty years has been this massive swing of attention towards Continental structuralism. There are, of course, still strongholds of dissent and resistance, still plenty

of academics in England and America (and elsewhere) who have convinced themselves that if they keep their heads down long enough the
whole structuralist fuss will blow over; or who, more valiantly, man the
periodical ramparts in defence of empiricism, humanism, the New
Criticism or whatever.* But if the allegiances of the brightest young
university teachers and graduate students are any guide, that battle has
already been lost (or won, according to your point of view), and the
question is what to do in the aftermath: how to work with structuralism, not only in the sense of applying it when it seems useful to do so,
but also in the sense of working *alongside* it, recognising its existence
as a fact of intellectual life without being totally dominated by it.
I have called this book *Working with Structuralism*, but it might as
well have been called *Living with Structuralism*.

Since the old criticism, like the old physics, appears to work perfectly well for most practical purposes, the common reader (and common student) understandably does not see why (s)he should be bothered
to master the difficult new one. For the professionals who know how
to operate the structuralist methodology, however, there is no question
of going back to something less precise, less powerful and less productive. The consequences have been damaging, both inside and outside the
academy. Inside, there is an increasing gap between teaching and research, the same individual giving bland, old-fashioned tutorials on
Middlemarch in the morning, and in the afternoon reducing it to something resembling algebra, or a treatise on phenomenology badly trans-
lated from the French, for the edification of a small peer group. Outside, there is an increasing discontinuity between the language of academic criticism and the language of ordinary reviewing and literary
journalism, so that the latter is no longer refreshed and stimulated by
exposure to whatever the best and brightest academic minds are thinking (or vice versa). This discontinuity is particularly marked in England,
whose literary intellectuals have always been hostile to literary theory.
Structuralism offers a very broad target to their animosity; and one
would have to go back to the eighteenth century to find a time at
which writers and literary journalists were as united in their fear and
loathing of academic criticism as they are now.

The essays and review articles gathered in this volume are the work
of someone who is actively involved in the practice of university teaching, academic criticism, literary journalism and writing novels: and
anxious to preserve connections and continuity between these different

---

*See, for example, Howard Erskine-Hill, 'Scholarship as Humanism', *Essays in
Criticism*, January 1979, and various articles by George Watson collected in his
Modern Literary Thought (Heidelberg, 1978).

discourses. The various items were written for a variety of occasions and audiences, over a period (the 1970s) when I personally experienced the impact of structuralism; and they represent my effort to assimilate that influence without paying the price of incomprehensibility to all but a small group of initiates. (Whether I have succeeded or not, others must judge.)

'Structuralism' is a very elastic label, stretched over a wide range of intellectual activities, but one might distinguish two main branches at present. One is the extension of what I would call classical structuralism. It is concerned with the analysis and understanding of culture as a system of systems, of which language is usually taken as the ideal model for explanatory purposes. This structuralism aims to do for literature – or myth, or food or fashion – what grammar does for language: to understand and explain how these systems work, what are the rules and constraints within which, and by virtue of which, meaning is generated and communicated. It is essentially formalist, and aspires to the status of science. The second branch of structuralism, perhaps more properly called poststructuralism, is ideological in orientation. It combines the anti-empirical methodology of classical structuralism with ideas derived from Marxism, psychoanalysis and philosophy, to analyse cultural institutions, such as literature, as mediations of ideologies. This structuralism is polemical and *engagé*. Jakobson, Lévi-Strauss, and Todorov would be representative figures of the first branch of structuralism; Foucault, Lacan, and Derrida of the second. Some individuals – notably Roland Barthes – have contributed at different times to both schools of thought, but ultimately these are opposed in aims and methods, and are often highly critical of each other. The structuralism 'applied' in this book is almost exclusively of the first kind. I have always been more interested in formalist than in ideological criticism – perhaps because as a novelist I would prefer to be on the sharp end of the former; and I am not at all sure that poststructuralist discourse is susceptible of being assimilated and domesticated in a critical vernacular. To open a book or article by, for instance, Derrida or one of his disciples is to feel that the mystification and intimidation of the reader is the ultimate aim of the enterprise.

Structuralism of the classical, formalist kind is, as it were, only accidentally mystifying and intimidating. It works at a high level of abstraction and uses a specialised jargon because its bent is essentially theoretical; but my own interest in it (no doubt reflecting an incorrigibly empirical English mentality) has been in applying its concepts and methods to concrete critical tasks. The essays in the first section of this book are mostly exercises of this kind, some concerned with the analysis and interpretation of particular texts, others with broad topics in literary history. The first essay gives a condensed and somewhat

simplified account of ideas expounded more elaborately in my book
The Modes of Modern Writing (1977); and the fifth essay locates the
argument of that book in the context of current debate about the
ideology and methodology of historiography in general and of literary
history in particular. The three essays in between are concerned with
the formal analysis of narrative – especially of realistic fiction – an area
in which structuralism has proved a particularly fertile influence. Two
of these essays stand in a symmetrical relation to each other, and not
merely because both are concerned with very short stories that have
one rather important element in common. In the first of these essays,
a structuralist method of analysis is applied to a cryptic text by an
acknowledged modern master of narrative in order to test the power of
the method; in the second, it is applied to a text of acknowledged
triviality in order to study the system of narrative itself. In general,
structuralism is probably most effective in such contexts – where literary value is either taken for granted or is irrelevant to the main object
of inquiry. But between these two essays I have included one (on *Hard
Times*) which addresses itself more directly to a question of evaluation.

Several of the concepts and terms introduced in this first section of
the book recur in subsequent sections – for instance, in the essays on
Hardy as a cinematic novelist, on the New Journalism, and on 'psychobabble'. My increasing interest in Hardy, evidenced by the three essays
on his work, itself no doubts reflects the influence of structuralist criticism, for no novelist demonstrates more strikingly the operation of that
fundamental aesthetic principle Jakobson calls 'equivalence'. In Hardy's
elaborate and ingenious – and sometimes tortuous – patterning of his
novels, we see that 'projection of equivalence from the axis of selection
into the axis of combination' taken to the very limits of what the
classic realist novel could tolerate without collapsing and re-forming
into the modernist novel.

Other essays collected here show little or no trace of structuralist
ideas, and some, like the mainly biographical studies of Evelyn Waugh
in Part III, run directly counter to the spirit of that movement. I make
no apology for this. The range of questions that may validly be posed
about literature and literary texts is very wide, and no single method
will answer them all. The eclecticism of this book is its point – and, I
hope, its justification.

Acknowledgments

Most of the pieces collected here have been published before in slightly or substantially different forms, and some have been revised more than once. 'Modernism, Antimodernism and Postmodernism' was an inaugural lecture and was published as such by the University of Birmingham; 'Analysis and Interpretation of the Realist Text' was originally presented as a paper to a conference organised by the Porter Institute for Poetics and Semiotics at the University of Tel Aviv, and was subsequently published in the institute's journal, *Poetics Today*; 'How Successful is *Hard Times*?' is an adaptation of a contribution to a volume of essays on this text, edited by Graham Storey for the British Council; 'Historicism and Literary History' was originally a paper delivered at the MLA Convention of 1978 and subsequently published by the journal *New Literary History*; the essay on *The Woodlanders* is an abridged version of my introduction to the New Wessex edition of Hardy's novel, published by Macmillan; 'Thomas Hardy as a Cinematic Novelist' started as a note in the journal *Novel*, and in its present form appeared in *Thomas Hardy after Fifty Years*, edited by Lance St John Butler and published by Macmillan; 'Pessimism and Fictional Form' was originally a recorded talk for the Open University and in its present form was published in *Critical Approaches to the Fiction of Thomas Hardy* edited by Dale Kramer, published by Macmillan; 'Evelyn Waugh: Habits of a Lifetime was originally published in the *New Review* and now incorporates part of an earlier essay, 'The Arrogance of Evelyn Waugh' published in the *Critic*; 'The Fugitive Art of Letters' was first published in *Evelyn Waugh and His World*, edited by David Pryce-Jones and published by Weidenfeld & Nicolson; 'Ambiguously Ever After' was delivered to the Royal Society of Literature as the Joyce Brown Memorial Lecture, 1978; 'Turning Unhappiness into Money' was originally published in *Encounter*; 'Crow and the Cartoons' was first published in the *Critical Quarterly*; 'Tom Wolfe and the New Journalism' was first published in the *New Review*; 'Where It's At' was originally published in *Encounter* and, in its present form, in *The State of the Language*, edited by Christopher Ricks and Leonard Michaels,

xi

published by California University Press. Grateful acknowledgment is made to these publishers and journals for permission to reprint these essays and reviews, and, in many cases, for the original opportunity and stimulus to write them.

'Cat in the Rain' from *In Our Time* and *The First Forty-Nine Stories* by Ernest Hemingway (Copyright 1925 by Charles Scribner's Sons; copyright renewed) is reprinted by permission of the Executors of the Ernest Hemingway Estate and the publishers, Charles Scribner's Sons and Jonathan Cape Ltd. The lines on pp. 167–74 from *Crow* by Ted Hughes (Copyright © 1971 by Ted Hughes) are reprinted by permission of Faber and Faber Ltd and Harper & Row, Publishers, Inc.

I am grateful to many people, inside and outside my own Department at Birmingham University, with whom I have profitably discussed the topics dealt with in these essays. Special thanks are due to Deirdre Burton, whose interest extended to helping me find an appropriate title, and even a jacket design, for the book: in this, as in much else, personifying everything the word 'colleague' should mean.

Part I

Applying Structuralism

1 Modernism, Antimodernism and Postmodernism

One prejudice against professors of English is that there is nothing particularly difficult about what they profess. The other is that in trying to make it appear difficult, they spoil the innocent pleasure of ordinary people who know what they like and enjoy reading. It is all too easy to find examples of this attitude to academic criticism. Let me quote a celebrated modern writer, D. H. Lawrence:

> Literary criticism can be no more than a reasoned account of the feeling produced upon the critic by the book he is criticising. Criticism can never be a science: it is, in the first place, much too personal, and in the second, it is concerned with values that science ignores. The touchstone is emotion, not reason. We judge a work of art by its effect on our sincere and vital emotion, and nothing else. All the critical twiddle-twaddle about style and form, all this pseudo-scientific classifying and analysing of books in an imitation-botanical fashion, is mere impertinence and mostly dull jargon.

I suspect that quite a few of my readers may have a secret – or not so secret – sympathy with Lawrence's sentiments; but I must try to persuade them that he is wrong – or at least, wrong in his conclusion. For the passage I quoted, which opens Lawrence's 1928 essay on John Galsworthy, is deeply characteristic of the author in the way it becomes increasingly polemical and extreme as it goes on. The opening proposition is fair enough: 'Literary criticism can be no more than a reasoned account of the feeling produced upon the critic by the book he is criticising.' But I would maintain – and I think most academic literary critics would share this view – that if the critical account is to be, in Lawrence's word, 'reasoned', it must involve the classifying and analysing which he dismissed so contemptuously, and even a certain amount of jargon.

No book, for instance, has any meaning on its own, in a vacuum. The meaning of a book is in large part a product of its differences from and similarities to other books. If a novel did not bear some

3

resemblance to other novels we should not know how to read it, and if it wasn't different from all other novels we shouldn't *want* to read it. Any adequate reading of a text, therefore, involves identifying and classifying it in relation to other texts, according to content, genre, mode, period, and so on. The fact that a literary taxonomy can never be as exact as a botanical taxonomy does not affect the basic principle: the classification of data into larger groups and categories – if only Animal, Vegetable and Mineral – is a primary act of human intelligence without which neither Nature nor Culture can be made intelligible. Likewise, even if we agree with Lawrence that the essential core of literary criticism is the effect of a book upon an individual reader, the fact that this effect, or 'feeling' as he calls it, is produced by language and by language alone, means that we cannot explain how it works unless we have some understanding of 'style and form'. In short, without some notion of literature as a system – a system of possibilities of which the corpus of literary works is a partial realisation – Lawrence's advice to critics to rely on their 'sincere and vital emotion and nothing else' is itself very likely to produce critical twiddle-twaddle, particularly from critics with less interesting sensibilities and more limited rhetorical skills than he possessed.

What I propose to do here, in a necessarily simplified and schematic fashion, is to suggest some ways in which the enormous mass of texts that make up modern English literature can be ordered and classified. It is, if you like, the sketch of a literary history of the modern period – which I take to be now about a hundred years old – but a history of writing rather than of writers, a history of literary style, fashion, or mode, of what contemporary French critics call *écriture*; and it will reflect my own particular interests in being biased somewhat towards the novel, in occasionally stepping over the boundary between English and American literature, and in applying concepts and methods of analysis drawn from the European structuralist tradition in linguistics and poetics.

I have already invoked that tradition in describing literature as a system of possibilities, of which the corpus of literary works is a partial realisation, for this is essentially the distinction made by Saussure between *langue* and *parole*, a language and individual speech acts in that language. Saussure defined the verbal sign, or word, as the union of a signifier (that is, a sound or written symbolisation of a sound) and a signified (that is, a concept) and asserted that the relationship between *significant* and *signifié* is an arbitrary one. That is, there is no natural or necessary reason why the sound *cat* should denote a feline quadruped in English and the sound *dog* a canine quadruped, and the English language would work equally well if *cat* and *dog* changed places in the system, as long as all users were aware of the change. This nucleus of arbitrariness at the heart of language means that it is the systematic relationships between words that enable them to communicate rather than the relationships between words and things; and it exposes the idea of any *resemblance* between words and things as an illusion. Since language provides a model for all systems of signs, the idea has profound implications for the study of culture as a whole. In brief, it implies the priority of form over content, of the signifier over the signified.

One way of defining the art that is peculiar to the modern period – which I shall distinguish by calling modern*ist* – one way of defining modernist art, and especially modernist literature, is to say that it intuitively accepted or anticipated Saussure's view of the relationship between signs and reality. Modernism turned its back on the traditional idea of art as imitation and substituted the idea of art as an autonomous activity. One of its most characteristic slogans was Walter Pater's assertion, 'All art constantly aspires to the condition of music' – music being, of all the arts, the most purely formal, the least referential, a system of signifiers without signifieds, one might say. The fundamental principle of aesthetics before the modern era was that art imitates life, and is therefore in the last analysis answerable to it: art must tell the truth about life, and contribute to making it better, or at least more bearable. There was always, of course, a diversity of opinion about the kind of imitation that was most desirable – about whether one should imitate the actual or the ideal – but the basic premise that art imitated life prevailed in the West from classical times till the late eighteenth century, when it began to be challenged by Romantic theories of the imagination. It was temporarily reinforced by the considerable achievement of the realistic novel in the nineteenth century, but by the end of that century it had been turned on its head. 'Life imitates art', declared Oscar Wilde, meaning that we compose the reality we perceive by mental structures that are cultural, not natural in origin, and that it is art which is most likely to change and renew those structures when they become inadequate or unsatisfying. 'Where, if not from the Impressionists,' he asked, 'do we get those wonderful brown fogs that come creeping down our streets, blurring the gaslamps and changing the houses into monstrous shadows?'

But if life imitates art, where does art come from? The answer given is: from other art, especially art of the same kind. Poems are not made out of experience, they are made out of poetry – that is, the tradition of disposing the possibilities of language to poetic ends – modified, to be sure, by the particular experience of the individual poet, but in no straightforward sense an expression of it. T. S. Eliot's essay 'Tradition and the Individual Talent' is perhaps the best-known exposition of the idea, but variations on it can be found easily enough in the writings of Mallarmé, Yeats, Pound and Valéry. It produced poetry of the kind we call Symbolist with a capital 'S' – poetry that distinguishes itself from ordinary referential discourse by violently dislocated syntax and bewildering shifts of register, poetry in which denotation is swamped by connotation, in which there are no narrative or logical climaxes but instead vibrant, suggestive, ambiguous images and symbols.

The emergence of the modernist novel was a little slower and more gradual, because of the impressive achievement of the realistic novel in the nineteenth century. What seems to happen, first in France, and then in England in the work of James, Conrad, Joyce, and in his own idio-syncratic way Lawrence, is that the effort to capture reality in narrative fiction, pursued with a certain degree of intensity, brings the writer out on the other side of 'realism'. The writer's prose style, however sordid and banal the experience it is supposed to be mediating, is so highly and lovingly polished that it ceases to be transparent but calls attention to itself by the brilliant reflections glancing from its surfaces. Then, pur-suing reality out of the daylight world of empirical common sense into the individual's consciousness, or subconscious, and ultimately the collective unconscious, discarding the traditional narrative structures of chronological succession and logical cause-and-effect, as being false to the essentially chaotic and problematic nature of subjective experience, the novelist finds himself relying more and more on literary strategies and devices that belong to poetry, and specifically to Symbolist poetry, rather than to prose: allusion to literary models and mythical arche-types, for instance, and the repetition of images, symbols, and other motifs – what E. M. Forster described, with another gesture towards music, as 'rhythm' in the novel.

This characterisation of modernist poetry and fiction is familiar enough; but not all writing in the modern period is modern*ist*. There is at least one other kind of writing in this period which, for want of a better term, I have designated in my title as antimodernist. This is writing that continues the tradition modernism reacted against. It believes that traditional realism, suitably modified to take account of changes in human knowledge and material circumstances, is still viable and valuable. Antimodernist art does not aspire to the condition of music; rather it aspires to the condition of history. Its prose does not approximate to poetry; rather its poetry approximates to prose. It regards literature as the communication of a reality that exists prior to and independent of the act of communication. To Wilde's half-serious assertion that our perception of fog derives from the Impressionists, the antimodernist would reply that on the contrary it derives from industrial capitalism, which built large cities and polluted their atmosphere with coal-smoke, and that it is the job of the writer to make this causal connection clear; or, if he must dwell on the picturesque distorting visual effects of fog, at least to make them symbols of a more fundamental denaturing of human life, as Dickens did. Antimodernist writing, then, gives priority to content, and is apt to be impatient with formal experiment, which obscures and hinders communication. The model of language it implies is the antithesis of Saussure's and may be represented by George Orwell's advice to writers in his essay 'Politics and the English Language':

What is above all needed is to let the meaning choose the word and not the other way about . . . Probably it is better to put off using words as long as possible and get one's meaning as clear as one can through pictures or sensations . . . afterwards one can choose – not simply accept – the phrases that will best cover the meaning. . .

It would be easy enough to refute Orwell's suggestion that we can think without using verbal concepts, but this fallacy does not necessarily undermine the validity of his own work. It is possible that without this naïve faith in finding the right word for a pre-existent meaning Eric Blair would not have been able to create the persona of that utterly sincere, reliable, truth-telling author, George Orwell. It would be just as easy, and just as pointless, to show that Philip Larkin is either deceiving himself or trying to deceive us when he says, 'Form holds little interest for me. Content is everything.' Antimodernist writers invariably put up a poor show as theorists and aestheticians in the modern period: in order to distinguish themselves from the modernists they tend to be forced into naïve, fallacious or philistine attitudes to the creative process. This is as true, for instance, of H. G. Wells and Arnold Bennett earlier in the period as it is of Orwell and Larkin later on. Antimodernist writing is invariably more interesting than the theory that supports it; of modernist writing, sometimes, the reverse is true.

I would suggest not only that these two kinds of writing, modernist and antimodernist, persist throughout the modern period, but that we can map out alternating phases of dominance of one kind or another. Modernism first comes to England at the very end of the nineteenth century, in the work of Wilde and the other so-called Decadents, in the early Yeats and Conrad, and the late Henry James. In the first decade and a half of the twentieth century there seems to be a reaction against this cosmopolitan *avant-garde*, and a return to more traditional native literary modes: the successful and prestigious poets of this phase are Kipling, Hardy, Bridges, Newbolt, and Georgians like Rupert Brooke. James and Conrad are neglected, and Joyce cannot get his work published. Yeats moves away from his Symbolist vein and towards a starker, more topical poetry of statement. This was the literary situation Ezra Pound set himself the task of modernising, particularly by promoting the work of T. S. Eliot and Joyce, whom he met in 1914. The war which began in the same year and caused such enormous cultural, social and psychological upheaval, may have created a climate favourable to the reception of modernist art. The immediate post-war period saw the appearance, within a few years of each other, of such masterpieces as *The Wild Swans at Coole, Hugh Selwyn Mauberley, Women in Love, The Waste Land, Ulysses, A Passage to India* and *Mrs Dalloway*. The 1920s were certainly dominated by modernism. But in the 1930s the pendulum began to swing back in the other direction. The young, politically *engagé* writers of this decade – Auden, Isherwood, Spender, MacNiece, Day Lewis, Upward – criticised the modernist writers of the previous generation for their elitist cultural assumptions, their refusal to engage constructively with the great public issues of the day and their failure to communicate to a wide audience. 'The poets of *New Signatures*', Louis MacNiece wrote in 1938, 'have swung back to the Greek preference for information or statement. The first requirement is to have something to say, and after that you must say it as well as you can' – Orwell's sentiments exactly. 'Realism' came back into favour in the 1930s. 'There is a tendency for artists today to turn outward to reality', said Stephen Spender in 1939, in a pamphlet called *The New Realism*, 'because the phase of experimenting in form has proved sterile.' The representative fiction writers of this decade – Orwell, Isherwood, Greene, Waugh – gradually shook off the influence of modernist fiction with its mythic and poetic bias, and refurbished the traditional novel with techniques learned from the cinema. History was no longer, as Stephen Dedalus described it, a nightmare from which the writer was trying to awake, but an enterprise in which he was keen to participate – the Spanish Civil War providing the exemplary opportunity. Thirties writing tended to model itself on historical kinds of discourse – the autobiography, the eye-witness account, the travel log: *Journey to a War, Letters from Iceland, The Road to Wigan Pier, Journey Without Maps, Autumn Journal*, 'Berlin Diary', are some characteristic titles.

In the 1940s, after World War II, the pendulum swung back again – not fully, but to a perceptible degree, towards the modernist pole. To say that the English novel resumed experiment would be an overstatement, but 'fine writing' certainly returned and an interest in rendering the refinements of individual sensibility rather than collective experience. There was a great revival of Henry James, and many people thought Charles Morgan was his modern successor. There was great excitement at the apparent renaissance of verse drama, especially in the work of T. S. Eliot and Christopher Fry. The most enthusiastically acclaimed younger poet was Dylan Thomas, who very obviously continued the tradition of modernist verse.

In the middle of the 1950s, a new generation of writers began to exert an opposite pressure upon the pendulum. They were sometimes referred to as 'The Movement', mainly in the context of poetry, and sometimes, more journalistically, as the 'Angry Young Men', mainly in the context of fiction and drama. Some of the key figures in these partially overlapping groups were Kingsley Amis, Philip Larkin, John Wain, John Osborne, John Braine, Donald Davie, D. J. Enright, Alan Sillitoe. These, and other writers who came to prominence in the 1950s, like C. P. Snow and Angus Wilson, were suspicious of, if not actually hostile to, efforts at experimentation in writing. Technically, the novelists were content to use, with only slight modifications, the conventions of 1930s' and Edwardian realism, and their originality was largely a matter of tone and attitude and subject-matter. For the poets – Dylan Thomas was made to stand for everything they detested: verbal obscurity, metaphysical pretentiousness and romantic rhapsodising. They themselves aimed to communicate clearly and honestly their perceptions of the world as it was, in dry, disciplined, slightly depressive verse. In short, these writers were antimodernist, and made no secret of being so in their essays and reviews.

Changes in literary fashion of the kind I have been discussing are usually explained in terms of the impact of external circumstances – social, political, economic circumstances – upon writers: the shock of the Great War, the emergence of totalitarianism in the 1930s, the deracinating effect of affluence and social mobility after World War II, and so on. But the *regularity* of the shifts between modernist and antimodernist dominance in modern English writing, which I have compared to the predictable movement of a pendulum, suggests that the process cannot be accounted for by reference to fortuitous external circumstances alone, but must have some cause within the system of literature itself. In this respect we can profit from the theories of the Russian Formalist critics of the 1920s and the Prague School of Linguisticians and aestheticians who succeeded them in the 1930s, especially their concepts of defamiliarisation and foregrounding. The Russian Formalist Victor Schklovsky maintained that the end and justification of all art is that it defamiliarises things which have become dulled and even invisible to us through habit, and thus enables us to perceive the world afresh.

Habitualisation devours objects, clothes, furniture, one's wife and the fear of war . . . Art exists to help us recover the sensation of life, it exists to make us feel things, to make the stone, *stony*. The end of art is to give a sensation of the object as seen, not as recognised. The technique of art is to make things 'unfamiliar', to make forms obscure, so as to increase the difficulty and duration of perception.

As formulated in that passage the concept of defamiliarisation is biased towards modernist, experimental writing – Schklovsky was at this time an apologist for the Russian artistic *avant-garde* in the immediately post-Revolutionary period; but it is implicit in the theory that literary modes, as well as clothes, furniture and wives, can fall victim to the dulling effect of habit. Experiment can become so familiar that it ceases to stimulate our powers of perception, and then more simple and straightforward modes of writing may seem wonderfully fresh and daring. To use the jargon of the Prague School: what is foregrounded by one generation of writers becomes background for the next. Thus, Eliot and Pound foregrounded their poetry, with its bewildering shifts of registers, dislocations of syntax and esoteric allusion, against the background of the orthodox poetic taste of the early twentieth century. The 1930s poets in turn foregrounded their poetry against the background of the Eliot–Pound modernist mode by adopting a more consistent tone of voice, deviating very little from orthodox syntax and filling their poems with ample reference to the facts of contemporary life. Dylan Thomas and the Apocalyptic School foregrounded their verse against the background of 1930s poetry by extravagantly mixed metaphors, tortured syntax, religious, esoteric and occult allusion. Larkin and the Movement poets foregrounded their verse against the background of the Apocalyptics by adopting a dry, unpretentious tone of voice, avoiding romantic rhetoric and choosing modest, quotidian themes. The process is an historical manifestation of Saussure's idea that signs communicate by virtue of the differences between them. Literary innovation is achieved by reacting against and contrasting with the received orthodoxy. If we wonder why this invariably seems to involve a return in some measure to the last orthodoxy but one, the answer may be found in another theory in the same structuralist tradition, namely Roman Jakobson's distinction between the metaphoric and metonymic poles of language.

According to Jakobson, a discourse connects one topic with another either because they are in some sense similar to each other, or because they are in some sense contiguous to each other in space–time; and in any individual speaker or writer one type of connection predominates over the other. Jakobson calls them metaphoric and metonymic respectively, because these figures of speech, metaphor and metonymy, are models or epitomes of the processes involved. Metaphor is a figure of substitution based on similarity, as when a king is described as a sun because of his power and importance to his subjects; while metonymy and the closely associated figure of synecdoche are derived from contiguity, substituting an attribute for the thing itself, cause for effect or part for whole or vice versa, as when a monarch is referred to as the crown, or the throne or the palace. Most discourse uses both types of figure, but you are more likely to find metaphorical references to royalty in Shakespeare, and metonymic references in newspaper reports because these modes of discourse are metaphoric and metonymic respectively in *structure*, in the way they connect one topic with another. Metaphor and metonymy are in fact rhetorical applications of the two fundamental processes involved in any utterance: selection and combination. To construct any sentence we select certain items from the paradigms of the language and combine them according to its rules. Metaphor juggles with selection and substitution; metonymy juggles with combination and context. Part of Jakobson's evidence for the primal importance of his distinction is that the pathology of speech displays the same binary character. Aphasics who have difficulty *selecting* the word they want fall back on combination, contiguity, context, and make metonymic mistakes, saying 'knife' when they mean 'fork', 'bus' when they mean 'train'; while aphasics who have trouble *combining* words correctly into larger units use quasi-metaphorical expressions, calling a gas-light a 'fire', for instance, or a microscope a 'spy-glass'. There was a *Horizon* television programme a couple of years ago, about experiments in teaching chimpanzees to communicate through sign language. The crucial breakthrough came when the chimps were able spontaneously to select and combine the signs they had learned in order to describe novel situations, and it was reported that one chimp, called Washoe, referred to a duck as 'water-bird' and another, Lucy, referred to a melon as a 'candy-drink': metonymic and metaphoric expressions respectively.

If those two chimps go on to write books, one might predict that Lucy would be a modernist and Washoe an antimodernist, for Jakobson's distinction corresponds pretty accurately to the one I have been making between two types of writing in the modern period. Consider, as two representative works of modernist writing, *The Waste Land* and *Ulysses*: both titles are metaphorical and invite a metaphorical reading of the texts. Eliot's poem, indeed, can be read in no other way. Its fragments are linked together entirely on the basis of similarity and ironic contrast (a negative kind of similarity), scarcely at all on the basis of narrative cause and effect or contiguity in space–time. *Ulysses* does have a story – an everyday story of Dublinfolk, one might say; but this story echoes and parallels another one – the story of Homer's *Odyssey*, Bloom re-enacting or parodying the part of Odysseus, Stephen that of Telemachus and Molly that of Penelope. The structure of Joyce's novel is therefore essentially metaphorical, based on a similarity between things otherwise dissimilar and widely separated in space and time. In contrast, the realistic, antimodernist novel – Arnold Bennett's *The Old Wives' Tale*, for example – is essentially metonymic: it tends to imitate, as faithfully as discourse can, the actual relations of things to each other in space–time. Characters, their actions and the background against which they perform these actions, are all knitted together by physical contiguity, temporal sequence and logical cause and effect, and are represented in the text by a selection of synecdochic detail – parts standing for the whole. Antimodernist poets push verse in the same direction, using metaphor frugally, and relying heavily on metonymy and synecdoche – for example, this evocation of the memories of retired race-horses:

> Silks at the start: against the sky
> Numbers and parasols: outside
> Squadrons of empty cars, and heat,
> And littered grass: then the long cry
> Hanging unhushed till it subside
> To stop press columns in the street.

Philip Larkin. But it could, I think, be mistaken for MacNiece, or Auden in a certain mood – even for one of the Georgians.

The metaphor/metonymy distinction, then, suggests why there is a cyclical rhythm to literary history, why innovation is often in some ways a regression to the last fashion but one; because, if Jakobson is right, there is nowhere for discourse to go except between these two poles.

There is, however, another kind of art, another kind of writing, in the modern period, which claims to be neither modernist nor anti-modernist, and is sometimes called postmodernist. Historically it can be traced back as far as the Dada movement which began in Zurich in 1916. Tom Stoppard's entertaining play *Travesties*, set in that time and place, portrays one of the founders of Dadaism, Tristan Tzara, and brings him into entertaining collision with James Joyce and Lenin, representing modernist and antimodernist attitudes to art, respectively. But as a significant force in modern writing, postmodernism is a fairly recent phenomenon, and more evident in America and France than in England, except in the field of drama. Postmodernism continues the modernist critique of traditional realism, but it tries to go beyond or around or underneath modernism, which for all its formal experiment and complexity held out to the reader the promise of meaning, if not of *a* meaning. 'Where is the figure in the carpet?' asks a character in Donald Barthelme's *Snow White*, alluding to the title of a story by Henry James that has become proverbial among critics as an image of the goal of interpretation; 'Where is the figure in the carpet? Or is it just . . . carpet?' A lot of postmodernist writing implies that experience is just carpet, and that whatever meaningful patterns we discern in it are wholly illusory, comforting fictions. The difficulty, for the reader, of postmodernist writing is not so much a matter of obscurity, which might be cleared up, as of uncertainty, which is endemic. No amount of patient study could establish, for instance, the identity of the man with the heavy coat and hat and stick encountered by Moran in Beckett's *Molloy*. We shall never be able to unravel the plots of John Fowles's *The Magus* or Alain Robbe-Grillet's *Le Voyeur* or Thomas Pynchon's *The Crying of Lot 49* because these novels are labyrinths without exits.

Stated most baldly, Jakobson's theory asserts that any discourse must connect its topics according to either similarity or contiguity, and will usually prefer one type of connection to the other. Postmodernist writing tries to defy this law by seeking some alternative principle of composition. To these alternatives I give the names: Contradiction, Permutation, Discontinuity, Randomness, Excess and The Short Circuit.

Contradiction could not be better epitomised than by the refrain and closing words of Samuel Beckett's *The Unnamable*: 'You must go on, I can't go on, I'll go on.' Each clause negates the preceding one, as, throughout the text, the narrator oscillates between irreconcilable desires and assertions. Leonard Michaels approaches this radically contradictory basis for the practice of writing when he says in one of his stories, 'It is impossible to live with or without fictions.' The religion of Bokonism in Kurt Vonnegut's *Cat's Cradle* is based on 'the heart-breaking necessity of lying about reality and the heart-breaking impossibility of lying about it.' One of the most powerful emblems of contradiction, defying the most fundamental binary system of all, is the hermaphrodite, and it is not surprising that the characters of postmodernist fiction are often sexually ambivalent – for instance the narrator of Brigid Brophy's *In Transit* who is suffering from amnesia in an international airport unable to remember what sex he or she is and unable to settle the question by self-examination in a public convenience without knowing what he/she desires to find out. At the climax of John Barth's allegorical fabulation *Giles Goat-boy*, the caprine hero and his beloved Anastasia survive the inquisition of the dreaded computer WESCAC when, locked together in copulation, they answer the question 'ARE YOU MALE OR FEMALE?' with two simultaneous and contradictory answers, 'YES' and 'NO'.

Both metaphor and metonymy involve selection and selection implies leaving something out. Postmodernist writers sometimes defy this law by permutating alternative narrative lines in the same text – for example John Fowles's *The French Lieutenant's Woman*, or John Barth's story *Lost in the Funhouse*. Beckett uses permutation of trivial data to make both life and storytelling seem absurd:

As for his feet, sometimes he wore on each a sock, or on the one a sock
and on the other a stocking, or a boot, or a shoe, or a slipper, or a
sock and boot, or a sock and shoe, or a sock and slipper, or a stocking
and boot, or a stocking and shoe, or a stocking and slipper

and so on for a page and a half of *Watt*. Probably the most famous example of permutation in Beckett is that passage in *Molloy* where the hero wrestles with the problem of distributing and circulating his sixteen sucking stones in his four pockets in such a way that he will always suck them in the same sequence. Beckett's characters seek desperately to impose a purely mathematical order upon experience in the absence of any metaphysical order.

Permutation subverts the continuity of texts, a quality we naturally expect from writing. It is the continuity of realistic fiction, derived from spatial and temporal contiguities, that enables the world of the novel to displace the real world in the reading experience. Modernist texts, like *The Waste Land*, look discontinuous only as long as we fail to identify their metaphorical unity. Postmodernism is suspicious of any kind of continuity. One obvious sign of this is the fashion for composing fictions in very short sections, often only a paragraph in length, often quite disparate in content, the textual breaks between sections being emphasised by capitalised headings, numerals, or other typographical devices. A further stage in the pursuit of discontinuity is the introduction of randomness into the writing or reading process: William Burroughs's cut-ups, or B. S. Johnson's loose-leaf novel which each reader shuffles into a different order.

Some postmodernist writers have deliberately taken metaphoric or metonymic strategies to excess, tested them, as it were, to destruction, parodied and burlesqued them in the process of using them, and thus sought to escape from their tyranny. Richard Brautigan's *Trout-Fishing in America*, for example, is notable for its bizarre similes, which frequently threaten to detach themselves from the narrative and develop into little self-contained stories – not quite like the heroic simile, because they never return to their original context. For example:

The sun was like a huge 50 cent piece that someone had poured kerosene on and lit with a match and said 'Here, hold this while I go get a newspaper' and put the coin in my hand, but never came back.

The title of this book is used to take the metaphorical process of substitution to an absurd extreme: Trout-Fishing in America can, and does, replace any noun or adjective in the text without any principle of resemblance being involved. It can be the name of the author, his characters and inanimate objects. It can mean anything Brautigan wants it to mean. The metonymic equivalent to this metaphoric overkill might be exemplified by the novels of Alain Robbe-Grillet, whose immensely detailed, scientifically exact and metaphor-free descriptions of objects actually prevent us from visualising them. By presenting the reader with more data than he can synthesise, the discourse affirms the resistance of the world to interpretation.

The literary text, whether it tends towards a metaphoric or a metonymic structure and texture, is always metaphoric in the sense that when we interpret it we apply it to the world as a total metaphor. According to the author, we say, the world is 'like that' – 'that' being *The Waste Land* or *The Old Wives' Tale*. This process of interpretation assumes a gap between the text and the world, between art and life, which postmodernist writing characteristically tries to short-circuit in order to administer a shock to the reader and thus resist assimilation into conventional categories of the literary. Ways of doing this include: combining in one work the apparently factual and the obviously fictional, introducing the author and the question of authorship into the text, and exposing conventions in the act of using them. These metafictional ploys are not themselves discoveries of the postmodernist writers – they are to be found in prose fiction at least as far back as Cervantes and Sterne – but they appear so frequently in postmodernist writing and are pursued to such lengths as to constitute a distinctively new development. In his novel *Breakfast of Champions* Kurt Vonnegut is describing a scene in a bar as perceived by an ex-convict called Wayne Hoobler.

'Give me a Black and White and water,' he heard the waitress say, and Wayne should have pricked up his ears at that. That particular drink wasn't for an ordinary person. That drink was for the person who had created all Wayne's misery to date, who could kill him or make him a millionaire or send him back to prison or do whatever he damn well pleased with Wayne. That drink was for me.

This not only displays the author's hand in his work; it throws the reader completely off balance by bringing the real, historic author on to the same plane as his own fictitious characters and at the very same time drawing attention to their fictitiousness. It thus calls into question the whole business of reading and writing literary fictions.

There is considerable disagreement among critics and aestheticians as to whether postmodernism is a really significant and distinctive kind of art, or whether, being an essentially rule-breaking activity, it must always be a minority mode, dependent on a majority of artists trying to keep to the rules. I have not the space to go into these arguments, and in any case it was not my intention to discriminate between the modernist, antimodernist and postmodernist modes in terms of value, but in terms of form. What I hope to have shown is that each mode operates according to different and identifiable formal principles, and that it is therefore pointless to judge one kind of writing by criteria derived from another. To make such distinctions clear, even if it does involve a certain amount of jargon, seems to me to be the proper aim of studying literature in an academic context, and one that is ultimately of service to writers, inasmuch as it broadens the receptivity of readers. And if it has occurred to the reader to wonder where I would place my own fiction in this scheme, I would answer, in the spirit of 'Animal, Vegetable or Mineral': basically antimodernist, but with elements of modernism and postmodernism. Rummidge is certainly a metonymic place name, but Euphoric State is a metaphor, and the ending of *Changing Places* is a short circuit.

2 Analysis and Interpretation of the Realist Text: Ernest Hemingway's 'Cat in the Rain'

I

It is a commonplace that the systematic study of narrative was founded by Aristotle, and scarcely an exaggeration to say that little of significance was added to those foundations until the twentieth century. Narrative theory in the intervening period was mainly directed (or misdirected) at deducing from Aristotle's penetrating analysis of the system of Greek tragedy a set of prescriptive rules for the writing of epic. The rise of the novel as a distinctive and eventually dominant literary form finally exposed the poverty of neoclassical narrative theory, without for a long time generating anything much more satisfactory. The realistic novel set peculiar problems for any formalist criticism because it worked by disguising or denying its own conventionality. It therefore invited – and received – criticism which was interpretative and evaluative rather than analytical. It was not until the late nineteenth and early twentieth centuries that something like a poetics of fiction began to evolve from the self-conscious experiments of novelists themselves, and was elaborated by literary critics. At about the same time, developments in linguistics, folklore and anthropology stimulated a more broad-ranging study of narrative, beyond the boundaries of modern literary fiction. For a long time these investigations were pursued on parallel tracks which seldom converged. In the last couple of decades, however, the Anglo-American tradition of formalist criticism, essentially empirical and text-based, theoretically rather underpowered but hermeneutically productive, has encountered the more systematic, abstract, theoretically rigorous and 'scientific' tradition of European structuralist criticism. The result has been a minor 'knowledge explosion' in the field of narrative theory and poetics of fiction.

The question I wish to raise in this essay is whether progress in theory and methodology means progress in the critical reading of texts. Is it possible, or useful, to bring the whole battery of modern formalism and structuralism to bear upon a single text, and what is

gained by so doing? Does it enrich our reading by uncovering depths
and nuances of meaning we might not otherwise have brought to
consciousness, help us to solve problems of interpretation and to
correct misreadings? Or does it merely encourage a pointless and self-
indulgent academicism, by which the same information is shuffled from
one set of categories to another, from one jargon to another, without
any real advance in appreciation or understanding? The analysis offered
here of a short story by Ernest Hemingway is intended to support a
positive answer to the first set of questions, a negative answer to the
second set. But first it may be useful to remind ourselves of the range
and variety of theories, methodologies and 'approaches' now available
to the critic of fiction. I would group them into three categories, according to the 'depth' at which they address themselves to narrative structure.

1   *Narratology and Narrative Grammar* – i.e. the effort to discover the
langue of narrative, the underlying system of rules and possibilities of
which any narrative *parole* (text) is the realization. With a few arguable
exceptions – e.g. Northrop Frye's *Anatomy of Criticism* (1957) and
Frank Kermode's *The Sense of an Ending* (1966) – this enterprise has
been almost exclusively dominated by European scholars – Propp,
Bremond, Greimas, Lévi-Strauss, Todorov and Barthes, among others.
Crucial to this tradition of inquiry are the ideas of function and transformation. In the theory of Greimas, for instance, all narrative consists essentially of the transfer of an object or value from one 'actant'
to another. An actant performs a certain function in the story which
may be classified as Subject or Object, Sender or Receiver, Helper or
Opponent, and is involved in doing things which may be classified as
performative (tests, struggles, etc.), contractual (establishment and
breaking of contracts) and disjunctional (departure and returns). These
functions are not simply identifiable from the surface structure of a
narrative text: for instance, several characters may perform the function of one actant, or one character may combine the functions of two
actants. All concepts are semantically defined by a binary relationship
with their opposites (e.g. Life/Death) or negatives (e.g. Life/Non-Life)
yielding the basic semiotic model A:B :: −A:−B (e.g. Life:Death ::
Non-Life:Non-Death), so that all narrative can be seen as the transformation into actants and actions of a thematic four-term homology.[1]
     It is often said that this kind of approach is more rewarding when
applied to narratives of a traditional, formulaic and orally transmitted
type, rather than sophisticated literary narratives; and the exponents of
narratology themselves frequently remind us that their aim is not the
explication of texts but the uncovering of the system that allows narrative texts to be generated and competent readers to make sense of
them. Narratology does, however, bring to the attention of the literary

critic factors involved in reading narrative that are important, but in a sense so obvious that they tend to be overlooked. Roland Barthes has very fruitfully applied to the analysis of literary fictions the idea, derived from structuralist narratology, that narrative is divisible into sequences that open or close possibilities for the characters, and thus for the reader. The interest of these openings and closures may be either retrospective, contributing to the solution of some enigma proposed earlier in the text (the hermeneutic code), or prospective, making the audience wonder what will happen next (the proairetic code).[2] Curiosity and suspense are therefore the two basic 'affects' aroused by narrative, exemplified in a very pure form by the classic detective story and the thriller, respectively, as Tzvetan Todorov observes.[3] A story of any sophistication will also, as Kermode points out in *The Sense of an Ending*, make use of what Aristotle called peripeteia, or reversal, when a possibility is closed in a way that is unexpected and yet plausible and instructive. The reversal tends to produce an effect of irony, especially if it is anticipated by the audience.

Two problems arise in applying this kind of approach to realistic fiction. If we segment a text into its smallest units of information, how do we identify those which are functional on the basic narrative level, and what do we do with those units (the majority) which are not? Roland Barthes suggests one solution in his 'Introduction to the Structural Analysis of Narratives' where, drawing his illustrations mainly from Ian Fleming's *Goldfinger*, he classifies the narrative units as either *nuclei* or *catalysers*. Nuclei open or close alternatives that are of direct consequence for the subsequent development of the narrative and cannot be deleted without altering the story. Catalysers are merely consecutive units which expand the nuclei or fill up the space between them. They can be deleted without altering the narrative, though not, in the case of realistic narrative, without altering its meaning and effect, since segments which connect not, or not only, with segments at the same level, but with some more generalised concept such as the psychological makeup of the characters, or the atmosphere of the story, function as *indices*, or (if merely factual) *informants*. Jonathan Culler has suggested that our ability to distinguish nuclei from catalysers intuitively and to rank them in order of importance is a typical manifestation of reader-competence, verified by the fact that different readers will tend to summarise the plot of a given story in the same way. The intuitive recognition or ranking of nuclei is 'governed by readers' desire to reach an ultimate summary in which plot as a whole is grasped in a satisfying form'.[4] In short, the structural coherence of narratives is inseparable from their meaning, and reading them is inseparable from forming hypotheses about their overall meaning.

2 *Poetics of Fiction* Under this head I include all attempts to describe and classify techniques of fictional representation. The great
breakthrough in this field in the modern era was undoubtedly the
Russian Formalists' distinction between *fabula* and *sjuzet*: on the one
hand, the story in its most neutral, objective, chronological form – the
story as it might have been enacted in real time and space, a seamless
continuum of innumerable contiguous events; and on the other hand,
the actual text in which this story is imitated, with all its inevitable (but
motivated) gaps, elisions, emphases and distortions. Work along these
lines in Europe, culminating in Gérard Genette's 'Discours du récit'
(1972), established two principal areas in which *sjuzet* significantly
modifies *fabula*: time, and what is generally called 'point of view' in
Anglo-American criticism – though Genette correctly distinguishes here
between 'perspective' (who sees the action) and 'voice' (who speaks the
narration of it). He also distinguishes most suggestively three different
categories in the temporal organisation (or deformation) of the *fabula*
by the *sjuzet*: order, duration and frequency. The first of these concerns the relation between the order of events in the *fabula*, which is
always chronological, and the order of events in the *sjuzet*, which, of
course, need not be. The second category concerns the relation between
the putative duration of events in the *fabula* and the time taken to nar-
rate them (and therefore to read the narration) in the *sjuzet*, which may
be longer, or shorter, or approximately the same. The third category
concerns the relationship between the number of times an event occurs
in the *fabula* and the number of times it is narrated in the *sjuzet*. There
are four possibilities: telling once what happened once, telling n times
what happened n times, telling n times what happened once, and telling
once what happened n times.[5]

The choices made by the narrative artist at this level are in a sense
prior to, or 'deeper' than his stylistic choices in composing the surface
structure of the text, though they place important constraints upon
what he can achieve in the surface structure. They are also of manifest
importance in the realistic novel which, compared to other, earlier
narrative forms, is characterised by a carefully discriminated, pseudo-
historical treatment of temporality, and a remarkable depth and flexi-
bility in its presentation of consciousness.

A good deal of Anglo-American critical theorising about the novel,
from Percy Lubbock's *The Craft of Fiction* (1921) to Wayne Booth's
The Rhetoric of Fiction (1961), was implicitly, if unconsciously, based
on the same distinction between *fabula* and *sjuzet*, between 'story' and
'way of telling it'. The cross-fertilisation of the two critical traditions
has produced much interesting and illuminating work, analysing and
classifying novelistic techniques and covering such matters as tense,
person, speech and indirect speech in fictional narrative; and we are

now, it seems to me, within sight of a truly comprehensive taxonomy of fictional form at this level. Two recent books which have made particularly valuable contributions in this respect are Seymour Chatman's *Style and Discourse: Narrative Structure in Fiction and Film* (1978) and the more narrowly focused *Transparent Minds: Narrative Modes for Presenting Consciousness in Fiction* by Dorrit Cohn (1978).

3   *Rhetorical Analysis*   By this I mean analysing the surface structure of narrative texts to show how the linguistic mediation of a story determines its meaning and effect. This is a kind of criticism in which Anglo-American tradition is comparatively strong, because of the close-reading techniques developed by the New Criticism. Mark Shorer's essays 'Technique as Discovery' (1948) and 'Fiction and the Analogical Matrix' (1949)[6] are classic statements of this approach. The stylistics that developed out of Romance Philology, represented at its best by Spitzer and Auerbach,[7] also belongs in this category. When I wrote my first book of criticism, *Language of Fiction* (1966), this seemed the best route by which to achieve a formalist critique of the realistic novel.

The underlying aim of this criticism was to demonstrate that what looked like redundant or random detail in realistic fiction was in fact functional, contributing to a pattern of motifs with expressive and thematic significance. Much of this criticism was therefore concerned with tracing symbolism and keywords in the verbal texture of novels. Though very few of the New Critics were aware of the work of Roman Jakobson, he provided a theoretical justification for this kind of criticism in his famous definition of literariness, or the poetic function of language, as 'the projection of the principle of equivalence from the axis of selection to the axis of combination'.[8] What the New Critics called 'spatial form'[9] was precisely a pattern of paradigmatic equivalences concealed in the narrative syntagm. Furthermore, as I tried to show in my book *The Modes of Modern Writing* (1977), in his distinction between metaphor and metonymy,[10] Jakobson provided a key to understanding how the realistic novel contrives to build up a pattern of equivalences without violating its illusion of life.

Metaphor and metonymy (or synecdoche) are both figures of equivalence,[11] but generated by different processes, metaphor according to similarity between things otherwise different, metonymy according to contiguity or association between part and whole, cause and effect, thing and attribute, etc. Thus, if I transform the literal sentence 'Ships sail the sea' into 'Keels plough the deep', *plough* is equivalent to 'sail' because of the similarity between the movement of a plough through the earth and a ship through the sea, but *keel* is equivalent to 'ship' because it is part of a ship (synecdoche) and *deep* is equivalent to 'sea' because it is an attribute of the sea (metonymy). In fact, metonymy is a non-logical (and therefore foregrounded or rhetorical) condensation achieved by transformations of kernel sentences by deletion (*the keels of the ships* condensed to *keels* rather than *ships, deep sea* to *deep* rather than *sea*). Metonymy thus plays with the combination axis of language as metaphor plays with the selection axis of language, and together they epitomise the two ways by which any discourse connects one topic with another: either because they are similar or because they are contiguous. Jakobson's distinction thus allows the analyst to move freely between deep structure and surface structure.

Realistic fiction is dominantly metonymic: it connects actions that are contiguous in time and space and connected by cause and effect, but since it cannot describe exhaustively, the narrative *sjuzet* is always in a metonymic (or synecdochic) relation to the *fabula*. The narrative text necessarily selects certain details and suppresses or deletes others. The selected details are thus foregrounded by being selected, and their recurrence and interrelation with each other in the narrative text becomes aesthetically significant (what the Prague School calls systematic internal foregrounding). Furthermore, these details may carry connotations, building up a still denser pattern of equivalences, especially (though not exclusively) when they are described in figurative language, using the verbal tropes of metonymy or metaphor. This is usually (and rather loosely) called 'symbolism' in Anglo-American criticism. Barthes calls it connotation, the process by which one signified acts as the signifier of another signified not actually named. Jakobson's distinction enables us to distinguish four different ways in which it operates in literary texts, two of which are especially characteristic of realistic fiction:

A   Metonymic Signified I metonymically evokes Signified II (e.g. the hearth fire in *Jane Eyre*, an invariably selected detail in any description of domestic interiors, signifying 'inhabited room', also symbolises comfort, intimacy, security, etc., cause evoking effect).
B   Metonymic Signified I metaphorically evokes Signified II (e.g. mud and fog at the beginning of *Bleak House*, signifying 'inclement weather', also symbolise the obfuscation and degradation of goodness and justice by the Law, because of the similarity between the effects of the elements and those of the institution).
C   Metaphoric Signified I metonymically evokes Signified II (e.g. the description of the night in Llaregyb, in Dylan Thomas's *Under Milk Wood*, as 'bible-black', symbolises the Protestant chapel-going religious culture of the community; part, or attribute, standing for the whole).
D   Metaphoric Signified I metaphorically evokes Signified II (e.g. in the opening lines of Yeats's poem, 'The Second Coming' –

> Turning and turning in the widening gyre
> The falcon cannot hear the falconer

where the metaphor *gyre* applied to the spiralling movement of the falcon also symbolises the cyclical movement of history).

Realistic fiction relies principally upon symbolism of types A and B, in which the primary signified is introduced into the discourse according to the metonymic principle of spatial or temporal contiguity with what has come before.

II

No choice of a text for illustrative purposes is innocent, and no analysis of a single text could possibly provide universally valid answers to the questions posed at the beginning of this essay. These questions will not be settled until we have a significant corpus of synthetic or pluralistic readings of narrative texts of various types. Two distinguished achievements of this kind come to mind: Barthes's *S/Z* and Christine Brooke-Rose's study of *The Turn of the Screw*.[12] The following discussion of Hemingway's short story 'Cat in the Rain' (1925)* follows the model of the latter in taking the problem of interpretation as its starting-point, but it is necessarily much more modest in scope and scale than either. Two considerations prompted the choice of this story, apart from its convenient brevity. (1) A staff seminar on it in my own department at Birmingham revealed that it presents certain problems of interpretation, though without being quite so heavily encrusted with the deposits of previous readings and misreadings as *The Turn of the Screw*. (2) It is both realistic and modern, cutting across that historicist and tendentious distinction between the *lisible* and the *scriptible* which I personally find one of the less helpful features of the work of Barthes and his disciples.[13] The implied notion of *vraisemblance* on which Hemingway's story depends, the assumed relationship between the text and reality, is essentially continuous with that of classic bourgeois realism, yet in the experience of readers it has proved ambiguous, polyvalent and resistant to interpretative closure.

This is what Carlos Baker, in the standard critical work on Hemingway, had to say about 'Cat in the Rain' (he discusses it in the context of a group of stories about men–women relationships):

'Cat in the Rain', another story taken in part from the woman's point of view, presents a corner of the female world in which the male is only tangentially involved. It was written at Rapallo in May, 1923. From the window of a hotel room where her husband is reading and she

*Reprinted at the end of this essay, pp. 33–6.

is fidgeting, a young wife sees a cat outside in the rain. When she goes to get it, the animal (which somehow stands in her mind for comfortable bourgeois domesticity) has disappeared. This fact is very close to tragic because of the cat's association in her mind with many other things she longs for: long hair she can do in a knot at the back of her neck; a candle-lighted dining table where her own silver gleams; the season of spring and nice weather; and of course, some new clothes. But when she puts these wishes into words, her husband mildly advises her to shut up and find something to read. 'Anyway', says the young wife, 'I want a cat. I want a cat. I want a cat now. If I can't have long hair or any fun, I can have a cat.' The poor girl is the referee in a face-off between the actual and the possible. The actual is made of rain, boredom, a preoccupied husband, and irrational yearnings. The possible is made of silver, spring, fun, a new coiffure, and new dresses. Between the actual and the possible, stands the cat. It is finally sent up to her by the kindly old inn-keeper, whose sympathetic deference is greater than that of the young husband.[14]

There are several things to quibble with in this account of the story. Most important perhaps is Baker's assumption that the cat sent up by the hotel keeper at the end is the same as the one that the wife saw from her window. This assumption is consistent with Baker's sympathy with the wife as a character, implied by his reference to her as 'the poor girl' and his description of the disappearance of the cat as 'very close to tragic'. The appearance of the maid with a cat is the main reversal, in Aristotelian terms, in the narrative. If it is indeed the cat she went to look for, then the reversal is a happy one for her, and confirms her sense that the hotel keeper appreciated her as a woman more than her husband. In Greimas's terms, the wife is the subject of the story and the cat the object. The hotel-keeper and the maid enact the role of helper and George is the opponent. The story is disjunctive (departure and return) and concerns the transfer of the cat to the wife.

The description of the tortoise-shell cat as 'big', however, suggests that it is not the one to which the wife referred by the diminutive term 'kitty', and which she envisaged stroking on her lap. We might infer that the padrone, trying to humour a client, sends up the first cat he can lay hands on, which is in fact quite inappropriate to the wife's needs. This would make the reversal an ironic one at the wife's expense, emphasising the social and cultural abyss that separates her from the padrone, and revealing her quasi-erotic response to his professional attentiveness as a delusion.

I shall return to this question of the ambiguity of the ending. One more point about Baker's commentary on the story: he says that the cat 'somehow stands in [the wife's] mind for comfortable bourgeois domesticity', and speaks of its 'association in her mind with many other things she longs for'. In other words, he interprets the cat as a metonymic symbol of type A above. Indeed he sees the whole story as turning on the opposition between two groups of metonymies. 'The actual is made of rain, boredom, a preoccupied husband, and irrational yearnings. The possible is made of silver, spring fun, a new coiffure, and new clothes.'

John V. Hagopian gives a very different reading of this story. It is, he says, about 'a crisis in the marriage . . . involving the lack of fertility, which is symbolically foreshadowed by the public garden (fertility) dominated by the war monument (death)' in the first paragraph. These again are metonymic symbols of type A, effect connoting cause; but Hagopian's reading of the story hinges on the identification of the cat as a symbol of a wanted child, and of the man in the rubber cape (lines ' 52–3) as a symbol of contraception – symbolism of type B, in which a metonymic signified evokes a second signified metaphorically, i.e. by virtue of similarity.

As [the wife] looks out into the wet empty square, she sees a man in a rubber cape crossing to the café in the rain . . . The rubber cape is a protection from rain, and rain is a fundamental necessity for fertility and fertility is precisely what is lacking in the American wife's marriage. An even more precise interpretation is possible but perhaps not necessary here.[15]

What Hagopian is presumably hinting at is that 'rubber' is an American colloquialism for contraceptive sheath, and that the wife notices the man in the rubber cape because of the subconscious association – a piece of classic Freudian 'symbolism'. It is an ingenious interpretation and all the more persuasive because there seems to be no very obvious reason for introducing the man in the cape into the story – he is not an actant in the narrative but an item of the descriptive background, and his appearance does not tell us anything about the weather or the square that we do not know already. Admittedly, the cape does signify, by contrast, the wife's lack of protection from the rain, thus emphasising the padrone's thoughtfulness in sending the maid with the umbrella. But if we accept Hagopian's reading then the umbrella itself, opening with almost comical opportuneness and effortlessness behind her, becomes a symbol of how the wife's way of life comes between her and a vital, fertile relationship with reality. Her later demands for new clothes, a new hairstyle, a candle-lit dining-table are, according to Hagopian, expressions of a desire that never reaches full consciousness, for 'motherhood, a home with a family, an end to the strictly companionate marriage with George'. And the cat, he says, is by this stage in the story 'an obvious symbol for a child'.

Unlike Baker, Hagopian sees the final reversal in the story as ironic:

The girl's symbolic wish is grotesquely fulfilled in painfully realistic terms. It is George, not the padrone, by whom the wife wants to be fulfilled, but the padrone has sent up the maid with a big tortoise-shell cat, a huge creature that swings down against her body. It is not clear whether this is exactly the same cat as the one the wife had seen from the window – probably not; in any case, it will most certainly not do. The girl is willing to settle for a child-surrogate, but the big tortoise-shell cat obviously cannot serve that purpose.[16]

The reason why this story is capable of provoking these two very different interpretations might be expressed as follows: although it is a well-formed narrative, with a clearly defined beginning, middle and end, the primary action is not the primary vehicle of meaning. This can be demonstrated by testing upon the story Jonathan Culler's hypothesis that competent readers will tend to agree on what is and is not essential to the plot of a narrative text. Before the seminar at Birmingham University, participants were invited to summarise the action of the story in not more than thirty words of continuous prose.[17] All the contributors mentioned the wife, the cat, the rain, and the hotel manager; most mentioned the nationality of the wife and her failure to find the cat under the table; about half mentioned the husband, located the story in Italy, and made a distinction between the two cats. None mentioned the maid, or the bickering between husband and wife.

These omissions are particularly interesting. The non-appearance of the maid is easily explained: on the narrative level her function is indistinguishable from that of the manager – both are 'helpers' and the narrative would not be significantly altered *qua* narrative if the maid were deleted from the story and her actions performed by the manager himself. She does contribute to the symmetry of the story both numerically and sexually: it begins by pairing husband and wife, then pairs wife and manager, then wife and maid, then (in the wife's thoughts) maid and manager, then wife and manager again, then wife and husband again, and ends by pairing husband and maid. But this seems to be a purely formal set of equivalences with no significance in the hermeneutic or proairetic codes (such as would obtain if, for instance, there were some intrigue linking the husband with the maid and the manager, the kind of plotting characteristic of the *lisible* text). The main function of the maid in the story is to emphasise the status of the wife as a client and expatriate, and thus to act as a warning or corrective against the wife's tendency to attribute to the padrone a deeply personal interest in herself.

Both Baker and Hagopian agree that the rift between husband and wife is what the story is essentially about, even if they disagree about the precise cause. That none of the synopses should make any allusion to the bickering between the couple is striking evidence that the meaning of the story does not inhere in its basic action. In trying to preserve what is essential to that action in a very condensed summary – the quest for the cat, the failure of the quest, the reversal – one has to discard what seems most important in the story as read – the relationship between husband and wife. Adopting Barthes's terminology in 'The Structural Analysis of Narratives', there are only four nuclei in the story, opening possibilities which might be closed in different ways: will the wife or the husband go to fetch the cat? will the wife get the cat? will she get wet? who is at the door? There is perhaps another possibility tacitly opened around line 115, and closed, negatively, at line 131: namely, that George will put down his book and make love to his wife. All the rest of the story consists of catalysers that are indexical or informational, and since most of the information is given more than once, these too become indexical of mood and atmosphere (for instance, we are told more than once that it is raining). One might indeed describe the story generically as indexical: we infer its meaning indexically from its non-narrative components rather than hermeneutically or teleologically from its action. Another way of putting it would be to invoke Seymour Chatman's distinction between the resolved plot and the revealed plot:

In the traditional narrative of resolution, there is a sense of problem solving . . . of a kind of ratiocinative or emotional teleology . . . 'What will happen?' is the basic question. In the modern plot of revelation, however, the emphasis is elsewhere, the function of the discourse is not to answer that question or even to pose it . . . It is not that events are resolved (happily or tragically) but rather that a state of affairs is revealed.[18]

Chatman offers *Pride and Prejudice* and *Mrs. Dalloway* as examples of each kind of plot. 'Cat in the Rain' seems to share characteristics of both: it is, one might say, a plot of revelation (the relationship between husband and wife) disguised as a plot of resolution (the quest for the cat). The ambiguity of the ending is therefore crucial. By refusing to resolve the issue of whether the wife gets the cat she wants, the implied author indicates that this is not the point of the story.

There are several reasons why this ending is ambiguous. One, obviously, is that the story ends where it does, for if it continued for another line or two, or moment or two, it would become apparent from the wife's response whether the cat was the one she had seen from the

window, whether she is pleased or disconcerted by its being brought
to her, and so on. In other words, the *sjuzet* tantalisingly stops just
short of that point in the *fabula* where we should, with our readerly
desire for certainty, wish it to. In other respects there is nothing especially striking about the story's treatment of time, though we may admire
the smooth transition in the first paragraph from summary of a state
of affairs obtaining over a period of days or weeks to the state of
affairs obtaining on a particular afternoon, and the subtle condensation
of durational time in the final scene between husband and wife, marked
by changes in the light outside the window. The order of events is
strictly chronological (characteristic, Chatman observes, of the resolved
plot). As regards what Genette calls frequency, the story tends towards
reiteration rather than summary, telling *n* times what happened *n*
times or *n* times what happened once rather than telling once what
happened *n* times. This is important because it reinforces the definition
of the characters according to a very limited repertoire of gestures.
Thus the wife is frequently described as looking out of the window, the
husband as reading, the manager as bowing (and the weather as raining).

The story of the quest for the cat involves four characters, and in
theory could be narrated from four points of view, each quite distinct
and different in import. The story we have is written from the point of
view of the American couple rather than that of the Italian hotel staff,
and from the wife's point of view rather than the husband's. We must
distinguish here between what Genette calls voice and perspective. The
story is narrated throughout by an authorial voice which refers to the
characters in the third person and uses the past tense. This is the standard mode of authorial narration and by convention the narrator is
authoritative, reliable and, within the fictional world of the discourse,
omniscient. The authorial voice in this story, however, renounces the
privilege of authorial omniscience in two ways, firstly by abstaining
from any comment or judgment or explanation of motive regarding the
behaviour of the characters, and secondly by restricting itself to the
perspective of only two of the characters, and for part of the story to
the perspective of only one. By this I mean that the narrator describes
nothing that is not seen by either husband or wife or both. Yet it is not
quite true to say that the narrator has no independent angle of vision:
he has. As in a film, we sometimes see the wife from the husband's
angle, and the husband sometimes from the wife's angle, but much of
the time we see them both from some independent, impersonal angle.

The first paragraph adopts the common perspective of the American
couple, making no distinction between them. With the first sentence
of the second paragraph, 'The American wife stood at the window
looking out', the narrative adopts her perspective but without totally
identifying with it. Note the difference between '*her* husband' in line

30, which closely identifies the narration with her perspective, and 'the husband' in line 33, 'the wife' in line 36, which subtly reasserts the independence of the authorial voice. From this point onwards, however, for the next fifty lines the narration identifies itself closely with the wife's perspective, following her out of the room and downstairs into the lobby, and reporting what she thinks as well as what she sees. The anaphoric sequence of sentences beginning 'She liked' (lines 45–50) affect us as being a transcription rather than a description of her thoughts because they could be transposed into monologue (first person/present tense) without any illogicality or stylistic awkwardness. Sentences in free indirect speech, 'The cat would be round to the right. Perhaps she could go along under the eaves' (54–5) and 'Of course, the hotel-keeper had sent her' (59), mark the maximum degree of identification of the narration with the wife's point of view. When she returns to the room the narration separates itself from her again. There is a lot of direct speech from now on, no report of the wife's thoughts, and occasionally the narration seems to adopt the husband's perspective alone, e.g. 'George looked up and saw the back of her neck, clipped close like a boy's' (109–10) and – very importantly:

Someone knocked on the door.
'Avanti,' George said. He looked up from his book.
In the doorway stood the maid. She held a big tortoise-shell cat . . .
(142–4)

We can now fully understand why the ending of the story is so ambiguous: it is primarily because the narration adopts the husband's perspective at this crucial point. Since he did not rise from the bed to look out of the window at the cat sheltering from the rain, he has no way of knowing whether the cat brought by the maid is the same one – hence the non-committal indefinite article, 'a big tortoise-shell cat'. If, however, the wife's perspective had been adopted at this point and the text had read,

'Avanti,' the wife said. She turned round from the window.
In the doorway stood the maid. She held a big tortoise-shell cat . . .

then it would be clear that this was not the cat the wife had wanted to bring in from the rain (in which case the definite article would be used). It is significant that in the title of the story, there is no article before 'Cat', thus giving no support to either interpretation of the ending.

Carlos Baker's assumption that the tortoise-shell cat[19] and the cat in the rain are one and the same is therefore unwarranted. Hagopian's reading of the ending as ironic is preferable but his assumption that the wife's desire for the cat is caused by childlessness is also unwarranted. Here, it seems to me, the structuralist notion of language as a system of differences and of meaning as the product of structural oppositions can genuinely help to settle a point of interpretation. Hagopian's interpretation of the man in the rubber cape as a symbol of contraception depends in part on the association of rain with fertility. Now rain *can* symbolise fertility – when defined by opposition to drought. In this story, however (and incidentally, throughout Hemingway's work), it is opposed to 'good weather' and symbolises the loss of pleasure and joy, the onset of discomfort and ennui. Hagopian's comments on the disappearance of the painters, 'The rain, ironically, inhibits creativity,'[20] is a strained attempt to reconcile his reading with the text: there is no irony here unless we accept his equation, rain = fertility.

The cat as a child-surrogate is certainly a possible interpretation in the sense that it is a recognised cultural stereotype, but again Hagopian tries to enlist in its support textual evidence that is, if anything, negative. He comments on the description of the wife's sensations as she passes the hotel-keeper for the second time: ' "very small and tight inside . . . really important . . . of supreme importance" all phrases that might appropriately be used to describe a woman who is pregnant'.[21] But not, surely, to describe a woman who merely *wants* to be pregnant. Indeed, if we must have a gynaecological reading of the story it is much more plausible to suppose that the wife's whimsical craving for the cat, and for other things like new clothes and long hair, is the result of her *being* pregnant. There is, in fact, some extratextual support for this hypothesis. In his biography of Hemingway, Carlos Baker states quite baldly that 'Cat in the Rain' was about Hemingway, his wife Hadley and the manager and chambermaid at the Hotel Splendide in Rapallo, where the story was written in 1923. He also states, without making any connection between the two items, that the Hemingways had left the chilly thaw of Switzerland and gone to Rapallo because Hadley had announced that she was pregnant.[22]

At about the same time, Hemingway was evolving 'a new theory that you could omit anything if you knew what you omitted, and the omitted part would strengthen the story and make people feel something more than they understood'.[23] This is, I think, a very illuminating description by Hemingway of his application of the metonymic mode of classic realism to modernist literary purposes. Metonymy, as I said earlier, is a device of non-logical deletion. Hemingway's word is 'omission'. By omitting the kind of motivation that classic realistic fiction provided, he generated a symbolist polyvalency in his deceptively simple stories, making his readers 'feel more than they understood'. It would be a mistake, therefore, to look for a single clue, whether pregnancy or barrenness, to the meaning of 'Cat in the Rain'. That the wife's (and, for that matter, the husband's) behaviour is equally intelligible on either assumption is one more confirmation of the story's indeterminacy.

Hemingway's stories are remarkable for achieving a symbolist resonance without the use of rhetorical figures and tropes. Not only does 'Cat in the Rain' contain no metaphors and similes – it contains no metonymies and synecdoches either. The story is 'metonymic' in the structural sense defined above: its minimal semantic units are selected from a single context, a continuum of temporal and spatial contiguities, and all foregrounded simply by being selected, repeated and related to each other oppositionally. Consider, for example, the opening paragraph, which establishes the story's setting in diction that is apparently severely denotative, with no metaphors or metonymies, similes or synecdoches, no elegant variation or pathetic fallacies, yet is nevertheless highly charged with connotative meaning.

There were only two Americans stopping at the hotel. Americans opposed to other nationalities: index of cultural isolation.

They did not know any of the people they passed on the stairs on their way to and from their room. Index of social isolation and mutual dependence – vulnerability to breakdown in relationship.

Their room was on the second floor facing the sea. Culture faces nature.

It also faced the public garden and the war monument. Culture paired with nature (public: garden) and opposed to nature (monument: garden). Pleasure (garden) opposed to pain (war).

There were big palms and green benches in the public garden. Culture and nature integrated. Benches same colour as vegetation.

In the good weather there was always an artist with his easel. Artists liked the way the palms grew and the bright colors of the hotels facing the gardens and the sea. Culture and nature happily fused. Image of euphoria.

Italians came from a long way off to look up at the war monument. Euphoria qualified. War monument attracts the living but commemorates the dead. Looking associated with absence (of the dead). 'Italian' opposed to 'American'.

It was made of bronze and glistened in the rain. Inert mineral (bronze) opposed to organic vegetable (palm). Rain opposed to good weather. Euphoria recedes.

It was raining. Rain dripped from the palm trees. Euphoria recedes further. Weather uninviting.

Water stood in pools on the gravel paths. Image of stagnation.

The sea broke in a long line in the rain and slipped back down the beach to come up and break again in a long line in the rain. Excess of wetness. Monotony. Ennui.

The motor cars were gone from the square by the war monument.
Across the square in the doorway of the café a waiter stood looking
out at the square. Images of absence, loss, ennui.[24]

The first paragraph, then, without containing a single narrative
nucleus, establishes the thematic core of the story through oppositions
between nature and culture, joy and ennui. Joy is associated with a
harmonious union of culture and nature, ennui is the result of some
dissociation or discontinuity between culture and nature. The wife,
looking out of the window at a scene made joyless by the rain, sees a
cat with whose discomfort she emotionally identifies. Her husband,
though offering to fetch it, implies his indifference to her emotional
needs by not actually moving. The husband is reading, a 'cultural'
use of the eyes. The wife is looking, a 'natural' use of the eyes. Her
looking, through the window, expresses a need for communion. His
reading of a book is a substitute for communion, and a classic remedy
for ennui. It is worth noticing that he is reading on the bed – a place
made for sleeping and making love; and the perversity of this behaviour
is symbolised by the fact that he is lying on the bed the wrong way
round. As the story continues, the contrast between looking and
reading, both activities expressing the loss or failure of love, becomes
more insistent. Denied the kitty, a 'natural' object (opposed to book)
which she could have petted as a substitute for being petted, the
wife looks in the mirror, pining for a more natural feminine self. Then
she looks out of the window again, while her husband, who has not
shifted his position (his immobility opposed to the padrone's punctilious bowing), reads on and impatiently recommends her to 'get something to read'. One could summarise this story in the style of Greimas,
as follows: loving is to quarrelling as stroking a cat is to reading a book,
a narrative transformation of the opposition between joy and ennui,
thus:

Loving (Joy):Quarrelling (Ennui) :: stroking a cat (Non-joy, a giving
but not receiving of pleasure):reading a book (Non-ennui).

Such a summary has this to recommend it, that it brings together the
overt action of the story (the quest for the cat) with its implicit subject
(the relationship between husband and wife). Whether it, and the preceding comments, enhance our understanding and appreciation of
Hemingway's story, I leave others to judge.

Cat in the Rain

There were only two Americans stopping at
the hotel. They did not know any of the people
they passed on the stairs on their way to and
from their room. Their room was on the second
floor facing the sea. It also faced the public
garden and the war monument. There were big
palms and green benches in the public garden.
In the good weather there was always an artist
with his easel. Artists liked the way the palms
grew and the bright colors of the hotels facing
the gardens and the sea. Italians came from a
long way off to look up at the war monument.
It was made of bronze and glistened in the rain.
It was raining. The rain dripped from the palm
trees. Water stood in pools on the gravel paths.
The sea broke in a long line in the rain and
slipped back down the beach to come up and
break again in a long line in the rain. The motor
cars were gone from the square by the war
monument. Across the square in the doorway
of the café a waiter stood looking out at the
empty square.

 The American wife stood at the window looking out. Outside right under their window a
cat was crouched under one of the dripping
green tables. The cat was trying to make herself
so compact that she would not be dripped on.

 'I'm going down and get that kitty,' the
American wife said.

 'I'll do it,' her husband offered from the bed.

 'No, I'll get it. The poor kitty out trying to
keep dry under a table.'

 The husband went on reading, lying propped
up with the two pillows at the foot of the bed.

 'Don't get wet,' he said.

 The wife went downstairs and the hotel owner
stood up and bowed to her as she passed the
office. His desk was at the far end of the office.
He was an old man and very tall.

 'Il piove,' the wife said. She liked the hotel-
keeper.

 'Si, si, Signora, brutto tempo. It is very bad
weather.'

He stood behind his desk in the far end of
the dim room. The wife liked him. She liked   45
the deadly serious way he received any com-
plaints. She liked his dignity. She liked the
way he wanted to serve her. She liked the way
he felt about being a hotel-keeper. She liked
his old, heavy face and big hands.   50
   Liking him she opened the door and looked
out. It was raining harder. A man in a rubber
cape was crossing the empty square to the café.
The cat would be around to the right. Perhaps
she could go along to the caves. As she stood   55
in the doorway an umbrella opened behind her.
It was the maid who looked after their room.
   'You must not get wet,' she smiled, speaking
Italian. Of course, the hotel-keeper had sent her.
   With the maid holding the umbrella over her,   60
she walked along the gravel path until she was
under their window. The table was there,
washed bright green in the rain, but the cat was
gone. She was suddenly disappointed. The
maid looked up at her.   65
   'Ha perduto qualque cosa, Signora?'
   'There was a cat,' said the American girl.
   'A cat?'
   'Si, il gatto.'
   'A cat?' the maid laughed. 'A cat in the   ⸗   70
rain?'
   'Yes,' she said, 'under the table.' Then, 'Oh,
I wanted it so much. I wanted a kitty.'
   When she talked English the maid's face
tightened.   75
   'Come, Signora,' she said. 'We must get
back inside. You will be wet.'
   'I suppose so,' said the American girl.
   They went back along the gravel path and
passed in the door. The maid stayed outside to   80
close the umbrella. As the American girl passed
the office, the padrone bowed from his desk.
Something felt very small and tight inside the
girl. The padrone made her feel very small and
at the same time really important. She had a   85

momentary feeling of being of supreme importance. She went on up the stairs. She opened
the door of the room. George was on the bed,
reading.

'Did you get the cat?' he asked, putting the   90
book down.

'It was gone.'

'Wonder where it went to,' he said, resting
his eyes from reading.

She sat down on the bed.   95

'I wanted it so much,' she said. 'I don't
know why I wanted it so much. I wanted that
poor kitty. It isn't any fun to be a poor kitty
out in the rain.'

George was reading again.   100

She went over and sat in front of the mirror
of the dressing table looking at herself with the
hand glass. She studied her profile, first one
side and then the other. Then she studied the
back of her head and her neck.   105

'Don't you think it would be a good idea
if I let my hair grow out?' she asked, looking
at her profile again.

George looked up and saw the back of her   110
neck, clipped close like a boy's.

'I like it the way it is.'

'I get so tired of it,' she said. 'I get so tired
of looking like a boy.'

George shifted his position in the bed. He   115
hadn't looked away from her since she started
to speak.

'You look pretty darn nice,' he said.

She laid the mirror down on the dresser and
went over to the window and looked out. It   120
was getting dark.

'I want to pull my hair back tight and smooth
and make a big knot at the back that I can feel,'
she said. 'I want to have a kitty to sit on my
lap and purr when I stroke her.'

'Yeah?' George said from the bed.   125

'And I want to eat at a table with my own
silver and I want candles. And I want it to be
spring and I want to brush my hair out in front

of a mirror and I want a kitty and I want some
new clothes.'   130
    'Oh, shut up and get something to read,'
George said. He was reading again.
    His wife was looking out of the window. It
was quite dark now and still raining in the palm
trees.   135
    'Anyway, I want a cat,' she said, 'I want a
cat. I want a cat now. If I can't have long
hair or any fun, I can have a cat.'
    George was not listening. He was reading
his book. His wife looked out of the window   140
where the light had come on in the square.
    Someone knocked at the door.
    'Avanti,' George said. He looked up from
his book.
    In the doorway stood the maid. She held a   145
big tortoise-shell cat pressed tight against her
and swung down against her body.
    'Excuse me,' she said, 'the padrone asked me
to bring this for the Signora.'

3 How Successful is *Hard Times*?

The so-called industrial novels of the Victorian period, like *Hard Times*, offer a special problem, or trap, for literary criticism. Because these novels comment directly upon contemporary social issues, they open themselves to evaluation according to the 'truthfulness' with which they reflect the 'facts' of social history. Modern criticism of *Hard Times* shows this tendency very clearly. Humphrey House, in *The Dickens World* (1941), for instance, argued that the novel was a failure because Dickens had taken on subject-matter that he either could not or would not treat adequately: Dickens did not understand Utilitarianism well enough to attack it effectively, and in handling the theme of industrial relations falsified his own observations, as recorded in his report on the Preston strike in *Household Words* (11 February 1854). Dr Leavis, in advancing a (then) startlingly high evaluation of the novel in *The Great Tradition* (1948), conceded Dickens's failure on the latter score, but minimised its significance. For him, the centre of the novel was its critique of Utilitarianism, through the characterisation of Gradgrind and Bounderby. In his treatment of the latter, Leavis claimed, 'Dickens . . . makes a just observation about the affinities and practical tendency of Utilitarianism, as, in his presentment of the Gradgrind home and the Gradgrind elementary school, he does about the Utilitarian spirit in Victorian education'.[1] John Holloway contested this view in his essay, '*Hard Times*, A History and a Criticism'. Documenting his case extensively from contemporary encyclopedias, textbooks and government reports, Holloway argued forcefully that Dickens's account of Utilitarianism, and of the various practices that derived from it, was both unfair and internally inconsistent; and as regards the industrial theme he followed House in stressing Dickens's 'deliberate falsification of what [he] knew from his visit to Preston'.[2] In his introduction to the Penguin English Library edition of the novel, the Marxist critic David Craig swung back to the opposite pole. Affirming the 'deep and manifold rootedness of *Hard Times* in its age', he sought to demonstrate the essential truthfulness of Dickens's critique of Gradgrind's philosophy of education by culling from the work of the

37

Hammonds and other social historians descriptions of contemporary board schools that correspond closely to the early chapters of *Hard Times*. 'The schooling systems favoured by go-ahead cotton masters', says Craig, 'were themselves like living satires on Utilitarianism in practice, even before Dickens had recreated them in the mode of satire'.[3] But the 'mode' of the novel is less acceptable to Craig when it comes to the treatment of the working class, and his claims for the novel's truthfulness become progressively more tortuous and equivocal as his introduction proceeds. His conclusion reads almost like a parody of Stalinist Socialist Realism: 'if one tried to imagine the great industrial novel that never did get written, one might suggest that the masters cried out to be satirized, the mass of the people presented with clear-eyed realism. Insofar as Dickens fails in the latter, his novel sags; insofar as he excels in the former, it succeeds . . .'[4]

The history of critical commentary on *Hard Times* demonstrates that no amount of comparison between a novel and its social-historical sources (whether specific or general) can ever settle the question of how successful it is as a work of art. The reason is not that criteria of empirical truthfulness are wholly irrelevant (they are not); but that in referring from fiction to fact and back again, the critics are ignoring a vitally important stage in the creative process by which narratives are composed, viz. the transformation of the deep structure of the text into its surface structure. We must consider, that is to say, not just the transformation of historical data into fictional narrative, but the transformation of the narrative *fabula*, a story potentially realisable in an infinite number of ways, into a particular *sjuzet*, or text.* It is in this process that the particular literary identity of a novel, and therefore the range of reader-responses appropriate to it, are determined.

In an earlier essay on *Hard Times*[5] I tried to mediate between conflicting evaluations of the novel by a formalistic analysis of its surface structure – that is, its characteristic style or rhetoric – suggesting that persuasiveness rather than truthfulness should be the criterion of success or failure. In this essay I aim to complement that earlier study by examining the novel's structure at a deeper level, that of narrative technique. The object is to answer the question, how successful is *Hard Times*, by answering another one: what kind of novel is *Hard Times*?

In advancing his very high estimate of the novel, Dr Leavis classified it as a 'moral fable', which he defined by saying that 'in it the intention is peculiarly insistent, so that the representative significance of everything in the fable – character, episode and so on – is immediately apparent as we read'.[6] But as Robert Garis pointed out, Dr Leavis's reading of *Hard Times* is not perceptibly different from his reading of

---

*These and other technical terms used in the remainder of this essay are explained in the preceding essay, 'Analysis and Interpretation of the Realist Text'.

other novels in *The Great Tradition*, and claims for it qualities which it hardly possesses.[7] Professor Garis's own term for the exuberant explicitness which Leavis characterised as 'moral fable' is 'theatre', but it is a quality *he* finds permeating all Dickens's writing, whereas most readers of *Hard Times* have felt that there is something quite distinctive about the 'feel' of this novel. In what follows I shall try to analyse in formal terms the moralised theatricality that is specific to *Hard Times*, beginning with the categories of time and 'point of view'.

The most significant aspect of Dickens's handling of time in his novel concerns what Gérard Genette calls 'duration', affecting the *pace* of the narrative. There is not much to comment on with regard to the *ordering* of events – we do not find in *Hard Times* that radical dislocation and rearrangement of chronological order that we encounter, for instance, in *Wuthering Heights* or the novels of Joseph Conrad. Dickens tells his story in a straightforward way, narrating events in the order in which they occurred (except for passages where he shifts attention from one set of characters to another, and must bring us up to date by a brief recapitulation). The pace of the narrative is, however, rapid – considerably more so than Dickens's other novels, and certainly more rapid than other 'industrial novels' of the period, like Mrs Gaskell's *Mary Barton* (1848) or Disraeli's *Sybil* (1845). This rapid pace is partly the result of the condensation of several years' doings into a relatively short text, but it is also the result of the drastic curtailment of *description*, compared with Dickens's usual practice. There are, of course, vivid and memorable descriptions of people and places in *Hard Times*, but they are highly compressed, and overtly symbolic rather than realistic in function. The description of Mr Gradgrind's physiognomy and physique (I,1) and house (I,2) in metaphorical terms of geometrical regularity, mercantile accountancy, etc., is representative. Location is described in the same way, with a few bold strokes: the brick-red and soot-black city of Coketown, with its ugly, uniform civic architecture, its anonymous crowds of workers moving backwards and forwards at fixed intervals between their mean, identical dwellings and the factories that are ironically likened to brightly lit palaces, in which the pistons of the steam engines 'worked monotonously up and down, like the head of an elephant in a state of melancholy madness' (I, 5). Dickens's often remarked technique of describing the animate in terms of the inanimate, and vice versa, here attains a stark, cartoon-like simplicity and economy of means. And since description always suspends the onward flow of narrative, this economy has the effect of speeding up the narrative tempo of *Hard Times* – an effect increased by the breaking up of the text into very short chapters. Authorial commentary, too, is more self-denying in terms of space than equivalent passages in, say, *Dombey and Son* or *Bleak House*. These features of

Hard Times were no doubt partly dictated by the weekly serial publication in *Household Words* for which it was originally written – but only partly. Other novels by Dickens originally published in the same way, such as *The Old Curiosity Shop* or *Great Expectations*, have quite different and more leisurely rhythms. The basic rhythm of *Hard Times* is the alternation of highly compressed and stylised authorial narration/description/commentary with dialogue between the characters, presented in a scenic or dramatic fashion, with comparatively little comment or analysis from the authorial voice. In these dialogue scenes, the tempo of the text approximates to that of 'real life', but it rarely becomes slower, because Dickens does not linger to examine motives and responses in great detail.

I turn now to 'point of view'. *Hard Times* is narrated by an authorial voice who occasionally refers to himself as 'I' and whom it is natural to regard as a literary persona of the 'Charles Dickens' whose name appears on the title page, In other words, he is a reliable narrator, whose values and opinions we are invited to adopt. He is also omniscient, in the sense that he knows all there is to be known about the characters and their actions, though he withholds or postpones the revelation of his knowledge in the interests of narrative. He is intrusive, constantly drawing attention to his mediation of the story by the highly rhetorical language he uses, and by making polemical, didactic comments from time to time on matters of education, politics, social justice, etc. The entire novel, considered as a discourse, is uttered by the authorial voice, except for the direct speech of the characters. But while the author reports everything, he frequently restricts himself to reporting what this or that particular character *perceives*. Thus, by restricting the narrative to the limited and fallible perspective of a character, suspense and mystery are generated, by making the reader share the uncertainty of the character.

The characters in the novel are grouped in various clusters:

1   the Gradgrind family
2   the Bounderby ménage
3   the workers
4   the circus folk

What the narrative does is to bring members of these clusters into contact with each other, and occasionally to shift them from one cluster to another (thus, Louisa and Tom move from 1 to 2, Sissy from 4 to 1, and Mrs Pegler from 3 to 2) in ways which generate enigma and suspense and at the same time illustrate in moral terms certain ideas about culture and society which are explicitly formulated by the authorial voice. Of these effects enigma is probably the least important. It would be a very slow-witted reader who did not guess that Tom committed the robbery, and that Mrs Pegler is Bounderby's mother, long before these facts are made plain to the characters. Compared with Dickens's other novels, the plot of *Hard Times* depends little upon mystery for its interest. The main source of simple narrative interest lies in suspense – in such questions as: will Louisa commit adultery? will Stephen be found and cleared of suspicion? will Tom escape from Bitzer? Most important of all is the didactic, illustrative import of the story, which is principally communicated by a series of ironic reversals or peripeteias. Thus the falsity of Mr Gradgrind's Utilitarian philosophy of life is demonstrated by the failure of his educational system as applied to his own children and to others. Louisa is so emotionally starved by her upbringing that she makes a loveless marriage and is thus rendered vulnerable to seduction by Harthouse, whom Gradgrind has himself introduced to Coketown in pursuance of his Utilitarian political interests; Tom grows up to be a wastrel and a thief, and when Mr Gradgrind tries to rescue him from public disgrace he is almost prevented by the model pupil of his own school, Bitzer, who produces impeccably Utilitarian reasons for his intervention.[8] Sissy Jupe, by contrast, who was ineducable by Gradgrind's system, has developed into a young woman of shining character on whom Gradgrind himself has come to depend heavily for moral support and practical assistance. The motif of ironic reversal permeates the whole novel. Mrs Sparsit's efforts to ingratiate herself with Mr Bounderby and vent her own spleen twice misfire – once in connection with Louisa's suspected elopement and a second time when she arrests Mrs Pegler, a scene which also constitutes a humiliating reversal for Bounderby himself.

The above description of the form of *Hard Times* does not, however, take us very far towards defining what is distinctive about this novel. Most of Dickens's novels concern several clusters of characters drawn from different ranks of society, between whom the plot sets up interesting and instructive connections, and most are narrated by an omniscient and intrusive authorial voice, who, however, often limits himself to articulating what is perceived by certain characters. Indeed, one might say this is the form of most classic English novels from Scott to George Eliot. *Hard Times* is unusual in that there are no characters whose pespectives dominate the novel, which is another way of saying that it has no hero or heroine: no character or pair of characters in whose fortune the reader develops an overriding interest. Sissy, Louisa and Stephen Blackpool are all possible candidates for such a role, but we are never allowed to share their perspectives in a sufficiently sustained way as to really identify with them. Indeed, we hardly ever get inside the girls' heads at all – they are primarily objects in the perceptual fields of other characters; and Stephen, though presented in a more interiorised fashion, is not in the foreground of the novel long enough to dominate it (out of thirty-seven chapters, he appears in only nine). The characters whose viewpoints are adopted by the narrator for any significant length of time are the morally unreliable characters like Mr Gradgrind in the early chapters of Book I, or Harthouse and Mrs Sparsit in Book II. But none of them is allowed to dominate the book either. The overall impression is of rapid and constant shifts of perspective, not only from one chapter to another, but often within a single chapter. No character is allowed to dominate, and no character is interiorised to any significant extent. We learn what they think and feel from what they say – aloud and to each other. The narrative is built up of scenes rather than episodes, explicit verbal interchanges between characters. The scene in the schoolroom, the scene at the Pegasus's Arms, the interview between Louisa and her father to discuss Bounderby's proposal, the corresponding scene in which she returns, a fugitive from Harthouse's attention, to reproach Gradgrind for the way she was brought up, the speeches at the workers' meetings and Stephen Blackpool's two confrontations with Bounderby, Harthouse's insidious *tête-à-têtes* with Louisa and Tom, and his verbal defeat by Sissy in his hotel – these and many similar scenes are the building blocks out of which *Hard Times* is constructed. Even the authorial voice is very much a speaking voice: not a ruminative essayist, or even a fireside conversationalist, but an orator, a pulpit-thumper, a Chorus.

Dickens's lifelong interest in the theatre and theatricals is well-known, and the theatrical quality of his literary genius has been remarked by more than one critic. That this influence is particularly evident in *Hard Times*, and that it can alienate readers who expect a more subtle and realistic representation of life in novels, was shrewdly observed by Dickens's great contemporary, John Ruskin:

The usefulness of that work (to my mind, in several respects, the greatest he has written) is with many persons seriously diminished because Mr Bounderby is a dramatic monster instead of a characteristic example of a worldly master; and Stephen Blackpool a dramatic perfection instead of a characteristic example of an honest workman. But let us not lose the use of Dickens's wit and insight, because he chooses to speak in a circle of stage fire.[9]

A sympathetic reading of *Hard Times*, then (which is not to say an uncritical reading), must recognise that its method is to a considerable extent borrowed from the popular theatre. The point may be illustrated by comparing Dickens's novel with that peculiarly British theatrical

institution, the pantomime. Originally a form of mime, with its roots in
the Italian Commedia del Arte, the pantomime became in the course of
the nineteenth century a mixed form of narrative drama, usually based
on some traditional story such as a fairy-tale, combining music, dance,
spectacle, broad humour, slapstick and strong melodrama, with audience participation in the form of hissing, booing and cheering. It is
still, of course, an extremely popular form of entertainment – indeed,
the annual visit to the Christmas pantomime is the only occasion on
which the average British family patronises the live theatre.

There are several reasons why it seems useful to invoke the pantomime in defining the distinctive quality of *Hard Times*. First of all,
something very like pantomime is actually represented in the novel. The
entertainment provided by Sleary's Horse-Riding is not, like our
modern circuses, pure spectacle, but has a strong narrative and dramatic
element. Sissy's father, for instance, plays the leading role in 'the novel
and laughable hippo-commedietta of the Tailor's Journey to Brentford'
(I, 4) and Tom is disguised as a black servant in a presentation of 'Jack
the Giant-Killer' (III, 7). Dickens, then, invites our approval not only of
the values which the circus folk embody (loyalty, generosity, spontaneity, etc.) but also of the art which they practice. Secondly, as I have
demonstrated elsewhere,[10] the text of *Hard Times* is saturated with
allusions to the world of fairy tale and nursery rhyme with which
pantomimes are characteristically concerned: ogres and witches and
dragons and fairies, old women on broomsticks, the cow with the
crumpled horn, Peter Piper, and so on. Mr Gradgrind's ruthless exclu-
sion of this kind of fantasy from his children's education is a primary
index of what is wrong with his system:

'And what,' asked Mr Gradgrind, in a still lower voice, 'did you
read to your father, Jupe?'
'About the Fairies, sir, and the Dwarf, and the Hunchback and the
Genies,' she sobbed out; 'and about – '
'Hush!' said Mr Gradgrind, 'that is enough. Never breathe a word of
such destructive nonsense any more. Bounderby, this is a case for
rigid training, and I shall observe it with interest.' (I, 8)

Thirdly, and perhaps most importantly, the characters themselves tend
to act out roles that derive from the same literary and dramatic traditions. Thus Louisa and Tom first figure as the brother and sister pair
who often appear in fairy tales (e.g. the Babes in the Wood, another
item in Sleary's repertoire) threatened by various dangers – in their
case, the 'ogre' their father (I, 8). Bounderby is a giant in a castle as
far as Stephen Blackpool is concerned ('Stephen . . . turned about and
betook himself as in duty bound, to the red brick castle of the giant

Bounderby' (II, 5)), but he also owes a lot to the very traditional comic figure of the Braggart or *miles gloriosus*, the boastful soldier who is really a coward. As the Gradgrind children grow up, Louisa becomes a princess threatened with enchantment by a bad fairy or witch (Mrs Sparsit, willing Louisa to descend the 'Giant's Staircase'), Tom is the thieving knave, and Harthouse a demon king invariably wreathed in smoke:

smoking his cigar in his own easy way, and looking pleasantly at the whelp, as if he knew himself to be a kind of agreeable demon who had only to hover over him, and he must give up his whole soul if required. (II, 3)

The way these characters interact is theatrical in a bold, explicit, conventionalised manner typical of pantomime and other forms of popular theatre. I will give three examples. First, the scene in which Sissy tells Harthouse that he must give up any hope of winning Louisa and leave Coketown immediately. Sissy combines, in the novel, the roles of Cinderella (at first the most despised, later the most valued member of the family) and Fairy Godmother (Mr Gradgrind, in III, 7, 'raised his eyes to where she stood, like a good fairy in his house'), and her success in dispatching the demon tempter Harthouse depends on our acceptance of these stereotypes rather than on the persuasiveness of her arguments or the plausibility of Harthouse's motivation. The second scene is the one in which the mysterious old woman who, Bounderby observes, 'seems to have been flying into the town on a broomstick now and then', and whom he suspects of being involved in the bank robbery, is revealed to be his mother and thus exposes the falsity of his claims to have dragged himself up from the gutter. The highly theatrical feature of this scene, apart from the fact that it is nearly all direct speech, is that a large number of townspeople pour into Bounderby's house to witness the confrontation. It is implausible that they should have been admitted in the first place and still more so that they are permitted to remain after Bounderby has recognised his mother. But realism is sacrificed to a theatrical denouement, the whole 'company' on stage to mark, ritually, Bounderby's exposure. The third scene is when Louisa returns to her father and reproaches him with his failure to educate her emotions in the past. Louisa is given lines and gestures that belong entirely to the stage, and the chapter (the last one in Book II) ends with a strong 'curtain line' and symbolic tableau in which the novel's primary theme is made heavily explicit:

'Now, father, you have brought me to this. Save me by some other means!'

He tightened his hold in time to prevent her sinking on the floor, but she cried out in a terrible voice, 'I shall die if you hold me! Let me fall upon the ground!' And he laid her down there, and saw the pride of his heart and the triumph of his system, lying, an insensible heap, at his feet.

This scene owes more to melodrama than to pantomime, and it is precisely in this respect that Dickens's reliance on the conventions of the popular stage creates most problems for his readers, especially modern ones. To treat the 'Condition of England' theme in the style of pantomime was a brilliantly imaginative stroke. First of all, it relieved Dickens of the obligation to present Utilitarianism, trade unionism or the workings of industrial capitalism, with any kind of objective, detailed verisimilitude – something he lacked the necessary experience and technical knowledge to accomplish in any case. Secondly, by invoking the world of fairy-tale *ironically*, making the inhabitants of this drab, gritty, Victorian mill town re-enact the motifs of folk-tale and legend, he drew attention to that repression or elimination of the human faculty of imagination (he calls it 'Fancy') which he believed was the culturally disastrous effect of governing society according to purely materialistic, empirical criteria of 'utility'. This double effect is epitomised by the recurrent description of the factories of Coketown as 'fairy palaces': instead of a realistic description of a factory, full of documentary detail, we get an ironic metaphor. To complain of the lack of realism is to miss the point of the metaphor. In *Hard Times* Dickens seems to be attempting something comparable to the 'alienation effect' of Bertolt Brecht's plays: to defamiliarise not merely the subject-matter of the story, so that we perceive it freshly, but also the method of presentation itself, so that instead of lapsing into a passive enjoyment of the illusion of life, instead of reacting emotionally to the story, we are compelled to recognise its artificiality and to consider its ideological implications. Dickens is not, however, so consistent and thoroughgoing as Brecht – and it would be anachronistic to expect him to be. In some parts of *Hard Times* – such as Louisa's scene with her father, or Stephen Blackpool's death scene – he exploits the techniques of popular theatre to encourage an emotional, indeed sentimental, response to the story, and seems to evade the awkward questions about class, capitalism and social justice that he himself has raised. *Hard Times* is not a totally satisfactory novel, but when we consider the boldness of Dickens's experiment, we should perhaps be more impressed by the degree of his success than by the novel's imperfections.

4 Oedipuss: or, The Practice and Theory of Narrative

Guess What Happened?
    a short story
'If anybody has forgotten anything', said Dorothy, as
their heavily laden car drew away from the house and
headed for the motorway, 'say so now, or for ever hold
your peace.'

'Will we be in time for the ferry?' said Susan, the   5
youngest of the three children on the back seat.

'We shall if we don't have to go back to turn off
the bathroom tap,' said her mother.

Last year it had been the bathroom tap. The year
before that, someone had broken a window just as they   10
were leaving. And the year they went camping, they
left a dozen tins of cat food behind for Ollie, but
took the tin-opener away with them, to the considerable
inconvenience of the neighbours who came in to feed
their pet. Holiday departures were always occasions of   15
stress and error. 'But this year', said Dorothy, 'we
seem to have got away without a hitch. Touch wood.'
She tapped the dashboard fascia.

'That's plastic,' observed her husband, Adrian, who
was driving.   20

'Never mind,' said Dorothy, 'I'm not superstitious.
By the way, what on earth were you doing half an hour
ago? I looked out of the front bedroom window and saw
you tearing off up the road in the car, and then about
ten minutes later I looked out of the back bedroom   25
window and you were in the garden, digging.'

'I'll tell you later,' said Adrian.

'That sounds suspicious,' said his eldest, Jonathan.

'What happened, Daddy?' said Rosemary, the middle
child.   30

46

'Try and guess,' said Adrian. 'It'll pass the time
on the journey. Scene One: man dashes out of house,
jumps into car loaded with holiday gear and drives off
like a bat out of hell. Scene Two, ten minutes later,
same man is observed digging in his back garden. Now   35
what connection could there be between the two events?'
   Nobody could guess, but Adrian refused to tell
them the answer, and after a while they grew bored with
the game and forgot all about it. Not until they were
driving back towards home three weeks later did he remind   40
them. The car was much less heavily laden now because
most of their luggage had been stolen during a stop in
Versailles. Jonathan's arm was in a sling, Dorothy could
not see properly because she had lost her contact lenses,
and the two girls were covered from head to toe with an   45
unidentified rash. It had not been a very successful
holiday.
   'You see,' said Adrian, 'half an hour before we were
due to leave, I discovered that we hadn't enough cat
food to leave behind for Ollie. So I jumped into the   50
car and rushed off to the shops to get some more tins.
Well, when I got back I found poor Ollie in the gutter,
dead. He'd been run over.'
   A wail of horror and grief rose from the back seat.
   '*You* ran him over!' said Jonathan accusingly.   55
   'Well, yes, I'm rather afraid I did.' said Adrian.
'On my way to the shops. Backed out of the drive a
bit too fast for him, I suppose. Of course, he was
getting old. . . Anyway, there was nothing to be done,
except bury him in the back garden.'   60
   At this point Susan began sobbing bitterly and
raining blows on the back of her father's head,
causing him to swerve off the road and into a ditch.
   'No wonder this holiday was cursed,' said Dorothy,
as they sat on the grass verge waiting for the break-   65
down truck. 'Killing our own cat for starters.'
   'I thought you weren't superstitious,' said Adrian.
   'Well, I mean, a black one, too,' said Dorothy. 'By
the way, what did you do with the cat food?'
   'Buried it with Ollie.'   70
   'Wasn't that a rather superstitious thing to do?'
   'I suppose it was,' said Adrian. 'Perhaps I should
have thrown in a tin-opener.'

I make no claims for the literary value of the story reproduced above.
I think it may seem less feeble when listened to than when read, because
I wrote it for radio; but it did not apparently please the BBC producer
to whom it was submitted, and as far as I know it was never broadcast.
Shortly after I wrote it I had to prepare a talk for an academic audience
on the theory of narrative; and since the genesis and composition of
this story were fresh in mind, and the various versions it had passed
through could be displayed in a small space, I decided to use it as an
illustrative case, combining authorial introspection with formal analysis
in the hope that this bifocal view of a narrative text might throw some
light on the laws of narrative in general and literary narrative in particular. If a certain egotism is inseparable from such an exercise, I hope it
will be mitigated by the manifest slightness of the text, in which no one
could pretend to take great pride. For the purpose of the exercise, it
is necessary only that the story should be 'well-formed' in the gram-
matical sense – i.e. acceptable as a story by competent readers of, or
listeners to, stories. That is as much as I am prepared to claim for
'Guess What Happened?'

The source of the story was an anecdote which I heard in the senior
common room at the University of East Anglia. A number of people
were sitting around drinking coffee, and the conversation had turned to
cats, and the problems of caring for pets at holiday times. One of our
number told the story of a friend who, just as her family were about to
depart for their annual holiday, looked out of the window of the front
bedroom of her house and saw her husband driving off up the road in a
great hurry, then a few minutes later looked out of the back bedroom
window and was surprised to see her husband digging in the garden.
'What had happened', explained the narrator, 'was that her husband had
discovered there wasn't enough cat food to leave behind for the neighbours to feed the cat with, so he rushed off to the shops to get some
more, and when he got back he found that he'd run over the cat. So he
had to take it into the back garden and bury it.' I cannot swear that
these were her exact words, but this was the full narrative content of
the story as far as I can remember. All of us present thought it was very
funny, and also poignant. When, a few months later, the producer of a
radio magazine programme invited me to write a piece of fiction that
would not take more than four minutes to read aloud, it seemed a
promising subject for a very short story.

   In comparing the *donné* of the story with the written text in all its
various stages (reproduced in the Appendix), the first and most obvious
point to emerge is the difference between telling a 'true story' and
producing a literary fiction. This difference can be broken down into
differences of *context* and of *motivation*. The context of the telling of

the original anecdote was real life as guaranteed by the physical presence of the narrator, whose human personality imparted to the story
much of its persuasive force, and compensated, as it were, for the lack
of specificity concerning the actors in the story. The motivation of the
original anecdote was to contribute to a conversation about pets,
holidays, etc., with a 'capping' effect. (No one could cap this story
and it brought the conversation to an end.) The same effect can operate
in literary fictions with multiple stories and story-tellers (e.g. *The
Decameron, The Canterbury Tales*) but it is never the *primary* motivation, attributable to the implied author of the whole work.

To turn an anecdote into a literary fiction is axiomatically to deprive
it of its original motivation and contextual support, and therefore the
author is obliged to supply alternative means of support that will be
internal to the text. The first obvious way of doing this is to give the
characters names, a certain amount of psychological and behavioural
individuality (very minimal, in this example, because of its extreme
brevity), and to fill out the basic action which gives rise to the story
(here, Going on Holiday) with some detail. The purpose of these moves
is to overcome the initial resistance and inertia of the reader or listener
(whose posture is quite unlike that of the already 'warmed-up' audience
of the original anecdote) and to create an illusion of reality so that the
reader/listener can get interested in the story, and believe in its plausibility, without any external authentication. In short, to give the narrative what French critics call *vraisemblance.*

The second thing that has to be done to turn an anecdote into a
literary fiction is to provide it with a motivation – an answer to the
reader's potential question: 'What's the point?' This is usually more
difficult than providing *vraisemblance*, but in this case the original anecdote already had an inherent literary motivation which might be expressed as the theme of Irony of Fate. It was the way in which the
symmetrical structure of the anecdote mirrored its ironic content –
the man who, going out to get food for his pet, returns to find that he
has killed it – which had caught my fancy in the first place. In the
original anecdote, too, the basic ironic contrast between intention and
performance was mirrored in the wife's puzzled observation of her
husband's strange behaviour, first from the front of the house and then
at the back. The anecdote, in short, involved enigma as well as irony,
and of course this is a very powerful combination in narrative. The
postponement of the recognition of irony by enigma gives the eventual
discovery additional force, and affords the reader the pleasure of being
vicariously in a state of uncertainty which, however, carries no practical
consequences for him (as it does for the characters), and which he is
confident of having resolved by the end of the narrative. In this respect,
and others, my story corresponds to what Roland Barthes calls the

lisible, or reader-oriented text. The composition of the story, and its modification through various drafts, could, then, be described as a process of trying to enrich the inherent literary motivation of the original anecdote, and making all the merely *vraisemblable* details contribute to that motivation.

The combination of enigma and irony in the basic narrative raises the interesting question – who is to be the subject of the story: the husband or the wife? The original anecdote was, in telling, rather biased towards the wife's point of view (perhaps because the teller was herself a woman) and the emphasis was on enigma. In retelling the anecdote it would have been quite easy to make the husband the exclusive subject of the story, presenting it from his point of view, perhaps using him as a first person narrator. This would preserve the irony, but sacrifice the enigma, and impoverish rather than enrich the motivation. I do not think I ever considered such a treatment. From the first draft I was quite sure I wanted to preserve the double subject – which, given the very compressed dimensions of the story, meant that the narration would be essentially objective-impersonal in mode, conveying only information which was shared by husband and wife, information which was not shared being conveyed from one to the other by direct speech. In Gérard Genette's terms, the 'voice' of the story is authorial and the perspective common to husband and wife; but since the authorial narrator speaks in the same idiom as the characters (an effect sometimes called 'stylistic contagion') there is no significant aesthetic distance between voice and perspective in this story.

My basic strategy in the first draft of the story ('MS' in the Appendix) was to extend the structure of the given anecdote in time, backwards and forwards. The departure for the holiday is established as one of a *set* of departures, each one of which has been marked by some mishap (lines 14–22). By delaying the revelation of the solution to the enigma, the element of irony is doubled, since Dorothy thinks that *this* holiday departure is an exception to the rule of mishap (3–4) but discovers later that it was not. A note of hubris is thus introduced at the beginning of the story, and acknowledged by Dorothy in her reference to touching wood. It is ominously as well as humorously ironic that there is no wood in the car. The element of enigma is heavily foregrounded by making Adrian turn Dorothy's casual question into a riddle for his children, and postpone giving the answer; also by the title, which I decided on at this stage. What the first version does, in short, is to multiply the structural components inherent in the original source, and make them contribute to a thematic pattern: Irony of Fate. There is also an addition to the characters in the source – the children. I think I introduced them in the first place in the interests of *vraisemblance*; but they proved to have a narrative function in the story which became steadily more important in the course of the various drafts. Even in the first draft, Adrian becomes a more isolated figure because of their presence, defined not only in terms of the opposition husband/wife, but also in terms of the opposition father/family. The children emphasise his guilt by their questions (31-3) and accusations (55-60).

Looking at the manuscript itself, I find a good deal of cancellation and revision of the passage around line 60 where Adrian, having confessed his deed, tries to minimise his guilt. I was evidently not sure at this point what weight to give to this theme of guilt. This uncertainty was probably connected to another problem, which continued to bother me right up to the final stage of revision: the question of how to end the story. I felt instinctively that to end the story where the original anecdote ended – with the solution of the enigma – would be anticlimactic. The reason perhaps is that as the story stands at this stage, no *consequences* follow from Adrian's confession – its import is all retrospective. I tried to get round this by what might be called the device of the double ending. That is, in order to take some of the weight of expectation off your 'real' ending, you carry on for a little and produce a second, rather more muted and enigmatic punch-line to deflect possible criticism that the 'real' ending is too neat, or too predictable, or too banal. In this case I reverted, for my second ending, to the tin-opener joke (18-22). This had been introduced in the first place as a way of conveying to the reader that the family had a cat, and that they had to leave cat food behind when they went away on holiday, without giving away the fact that these items of information would be crucial to the solution of the enigma. This is a very familiar device in all mystery stories: item A, which is a clue to enigma C, is disguised as an instance of B, thus permitting a later discovery that is both surprising and convincing. The little joke about the cat not being expected to open the tins himself was a mere decorative flourish, but in looking for my second punch-line I reverted to it: if it is humorously paradoxical to make a cat dependent for sustenance upon food sealed in tins, it is still more paradoxical, indeed irrational, to supply a dead cat with tinned food. Adrian, pressed by Dorothy, says he does not know why he buried the tins of food with the cat. Dorothy suggests a quasi-religious, ritualistic motive which Adrian in the MS seems to parody rather than endorse with his reference to a tin-opener. This repetition of reference to the tin-opener may be said to illustrate another characteristic feature of literary narrative, the principle of economy – of making one semantic unit perform more than one function. It still made what seemed to me a rather lame ending to my story.

The next version of the story ('1st TS' in the Appendix) modified the treatment of the solution of the enigma in two respects. Firstly, Adrian's explanation that he was digging in the back garden because he was burying the cat is brought forward from after Susan's assault to before – I think on the grounds that the reader would instantly guess that this was the case as soon as Adrian confessed to killing the animal. Secondly, there is a significant modification to Adrian's speech at lines 60–64 in the MS. This now reads (lines 56–9 in the 1st TS):

Conscious of a shocked and reproachful silence in the car, he added: 'I was pretty upset at the time, I can tell you. I mean, it's no way to start a holiday, running over your own cat, a black one, too.'

Before writing this I had not given any thought to the colour of the cat. The motivation for doing so now was, I think, to emphasise Adrian's moral isolation. Having made his confession, he finds that the moral disapproval of his family is more intense than he had anticipated. Trying to excuse himself or mitigate the offence, he merely adds to it. He claims to have been upset by the discovery that he had killed the cat, but when he says, 'a black one, too', he reveals that his regret is purely selfish (fear of incurring bad luck) and he reduces the family pet to the status of a mere object or fetish. It is this callous phrase which triggers off Susan's violent reaction.

But this phrase about the black cat now exerted a fatal fascination on me, by suggesting a new motivation for the whole story, namely Nemesis, the working out of a curse. Suppose Adrian's misgivings should have been spectacularly confirmed by events during the holiday, and then further confirmed immediately after he made his confession? The second typescript revised the story in this way. The passage beginning at line 40 in the first typescript was changed to read: 'The car was much less heavily laden now because they had had most of their luggage stolen in France. Jonathan's arm was in a sling, etc.' This seemed to me a great improvement on the grounds of economy, since it replaced a passage of rather inert realistic detail (sand, shells, orange peel, *etc.*) designed merely to signify Homecoming from Holiday. In this version, Adrian's reflection about the cat being black is postponed to provide the second punch-line, and the second reference to the tin-opener is deleted.

This, of course, constituted a considerable change in the motivation of the story. In this version, Adrian is the possessor of unwelcome knowledge of which the rest of the family is ignorant: that their holiday is cursed before it has properly begun. The action thus falsifies Dorothy's confidence that they had got away without a hitch, and also falsifies her scepticism about superstition. To emphasise this point, I added to her remark 'I'm not superstitious' the words 'like you' (lines 21–2).

I tried this version of the story out on my two teenage children and as a result of a comment from one of them, I decided to change the name of the cat from Moggins to Ollie. Moggins, it seemed, was too arch, too Enid Blytonish a name. Ollie is a more individual, more human name, which makes the cat seem more like a member of the family, and this strengthened the motivation for the children's shocked reaction at his death. I was beginning dimly to perceive, though I had not fully worked it out, that the story, like its source, was essentially a story of filicide, rather than felicide, the cat being a kind of surrogate child; and that it had certain similarities with myths, like the Oedipus myth, which deal with the consequences of accidentally undervaluing a blood-relationship.

In this form,* then, the story was sent off to the BBC producer who had invited it. She was not very happy with the story, and had reservations, especially about the ending. She said that she found the punchline about the black cat a let-down. After some argument and thought I came to the conclusion that she was right, for two reasons: first, the new ending narrowed and limited the import of the story by seeming to endorse a merely proverbial superstition about black cats. It implied that if the cat had not been black the family would have been all right, whereas the earlier drafts of the story had suggested that a much deeper and more important taboo had been broken: the act of killing *one's own* cat – a kind of filicide. Second, the new ending damaged the psychological consistency of the characterisation of Adrian, who, if he had been truly superstitious, would not have turned the killing of the cat into a rather heartless guessing game in the car.

Perhaps because my thoughts were already turning towards the paper on narrative theory that would soon be due, I was more and more struck by similarities between my story and the Oedipus legend, a story which has fascinated narratologists from Aristotle to Lévi-Strauss. Oedipus, who leaves Corinth to avoid killing his father and marrying his mother, unknowingly commits both these unnatural acts as a result of that departure. Adrian, going out of his house to get food to keep his cat alive, by that very action kills it. Oedipus' acts, though unintentional, bring plague and misfortune upon his family. So, apparently, does Adrian's deed. (The plague-like associations of the unidentified rash, which I inserted into the text before I became consciously aware of parallels with the Oedipus story, are particularly interesting.) In the myth, Oedipus solves a riddle and

---

*As the change of the cat's name is the only difference between the second and third typescripts, they have been conflated in the Appendix.

brings about the death of the Sphinx who proposed it, but when he inquires into the riddle of his own origins, the answer proves to be his own condemnation. Adrian proposes a riddle to his family, the answer to which is, more simply, his own condemnation. The car accident which follows the revelation of Adrian's guilt is parallel to the disasters which overtake Oedipus, Jocasta and their children.

These parallels would seem to support Northrop Frye's contention that all literary texts, however modern and 'realistic', are always displaced variations on certain mythical archetypes. In the case of my story, of course, the degree of displacement is enormous, but it still seems plausible that the reason the original source-anecdote had impressed me was that it exhibited the same symmetrical pattern of ironies, involving a matter of life and death, as the Oedipus legend; and that, like the Oedipus legend, though more faintly, it carried the same implication: that we are not masters of our own destinies. If my story was, then, alluding unconsciously over the space of centuries, from a civilisation of advanced technology, empiricism and materialism (represented metonymically by motor cars, canned food, plastic fascia boards, contact lenses, etc.) to a civilisation still essentially religious and magical in its world view, regulating life according to ritual and taboo, then it was also about the irruption of that older, more primitive consciousness, with its associated emotions of religious fear and awe, into the secularised world of the twentieth century; it was about the 'return of the repressed', in an occurrence which seems to invite a magical rather than a rational response. The story was, in essence, a play of two alternative views of reality, the rational and the religious (which in our culture goes by the name of superstition).

Even in the first paragraph of the first draft of the story, the note of superstition is introduced in Dorothy's reference to touching wood, and further reinforced in the first typescript by her quasi-ritualistic injunction to the family to own up to any sin of omission, or 'forever hold their peace'. Therefore, it seemed to me, as I meditated on the final revision of my story, my first thought about ending it with some reference to pagan burial customs had not been misdirected: by merely burying the cat, Adrian does no more than perform a hygienic act, but by burying the *cat food* with it he invests this act with some ritualistic significance, and perhaps reveals his own unacknowledged guilt and fear about what he has done. (It is perhaps relevant to recall here that in the sequel to the story of Oedipus, concerning the fate of his sons Eteocles and Polynices and his daughter Antigone, the question of proper burial is crucially important.) So, in my final revision of the ending, I went back to the original ending, but reworked it somewhat – made the allusion to pagan burial customs less specific than the reference to the Pharaohs in the MS, and tried to bring out the hesitation of both Dorothy and Adrian between the rational and the superstitious in the final dialogue between them. (In the absence of any authorial guidance, this hesitation should be felt by the reader/listener; in this respect the story conforms to the rule of the genre Tzvetan Todorov calls the Fantastic, in which every event is capable of a double explanation, and the ambiguity is never resolved.) Adrian's last remark is on one level a jocular allusion to the previous occasion on which they left the cat with tinned food and no tin-opener, but it also plays with the idea that the outraged spirit of the dead cat is pursuing them because the burial rites were not properly performed – Adrian 'forgot' something after all, though he was silent when Dorothy invited them all to confess any such lapse.

What, then, do I think I have learned from this exercise in narrative self-analysis? Firstly, though not for the first time, the lesson that the operations involved in writing narrative, as in using language itself, are so complex and multilayered as to make it impossible for all the choices and decisions involved to be conscious. This is a vindication of the structuralist paradox that it is not so much man that speaks language as language that speaks man; not so much the writer who writes narrative as narrative that writes the writer. Secondly, it seems to me, the exercise vindicates Roman Jakobson's assertion that literariness – that which makes a text literary, or allows it to be read as literary – is the projection of 'the principle of equivalence from the axis of selection into the axis of combination'. Stated less abstractly, this means that literary discourse is characterised by symmetry, parallelism, repetition of every kind and on every level. It is not hard to discern the recurrence of certain motifs in 'Guess What Happened?', and to group them into binary oppositions with thematic significance. Thus the motifs of departure and return are multiplied by framing the core action of Adrian's errand to the shops and his return to the house within the family's departure to and return from their holiday, and by making Adrian repeat the sequence of departure–return in formulating the riddle – a further 'embedding' of the small-scale action within the larger. The opposition between the front of the house and the back of the house in the core action is echoed by the contrast between front seat and back seat in the frame action. Adrian acts, impetuously, at the front of the house; at the back he tries to expiate the disastrous consequences of his action. In the front seat of the car he continues to act as though nothing had happened, while from the back seat his righteous children first probe his guilty conscience and then become outraged, punishing Furies. Digging is opposed to driving, and the cat's grave is equivalent to the ditch which nearly becomes the grave of Adrian and his family.

Examined in the light of Jakobson's distinction between metaphoric and metonymic discourse, 'Guess What Happened?' is readily classified as metonymic, in that it conforms structurally to the type of linguistic transformation that produces metonymy and synecdoche: deletion from and rearrangement of a syntagmatic chain of naturally contiguous items. Considered sentence by sentence, the story seems to be indistinguishable from a literal, referential report; but when one considers the 'syntax' of the narrative as a whole – the selection and ordering of its basic elements – one can see that a natural or logical sequence has been chopped up and rearranged so as to foreground those elements which are thematically important.

It may be useful at this point to introduce the distinction between *fabula* and *sjuzet* that is so central to structuralist analysis of narrative: on the one hand the story as a sequence or matrix of actions that we can conceptualise as enacted in real time and space, and on the other hand the actual narration of a story in particular words, entailing choices of order, point of view, etc. It is important to realise that the *fabula* is not the same as the source of a story (e.g. the anecdote on which 'Guess What Happened?' was based), but a hypothetical extrapolation from the *sjuzet*. Thus the *fabula* of my story would begin something like this:

Adrian, Dorothy and their three children had a cat, Ollie. Every year they took a holiday. One year they went camping, and they left some tins of cat food behind for a neighbour to feed their pet, but made the mistake of taking the tin opener away with them. Another year one of them broke a window just as they were leaving. The year after that someone left a bathroom tap running. When this was remembered they had to go back to turn it off and were late for the cross-Channel car ferry. The year after that, just before they were about to depart for their holiday, Dorothy saw, from the front bedroom window of the house, Adrian driving away rapidly in the already loaded car . . .

Most of these events did not appear in the original anecdote, but were 'invented' in the composition of the *sjuzet*. By conceptualising the *fabula* one can see how they have been arranged in the *sjuzet* to emphasise the theme of departure and raise at the very beginning the question of whether the pattern of mishaps associated with departure is going to be repeated on one particular occasion. It would be possible to go on inferring the *fabula* from the *sjuzet* in this way until one reaches that point in the story where Adrian proposes the riddle and none of the family can guess the answer (line 39 in the final text). At this point one would have to start *inventing* the *fabula*, because at no point in the composition of the *sjuzet* was it necessary to establish anything

about the holiday except its duration and the fact that it involved passing through France, and that various injuries, afflictions and losses were
incurred by all the party except Adrian. But in the realm of the *fabula*
there would, of course, have been much more specificity to the holiday: a destination, an itinerary, a sequence of actions, choices and
decisions which resulted in the various misfortunes. In other words, we
have in the *sjuzet* at this point, a massive deletion from the *fabula*. The
holiday itself has been removed from its proper chronological place, at
line 39, between the sentence that ends 'after a while they grew bored
with the game and forgot all about it' and the sentence that begins 'Not
until they were driving back. . . '. And when the holiday *is* described,
it is in a highly selective list of personal misfortunes, which are in
effect synecdoches for Calamitous Holiday.

This displacement and condensation of the narrative sequence Holiday comes approximately halfway through the text, and is to my mind
its most striking structural feature. It very obviously has the effect of
foregrounding the motif of departure and return, since in one sentence
the characters are still departing and in the next they are already
returning, and this same motif was foregrounded by the way the story
opened. In Greimas's terms, the action of the story is disjunctive –
i.e. concerned with departure and return, rather than performative or
contractual. And it is, of course, a feature of the institution of the
Holiday in our culture that the main point of the departure *is* the
return: one is supposed to come back to 'normal life' (i.e. work)
refreshed and renewed by a change of scene and temporary devotion
to nonproductive play. Yet experience teaches us that holidays are
often occasions of anxiety, discomfort, disappointment and loss which
would not have occurred if one had stayed at home. The institution of
the holiday is therefore riddled with contradiction, and Lévi-Strauss has
taught us that myths are man's way of coming to terms with contradictions between experience and belief.

Adrian would not have killed his cat if he had not been going on
holiday. Going out to get food for the cat, he kills it; by burying the
food with the cat he tries symbolically to fulfil the frustrated intention
and relieve the intolerable contradiction between intention and performance. Using the methodology of Greimas (see above, p. 18) the
story can be analysed as a narrative transformation of the four-term
homology, Life:Death :: Non-Life:Non-Death, as follows: foraging for
the cat is to killing the cat as driving is to digging. Foraging for the cat
is 'Life', and killing the cat is 'Death'; driving is 'Non-Life' because it is
aggressive (Adrian 'tears up the road'), artificial (the fascia is plastic)
and dangerous (the accident in the ditch); digging is 'Non-Death'
because it is associated firstly with growth, seasonal renewal, etc., in
the garden, and secondly with piety, resurrection, the afterlife, etc.

(the grave). In the accompanying diagram, the numbered arrows show the sequence of actions by which Adrian encounters contradiction and seeks to resolve it.

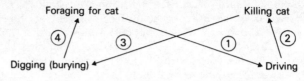

Speaking personally, I have always found family holidays a great strain.

Appendix

Guess What Happened?

MS
'Well,' said Dorothy, as the heavily loaded Cortina
drew away from the house and headed for the motorway, 'we seem to have got away without a hitch for
once. Touch wood.' She looked round the furnish-
ings of the car but there wasn't any. Adrian, in   5
the driver's seat beside her, grunted – a purely
phatic grunt indicating neither agreement nor disagreement, merely that he had heard her remark.
       'Will we be in time for the ferry?' said Susan,
the youngest of their three children, from the   10
back seat.
       'If we don't have to go back to turn off the
bathroom tap,' said Dorothy.
       Holiday departures were invariably times of
great stress, when it was easy to make mistakes   15
and forget things. Last year it had been the
bathroom tap. The year before that they had left
twelve tins of cat food for their cat, but no

2nd/3rd TS
'If anybody has forgotten anything', said Dorothy, as
their heavily laden car drew away from the house and
headed for the motorway, 'say so now, or for ever
hold your peace.'
       'Will we be in time for the ferry?' said Susan,   5
the youngest of the three children on the back seat.
       'We shall if we don't have to go back to turn off
the bathroom tap,' said her mother.
       Last year it had been the bathroom tap. The year
before that, someone had broken a window just as they   10
were leaving. And the year they went camping, they
left a dozen tins of cat food behind for Ollie, but
took the tin-opener away with them to the considerable
inconvenience of the neighbours who came in to feed
their pet. Holiday departures were always occasions   15
of stress and error. 'But this year,' said Dorothy,
'we seem to have got away without a hitch. Touch
wood.' She tapped the dashboard fascia.

Guess What Happened?

1st TS

'If anybody has forgotten anything', said Dorothy, as
the heavily laden car drew away from the house and
headed for the motorway, 'say so now, or for ever hold
your peace.'

    'Will we be in time for the ferry?' said Susan, the   5
youngest of the three children on the back seat.

    'If we don't have to go back to turn off the
bathroom tap,' said her mother.

    Last year it had been the bathroom tap. The year
before that, someone had broken a window just before   10
they were due to leave. And the year they went
camping they left a dozen tins of cat food behind for
Moggins, but took the tin-opener with them, to the
considerable inconvenience of the neighbours who
came in to feed him. Holiday departures were always   15
occasions of stress and error. 'But this year we seem
to have got away without a hitch,' said Dorothy, 'touch
wood.' She tapped the fascia.

Final text

'If anybody has forgotten anything', said Dorothy, as
their heavily laden car drew away from the house and
headed for the motorway, 'say so now, or for ever hold
your peace.'

    'Will we be in time for the ferry?' said Susan, the   5
youngest of the three children on the back seat.

    'We shall if we don't have to go back to turn off
the bathroom tap,' said her mother.

    Last year it had been the bathroom tap. The year
before that, someone had broken a window just as they   10
were leaving. And the year they went camping, they
left a dozen tins of cat food behind for Ollie, but
took the tin-opener away with them, to the considerable
inconvenience of the neighbours who came in to feed
their pet. Holiday departures were always occasions of   15
stress and error. 'But this year', said Dorothy, 'we
seem to have got away without a hitch. Touch wood.'
She tapped the dashboard fascia.

MS

tin-opener. Not that Moggins was expected to
open the tins himself – but the neighbour who   20
came in to do so had been seriously inconvenienced
since her own can-opener was attached to a wall.
    'Oh, by the way,' said Dorothy to Adrian, 'what
on earth were you doing about half an hour ago, when
I was seeing to the last-minute packing? I looked   25
out of the front bedroom window and saw you drive off
in the car like a man possessed, and then ten minutes
later I looked out of the back bedroom window and you
were in the garden, digging.'
    'I'll tell you later,' said Adrian.   30
    'It must be something bad,' said his eldest,
Jonathan, suspiciously.
    'What was it, Daddy?' said Rosemary, the middle
child.
    'Try and guess,' said Adrian. 'It will pass the   35
time on the motorway. Try and guess what happened.
Scene One: man dashes from house, jumps into car
loaded with holiday gear, drives off like a bat out

2nd/3rd TS

    'That's plastic,' observed her husband, Adrian,
who was driving   20
    'Never mind,' said Dorothy, 'I'm not super-
stitious, like you. By the way, darling, what on
earth were you doing half an hour ago? I looked
out of the front bedroom window and saw you tearing
off up the road in the car, and then about ten   25
minutes later I looked out of the back bedroom
window and you were in the garden, digging.'
    'I'll tell you later,' said Adrian.
    'That sounds suspicious,' said his eldest,
Jonathan.   30
    'What happened, Daddy?' said Rosemary, the
middle child.
    'Try and guess,' said Adrian. 'It'll pass the
time on the journey. Scene One: man dashes out of
house, jumps into car loaded with holiday gear and   35
drives off like a bat out of hell. Scene Two, ten
minutes later, same man is observed digging in his
back garden. Now, what connection could there be

1st TS

'That's plastic,' observed her husband, Adrian, who
was driving.   20
'Never mind,' said Dorothy, 'I'm not superstitious.
By the way, darling, what on earth were you doing half
an hour ago? I looked out of the front bedroom window
and saw you drive off in the car in a tearing hurry,
and then about ten minutes later I looked out of the   25
back bedroom window and you were in the back garden,
digging.'
'I'll tell you later,' said Adrian.
'That sounds suspicious,' said his eldest, Jonathan.
'What happened, Daddy?' said Rosemary, the middle   30
child.
'Try and guess,' said Adrian, 'it will pass the time
on the motorway. Scene One: Man dashes out of house,
jumps into car loaded with holiday gear, drives off
like a bat out of hell. Scene Two: ten minutes later,   35
same man is observed digging in his back garden. What
connection could there be between the two events?'
Nobody could guess, but Adrian refused to tell them

Final text

'That's plastic,' observed her husband, Adrian, who
was driving.   20
'Never mind,' said Dorothy, 'I'm not superstitious.
By the way, what on earth were you doing half an hour
ago? I looked out of the front bedroom window and saw
you tearing off up the road in the car, and then about
ten minutes later I looked out of the back bedroom   25
window and you were in the garden, digging.'
'I'll tell you later,' said Adrian.
'That sounds suspicious,' said his eldest, Jonathan.
'What happened, Daddy?' said Rosemary, the middle
child.   30
'Try and guess,' said Adrian. 'It'll pass the time
on the journey. Scene One: man dashes out of house,
jumps into car loaded with holiday gear and drives off
like a bat out of hell. Scene Two, ten minutes later,
same man is observed digging in his back garden. Now   35
what connection could there be between the two events?'
Nobody could guess, but Adrian refused to tell
them the answer, and after a while they grew bored with

MS

of hell. Scene Two, ten minutes later, same man is
observed digging in his back garden. Now. What   40
possible logical connection could there be between
the two events?'

    Nobody could guess, but Adrian refused to tell
them the answer and after a while they grew bored
with the game and forgot all about it. Not until they   45
they were driving back along the M1 three weeks
later, in a car littered with sand, shells, orange
peel and sweetpapers, did Adrian remind them.

    'You see,' he said, 'half an hour before we left
I suddenly discovered that we hadn't got enough cat   50
food to leave behind for feeding Moggins. So I dashed
out of the house and drove off to the shops to get some.
Well, when I came back I found poor old Moggins in the
gutter, dead. He'd been run over.'

    A wail of horror and grief rose from the back seat.   55

    '*You* ran him over,' said Jonathan accusingly.

    'Well, yes, I'm rather afraid I did,' said Adrian.
'Backed out of the drive a bit too fast for him, I

2nd/3rd TS

between the two events?'

    Nobody could guess, but Adrian refused to tell   40
them the answer, and after a while they grew bored
with the game and forgot all about it. Not until
they were driving back towards home three weeks later
did he remind them. The car was much less heavily laden
now because most of their luggage had been stolen   45
during a stop in Versailles. Jonathan's arm was in
a sling, Dorothy could not see properly because she
had lost her contact lenses, and the two girls were
covered from head to toe with an unidentified rash.
It had not been a very successful holiday.   50

    'You see,' said Adrian, 'half an hour before we
were due to leave, I discovered that we hadn't enough
cat food to leave behind for Ollie. So I jumped into
the car and rushed off to the shops to get some more
tins. Well, when I got back I found poor Ollie in the   55
gutter, dead. He'd been run over.'

    A wail of horror and grief rose from the back seat.

    '*You* ran him over!' said Jonathan accusingly.

1st TS
the answer, and after a while they grew bored with the
game and forgot all about it. Not until they were   40
driving back three weeks later, in a car carpeted with
sand, shells, orange peel and sweetpapers, did he remind
them.

'You see,' he said, 'half an hour before we were due
to leave, I discovered that we hadn't enough cat food to   45
leave behind for Moggins. So I dashed out of the house
and drove up to the High Street to get some more tins.
Well, when I got back I found poor old Moggins in the
gutter, dead. He'd been run over.'

A wail of horror and grief rose from the back seat.   50
'*You* ran him over!' said Jonathan accusingly.
'Well, yes, I'm rather afraid I did,' said Adrian.
'Backed out of the drive a bit too fast for him, I
expect. Of course, he was getting old . . . Anyway, there
was nothing to be done except bury him, in the back   55
garden.' Conscious of a shocked and reproachful silence
in the car, he added: 'I was pretty upset at the time,
I can tell you. I mean, it's no way to start a holiday,

Final text
the game and forgot all about it. Not until they were
driving back towards home three weeks later did he remind   40
them. The car was much less heavily laden now because
most of their luggage had been stolen during a stop in
Versailles. Jonathan's arm was in a sling, Dorothy could
not see properly because she had lost her contact lenses,
and the two girls were covered from head to toe with an   45
unidentified rash. It had not been a very successful
holiday.

'You see,' said Adrian, 'half an hour before we were
due to leave, I discovered that we hadn't enough cat
food to leave behind for Ollie. So I jumped into the   50
car and rushed off to the shops to get some more tins.
Well, when I got back I found poor Ollie in the gutter,
dead. He'd been run over.'

A wail of horror and grief rose from the back seat.
'*You* ran him over!' said Jonathan accusingly.   55
'Well, yes, I'm rather afraid I did,' said Adrian.
'On my way to the shops. Backed out of the drive a
bit too fast for him, I suppose. Of course, he was

MS

suppose. He was getting old, of course.'

    A shocked silence fell in the car. 'It was a   60
complete accident,' said Adrian defensively. 'After
all, it was for his sake that I was rushing out to
the shops.'

    At this point Susan began raining blows on the
back of her father's neck at some risk to his control   65
of the car, and had to be restrained by the rest of
the passengers.

    'So what you were doing in the garden,' Dorothy
said later, 'was burying the cat?'

    'That's right.' There wasn't time to explain   70
what had happened.

    'What did you do with the cat food?'

    'Buried it with him.'

    'Whatever for?'

    'I don't know, really.'   75

    'Just like the Pharaohs.'

    'What?'

    'Didn't they bury the Pharaohs with food beside
them? For their journey to the underworld.'

    Adrian thought for a moment. 'I should have put   80
a tin-opener in the grave in that case,' he said.

2nd/3rd TS

    'Well, yes, I'm rather afraid I did,' said
Adrian. 'On my way to the shops. Backed out of the   60
drive a bit too fast for him, I suppose. Of course,
he was getting old . . . Anyway, there was nothing to
be done, except bury him in the back garden.'

    At this point Susan began sobbing bitterly and
raining blows on the back of her father's head,   65
causing him to swerve off the road and into a ditch.

    'I knew it was going to be a rotten holiday,' said
Adrian, as they sat on the grass verge waiting
for the breakdown truck. 'Running over our own cat
for starters. A black one, too.'   70

1st TS
running over your own cat, a black one, too – '
    At this point Susan began screaming and raining   60
blows on the back of her father's neck, and had to be
forcibly restrained by the other passengers.
    Later, Dorothy asked Adrian what he had done with
the cat food.
    'Buried it with Moggins,' he replied.   65
    'Whatever for?'
    'I don't know, it seemed the natural thing to do.'
    'Like the Egyptians. Didn't they bury the Pharaohs
with food for their journey to the afterlife?'
    Adrian reflected for a moment. 'I should have   70
put a tin-opener in the grave in that case,' he said.

Final text
getting old . . . Anyway, there was nothing to be done,
except bury him in the back garden.'   60
    At this point Susan began sobbing bitterly and
raining blows on the back of her father's head,
causing him to swerve off the road and into a ditch.
    'No wonder this holiday was cursed,' said Dorothy,
as they sat on the grass verge waiting for the break-   65
down truck. 'Killing our own cat for starters.'
    'I thought you weren't superstitious,' said Adrian.
    'Well, I mean, a black one, too,' said Dorothy. 'By
the way, what did you do with the cat food?'
    'Buried it with Ollie.'   70
    'Wasn't that a rather superstitious thing to do?'
    'I suppose it was,' said Adrian. 'Perhaps I should
have thrown in a tin-opener.'

5 Historicism and Literary History: Mapping the Modern Period

Like many terms that we use in the study of literature – including the term *literature* itself – *modern* and *period* are at the same time indispensable and highly problematical. Put together in a single phrase – *the modern period* – they are paradoxical. *Period* implies an end, yet in some senses we still feel that we are living in the modern period. 'When will the Modern Period end?' Ihab Hassan has asked. 'Has ever a period waited so long? When will modernism cease and what comes thereafter?'[1] One answer is that the modern period has already ended and that we are now living in the postmodern period. Hassan himself, in the essay from which I quote, makes a useful contribution to the definition of postmodernism, but regards it as a change or development in modernism rather than a decisive break with it. In any case, the question, what comes hereafter, remains. 'The end of periodization? The slow arrival of simultaneity?' are among Hassan's apocalyptic suggestions. The Parisian *savants* of our day would I think, applaud this prospect. Lévi-Strauss, for instance, has offered the utopian vision of a world in which automation would free man to enjoy all the advantages of a timeless primitive existence and none of its disadvantages: 'Henceforth history would make itself by itself. Society, placed outside and above history, would be able to exhibit once again that regular and, as it were, crystalline structure which the best preserved of primitive societies teach us is not antagonistic to the human condition.'[2] If such a society read literary texts at all, it would surely approach them in the spirit of the *nouvelle critique*, as semantic playgrounds rather than as historical expressions or representations.

In such a society, it is safe to assume, there would be no university courses in literature, no scholarly journals, and no MLA Conventions, all of which institutions are heavily dependent on periodization for the conceptual organization of their subject-matter. The question of periodization is therefore part of a larger question about history as a mode of knowledge and its application to literature: is literary history possible, or desirable? I would say that it is certainly unavoidable, in the sense that even those writers and critics who seek to escape from or deny the historicity of literature do so on grounds that are in one sense of the word, historicist.

There are two kinds of historical consciousness which have made imperialistic claims in the modern era. Both have been vigorously attacked, and have attacked each other. Confusingly, both go under the name of historicism. It is necessary to distinguish between these two historicisms, and to identify their characteristic limitations, before questioning more closely the concept of the modern period in literature.

The first kind of historicism assumes that all human phenomena are unique and must be interpreted by reference to their historical contexts by means of a positivistic historical science. This kind of historicism has been attacked for being ideological, i.e. pretending to an objectivity and neutrality which in fact conceal specific political, economic, and intellectual prejudices. Roland Barthes's attack on the orthodox French literary history of Lanson is a well-known example of such a critique.[3] Another related objection to this kind of historicism is that it seeks artificially to restrict the infinite play of meaning that is potentially inherent in any literary text. Scholars and critics in the heyday of the Anglo-American New Criticism frequently clashed on this issue. A fundamental objection to positivistic literary historicism is that literary works are not, like the events of history, discrete, unique facts, but events that are realized in reading, and realized again and again in every reader's experience. Lately, Hans Robert Jauss has proposed taking account of this dimension of the institution of literature by means of 'reception aesthetics', investigating the ways in which specific works challenged and altered the horizon of expectations of their immediate audience, and comparing this with the place of the work in the literary historian's own horizon of expectations.[4] This is an attractive project, though perhaps more selective and less systematic in method than it admits to being. It owes a good deal to Karl Popper's philosophy of science, but literary texts are clearly very different things from scientific theories, and their impact much more difficult to measure.

The other kind of historicism is that described and attacked by Karl Popper himself. In the introduction to *The Poverty of Historicism* he defines it as 'an approach to the social sciences which assumes that *historical prediction* is their principal aim, and which assumes that this aim is attainable by discovering the "rhythms," the "patterns," the "laws" or the "trends" that underlie the evolution of history'.[5] As Popper points out, the concept of period is crucial to this kind of historicism. 'Historicism claims that nothing is of greater moment than the emergence of a really new period',[6] and that 'the only universally valid laws of society must be ... the *laws of historical development* which determine the transition from one period to another'.[7] In so far as historicism of the first kind uses the concept of period, therefore, it is borrowing from the historicism of the second kind, and to some extent compromising its own positivist claims, since a truly empirical history would be a mere chronicle with no period classifications. The important difference between the two kinds of historicism is that the one described by Popper invests the emergence of new periods with inevitability and thus a kind of imperative moral authority. According to this historicism, one should adjust one's values so as to assist and conform to the impending changes in society. Projected into the field of politics, this leads to various kinds of totalitarianism, against which Popper's book is primarily directed. But he comments that 'this historicist moral theory, which could be described as "moral modernism" or "moral futurism" . . . has its counterpart in an aesthetic modernism or futurism'.[8] Which brings me back to my subject.

There is no doubt that modernism as an aesthetic movement is historicist in Popper's sense.[9] Its major exponents have always been fond of issuing manifestos affirming the unique novelty of the modern period, and the consequent need for a radically new art. Virginia Woolf's famous saying, 'On or about December 1910, human character changed', was a consciously extravagant, but quite serious statement of a widespread modernist assumption. The precise dating of the rupture between past and present varies, of course, from one spokesman to another, as does its diagnosis. The alleged cause might be the death of God or the theory of relativity, the discovery of the unconscious or the advent of mass society, but the unanimity of opinion that modern experience is distinctively different from anything that has come before, and that modern art must revolutionize itself in response, is striking. Rimbaud's 'il faut être moderne', Pound's 'Make it new!', Eliot's 'Poets in our civilization, as it exists at present, must be difficult', are all expressions of the same imperative: to historicize the aesthetic, to aestheticize the historic. In some writers – Nietzsche, Yeats, and Lawrence come to mind – this urge tended to generate messianic delusions of grandeur and outpourings of apocalyptic prophecy. As has often been pointed out, many of the key figures in the modern movement were attracted to totalitarian political systems such as Popper associates with historicism in the social sciences, especially fascism. This has long been a puzzle and scandal to their critical admirers, who tend to be liberal or leftist. Perhaps one reason may be that there is a strong element of nihilism in fascism and modernism alike. Modernism is not content merely to serve the historical process, as the Marxist version of historicism prescribes. It is impatient to escape from history altogether. 'History is a nightmare from which I am trying to awake,' says Stephen Dedalus in *Ulysses*, and smashes the chandelier in the brothel with a cry of '*Nothung!*' causing 'Time's livid final flame' to leap. Paul de Man has culled a striking passage from Nietzsche's *Thoughts out of Season* in which the historical sense is seen as the enemy of authenticity, represented by a purely animal existence: 'the animal lives unhistorically: it hides nothing and co-incides at all moments exactly with that which it is; it is bound to be truthful at all times, unable to be anything else . . . we will therefore have to consider the ability to experience life in a non-historical way as the most important and original of experiences, as the foundation on which right, health, greatness and anything truly human can be erected'.[10] The animal here seems to enjoy the same enviable status as the primitive in the thought of Lévi-Strauss.

Now the characteristics of modernist art in general, and of modern-ist writing in particular, have been often enough described: formal experiment, dislocation of conventional syntax, radical breaches of decorum, disturbance of chronology and spatial order, ambiguity, polysemy, obscurity, mythopoeic allusion, primitivism, irrationalism, structuring by symbol and motif rather than by narrative or argumenta-tive logic, and so on. And it is easy to see how these strategies and themes reflect the sense that the modern period has a special historic destiny, perhaps to abolish history itself. The problem is that the modern period considered as a cultural entity, whatever precise chrono-logical boundaries we ascribe to it, includes a good deal of writing that is not modernist; and to accept the historicist conception of the modern period involves us in the literary equivalent of totalitar-ian politics, that is, rejecting and suppressing what does not coincide with the alleged historical necessity. An example of a literary critic who is quite happy to do this would be Roland Barthes. In *Writing Degree Zero* he proposed a typically historicist version of modern literature according to which, as a result of the failure of the 1848 revolution, 'classical writing disintegrated, and the whole of litera-ture from Flaubert to the present day, became the problematics of language'.[11] The only modern writing which is authentic in this scheme is therefore writing which is conscious of its problematical status, the *scriptible* rather than the *lisible*. As Barthes says in *S/Z*: 'On the one hand there is what it is possible to write, on the other hand what it is no longer possible to write.'[12]

Towards the end of *The Poverty of Historicism*, Popper says that the trouble with historicists is that they mistake trends for laws, and their interpretations for testable theories. Classical historians, on the other hand (by whom Popper means exponents of the first kind of histori-cism I described), make no claims to theory, but conceal their own reliance on interpretation. 'The way out of this dilemma, of course,' he says, 'is to be clear about the necessity of adopting a point of view;

to state this point of view plainly, and always to remain conscious that it is one among many, and that even if it should amount to a theory, it may not be testable.'[13] I will try to follow these injunctions in briefly outlining my own approach to the modern period in literature.

First of all, I should make clear that I am a novelist as well as a critic, a novelist who has written several books of the kind that Roland Barthes says it is no longer possible to write, i.e. novels that are continuous in technique with 'classic realism'. One reason for this, no doubt, is that I came of age in the 1950s, which happened to be a dominantly antimodernist phase in modern British literary history. There have been other dominantly antimodernist phases, or subperiods, within the larger category of the Modern Period – the 1930s, and, I would suggest, the first decade and a half of this century, between the collapse of the Decadence and the emergence of the Pound–Eliot group as a force in English letters.

Although I found the neo-realist climate of the 1950s in England congenial to my own early efforts as a novelist, I did not as a *reader* of literature accept the antimodernist polemics of Amis, Wain, Snow, Larkin, and other representative figures of the time. James, Yeats, and Joyce gave me my most rewarding and exciting literary experiences when I was a student and continued to do so when I became a teacher. As far as I am concerned, therefore, any literary historical account of the Modern period must recognize the coexistence, within its span, of at least two kinds of writing, only one of which is modernist. Stephen Spender's book, *The Struggle of the Modern* (1963), with its useful distinction between Moderns and Contemporaries, was a step in the right direction, but it did not explain the oscillating pattern of dominance by first one group and then the other. And in Spender's discussion, as in most accounts of the modern period, the two kinds of writing tended to be polarized on the form–content axis: research into form, technique as discovery, being the exclusive province of the moderns or modernists, while the contemporaries, or antimodernists, were taken at their word when they claimed to have no interest in form other than making it as transparent a medium as possible for communicating a content discovered in the real world. This polarization naturally invites partisan attitudes, the endorsement of one kind of writing at the expense of the other, that which it is possible to write and that which it is no longer possible to write.

What is needed, it has always seemed to me, is a way of mapping the literary history of the modern period which describes all the varieties of writing in it within a single conceptual scheme, without prejudging them. In *The Modes of Modern Writing* (1977), I applied Roman Jakobson's distinction between metaphoric and metonymic modes of discourse to this problem.* Like all structuralist ideas, this one presupposes that perception and cognition are relational: a phenomenon can only be identified and classified by virtue of its relations of similarity and difference with items in the same system. Metaphoric or metonymic dominance can only be established by comparison of data at the same level. Thus we might say that the modernist novel is broadly speaking dominantly metaphoric compared to the Victorian novel, but that among the major Victorians, Dickens is metaphoric compared to the more metonymic Thackeray; that early Dickens is metonymic by comparison with the later Dickens, and that the authorial chapters of *Bleak House* are dominantly metaphoric, Esther's narrative metonymic. In the same way, among the modernists Joyce is more metaphoric than, say, Lawrence; Joyce's late work more metaphoric than his early work, Stephen's stream-of-consciousness more metaphoric than Bloom's. We must take into account, too, that different genres are inherently biased towards one pole or the other, narrative being an essentially metonymic mode and lyric verse being essentially metaphoric. Modernist fiction thus displaces narrative from its natural place on the metaphor-metonymy axis; modernist poetry pushes the inherently metaphoric bias of verse to extremes.

The congruence of a dominantly metaphoric mode with that paradoxical combination of historicism and the yearning to escape from history which I mentioned earlier as being characteristic of the modernist sensibility from Nietzsche to Lévi-Strauss, may be suggested by a quotation from D. H. Lawrence's *Apocalypse*: 'To appreciate the pagan manner of thought, we have to drop our own manner of on-and-on, from a start to a finish, and allow the mind to move in cycles, or to flit here and there over a choice of images.'[14] Parts of that statement apply as well to the technique of Joyce, Yeats, Woolf, and Eliot as they do to Lawrence's own work. Antimodernist writers, on the other hand, Spender's 'contemporaries', cultivate the innately metonymic tendency of realistic art. Their novels – Bennett, Orwell, Amis would be examples taken from different generations – try to imitate as faithfully as possible the actual relations of things to each other in space–time. Characters, their actions, and the background against which they perform their actions are all knitted together by physical contiguity, temporal sequence, and logical cause and effect, and are represented in the text by a selection of synecdochic detail. Antimodernist poets – Kipling, Auden, Larkin – push verse against its natural grain in the same direction, affecting a prosaic or conversational or oratorical tone of voice,

*See also the first essay in this collection, 'Modernism, Antimodernism and Postmodernism'.

and respecting the combinational rules of orthodox logic and grammar which modernist verse delights to disrupt.

If we combine Jakobson's typology of discourse with the Russian Formalist theory of literary dynamics as a process driven by the automatization and defamiliarization of perception, a new style being developed because the old style has exhausted its expressive possibilities, then we have an explanation of why there seems to be a cyclical rhythm to literary history; why innovation is so often a return to the last fashion but one in some respects; why, within the modern period, phases of metaphoric experiment seem to alternate with phases of metonymic realism. If Jakobson is right, there is nowhere for writing to go except between these two poles.

To talk of rhythms and cycles in literary history, I am aware, sounds suspiciously close to Popper's characterization of historicism. But as long as the structuralist approach to literary history remains true to its formalist origins, it does not, I think, fall foul of Popper's critique. It is not intolerant, exclusive, prescriptive. On the contrary, it is inclusive and evenhanded. Its predictive power is limited to the claim that sooner or later the dominant literary mode will give way to something that is in some ways its opposite, but the texts in which this change will be manifested cannot be predicted or even imagined.

Prediction seems particularly hazardous at present, because it is difficult to say what the dominant literary mode *is* now, certainly in England, and perhaps in America, or to place it on the metaphor-metonymy axis. This may be a familiar problem of perspective, that we are too close to our own art to distinguish the important from the trivial. Or it could be that our liveliest writers, having consciously or intuitively grasped the structural principles of the literary system, have ganged up to cheat it: refusing to choose between a dominantly metaphoric or metonymic mode of writing, they employ both, in extreme, contradictory, often absurd or parodic ways, within the same work or body of work. If this is the case, it would be consistent with another of Popper's axioms, namely, that in the field of human culture prediction is impossible because, however well-founded, it is bound to provoke actions designed to upset it.

To sum up: the concept of a period, whether in history at large or in literary history, is not a fact, but an interpretation, a human selection and grouping of facts for human purposes, collectively generated and modified by an endless process of redescription. A distinctively *literary* history ought to be founded in the description of literary form, but there is no single characterization of literary form that will account for all that is literature in the modern period. If there is one modern period that begins some time in the late nineteenth century and still goes on, the terms of its definition must be sought beyond boundaries of the arts, in the alteration of human consciousness by developments in science, applied science, philosophy, and psychology. Different writers and groups of writers have responded to the experience of this larger modernity in different ways at different times and places. There is no single period style for the modern period, but a variety of styles. But this variety can be reduced to an intelligible order if we refer it to what is constant and finite in literature as a signifying system, mapping the diachronic on the grid of the synchronic.

Part II

Reading Hardy

6 The Woodlanders:
A Darwinian Pastoral Elegy

In the chronology of Thomas Hardy's fiction *The Woodlanders* (1887) comes between *The Mayor of Casterbridge* (1886) and *Tess of the d'Urbervilles* (1891). In his later years Hardy often said that it was 'in some respects . . . his best novel',[1] yet of his major works it is probably the least well known, and has certainly attracted least attention from scholars and critics. It is difficult to account for this relative neglect, for if *The Woodlanders* is not quite 'the finest English novel', as Arnold Bennett roundly declared,[2] it is demonstrably a work of mature, original artistry and considerable charm. Perhaps the reason is that among the 'Novels of Character and Environment' to which it belongs in the canon of Hardy's work it keeps a fairly low profile. 'Subdued' was the word one of its earliest reviewers used.[3] Despite the hint in the first chapter that we are to behold a drama of 'a grandeur and unity truly Sophoclean', *The Woodlanders* belongs to the genre of pastoral elegy rather than tragedy. There is no attempt to build the characters up into heroic proportions; the principal catastrophe (the death of Giles) generates pathos rather than pity and fear; and such violent, passionate deeds as the plot demands (like the death of Mrs Charmond) take place at a distance. *The Woodlanders* is, by Hardy's own standards, a novel in a muted key: quiet, meditative, as gentle-paced as Mrs Dollery's van; deliberately restricted to an enclosed, homogeneous environment which is observed with patient and eloquent attentiveness; not forcing the characters to represent more than they legitimately can; not (as Hardy was previously tempted to do) playing off high romantic drama against broad rustic comedy, but subtly blending the two, so that there is always a tinge of the comic, or potentially comic, about even the most sombre moments of the action and a grim sardonic strain in its lightest moments.

Like the woods themselves, the book encloses the reader and lays a strange enchantment upon him. We move through the story as though in a dream, led on irresistibly, but along unpredictable paths; sometimes we may feel, as one episode strongly reminds us of another, that, like Grace and Mrs Charmond in Chapter 33, we are travelling in circles;

and when we finally emerge it is in a place at once familiar and unexpected. Hardy's development as a novelist – it is what makes him, in
the last analysis, a modern rather than a Victorian – was directed towards a mode of writing in which every scene, gesture and image would
function simultaneously on several different levels: as a vivid and precise imitation of actuality, as a link in a chain of causation, as symbolic
action and as part of a formal pattern of parallels, contrasts and corres-
pondences. In *The Woodlanders* he came closer to achieving this perfect
fictional economy than in *Tess*, without – as in the case of *Jude* – sacrificing the lyricism, the sensuous celebration of nature and the humour,
for which his work is loved and admired.

As its title suggests, *The Woodlanders* is a novel especially characterised by 'unity of place'. From the very first paragraph Hardy saturates
our senses with impressions of the woods, the abundance and variety of
their foliage. 'Trees, trees, undergrowth, English trees! How that book
rustles with them,' exclaimed E. M. Forster, whose appreciation of the
novel was enhanced by reading it against the background of a bumpy,
burned-up Indian landscape.[4] The woods and paths are deep in dead
leaves, the interlocking branches make even summer noon into a kind
of twilight. Like all Hardy's landscapes, this woodland is a little more
intensely, vividly, 'there' than any real wood could possibly be: it grows
on the border between actuality and myth. The human habitations
within it are almost buried in the vegetation, and the traditional work
that goes on here – tree-planting and felling, barking, spar-making,
hurdle-making and hollow-turning – makes little impression upon the
organic, abundant life of the woods. Little Hintock is described in the
first chapter as 'one of those sequestered spots outside the gates of the
world', but the effect of the novel is rather to make us think of the
world as being outside the leafy, rooted 'gates' of the woodland. As
readers of the novel we are situated in the semi-wild heart of the woods,
where human life corresponds more closely to the primitive, in the
anthropological sense of the word, than perhaps anything else in Hardy
('primitive' is, indeed, a word used in the novel on certain important
occasions). Around the woods there is a belt of ordered, cultivated
nature in the form of apple-orchards; beyond the orchards there are
country towns like Abbot's Cernel and Sherton Abbas, and beyond
them Brighton, Cheltenham, London, the Continent – civilisation.

From out of this civilised world, into the woods, like the courtiers
of Shakespeare's pastoral comedy *As You Like It*, come strangers,
bringing with them habits, attitudes and values that disturb and un-
settle the traditional life of the woodland. Hardy's original title for
the novel, 'Fitzpiers at Hintock', indicates that this was, for him, the
central source of conflict and interest in the story. But Fitzpiers,
though the most important, is not the only interloper. There is Mrs

Charmond, a landowner with no real roots in her property; and there is Mr Percomb, the barber, who in the superb opening chapters acts out an illustrative prologue to the main action. Percomb's mission on that occasion is to persuade poor hard-pressed Marty to sell her crowning glory to make a wig for Mrs Charmond – or, in mythical terms, he is a demonic figure (compared to Mephistopheles by Marty and to the Scandinavian demon Loki by the narrator) who rapes the locks of the tutelary nymph of the woods. In many respects Percomb is a parallel figure to Fitzpiers (who is also ill-at-ease in the woods, excites attention from the local people, violates their values and their women, and is associated by them with the devil), while he acts as an agent for Mrs Charmond and her worldly preoccupations with physical vanity, money, social status and illicit sex. Typically, Hardy forges a causal as well as a symbolic link between Percomb and this mischievous pair, for it is partly through Percomb's success in obtaining Marty's hair that Mrs Charmond is later able to work her seductive spell upon Fitzpiers, and it is the latter's discovery of the truth about this hair that brings their affair to its violent conclusion.

Fitzpiers is a kind of third-rate Shelley (a poet he is fond of quoting): an idealist, a dabbler in science, philosophy, literature; idle, fickle, egocentric, selfish as a child. What attracts him, he must have; when he has it, he loses interest – especially where women are concerned. Preening himself on his superior birth and breeding, he is in fact crassly insensitive to the feelings of others, and never scruples to exploit their generosity (especially Melbury's). His 'modern, unpractical mind' has no real instinctive sympathy with the woodland or its denizens. The minute changes of appearance in the woods in winter do not register on his consciousness and he 'hate[s] the solitary midnight woodland through which he is obliged to make occasional journeys. His transient impulse to settle down with Grace in Little Hintock, 'sacrificing all practical aims to live in calm contentment here ... to accept quiet domesticity according to oldest and homeliest notions, is a piece of pastoral affectation betraying equal ignorance of himself and of the woodlands. This ignorance and insensitivity is perhaps most dramatic-ally manifested by his medical treatment of John South. Unable to appreciate the totemic significance of the tree for the old peasant, he briskly and confidently orders it to be felled. 'Damned if my remedy hasn't killed him!' is his somewhat callous response to the result. By causing the death of old South, Fitzpiers also indirectly causes the ruin of Giles Winterborne, and although this is unintentional it is not attended by any remorse, or even by an expression of regret when the opportunity offers itself.

Mrs. Charmond is in many ways like Fitzpiers. A slightly shop-soiled visitant from the beau-monde, she also dislikes the woods, finding them dull, depressing and, when she is lost in them, terrifying. As lady of the manor she controls the economic lives of the woodlanders, and oppresses them by pursuing a policy of enclosure. She is insulated from contact with them by her rank, her carriage and her fine house, its curtains drawn in daytime and candles lit within. When Melbury breaks through these defences and attempts an honest personal encounter, she writhes with embarrassment.

Opposed to this pair are Giles and Marty, who are everything that Fitzpiers and Felice Charmond are not: humble, good and in complete accord with their natural environment. From her first introduction, working late into the night to complete her sick father's work, Marty is the personification of selfless, unostentatious heroism; while Giles, generous, chivalrous and scrupulously honest, fully earns Marty's epitaph, 'you was a good man and did good things'. This ethical superiority of Marty and Giles is associated with their sympathetic bond with the woods themselves. Giles is constantly identified with trees by a number of delightful, typically Hardyesque touches: for instance, going off to meet Grace with his specimen apple-tree tied across the gig, 'the twigs nodding with each step of the horse', standing with it in the market-place of Sherton Abbas, bringing 'a delightful suggestion of orchards into the heart of the town' and being unable to advance to greet Grace because 'fixed to the spot by his apple-tree'. The narrator observes of Giles, 'He had a marvellous power of making trees grow . . . there was a sort of sympathy between himself and the fir, oak or beech that he was operating on'; and, significantly, when we see him employed on this task he is assisted by Marty. 'You and he', Grace tells Marty towards the end of the novel, 'could speak in a tongue that nobody else knew – not even my father . . . the tongue of the trees and fruits and flowers themselves'.

Grace Melbury is, of course, the catalyst in the situation. Without her, we may speculate, Fitzpiers might have married his old flame Felice Charmond, and Marty's love for Giles might have been requited. But, as it is, Giles loves Grace, and Fitzpiers at times also loves Grace, especially when he thinks that Giles loves her, and at other times loves Mrs Charmond. Meanwhile, Marty loves Giles and Mrs Charmond loves Fitzpiers – or at least loves the idea of being loved by him. As for Grace, she finds it fatally difficult to make up her mind whom she loves, though she undoubtedly needs to be loved by someone. It is this network of conflicting and criss-crossing romantic and erotic attraction (hearts 'ill affin'd', as the epigraph has it) that complicates the simple antithesis of Giles/Marty and Fitzpiers/Mrs Charmond, and brings the two worlds represented by these pairs into a volatile state of fusion. Grace is the catalyst because she belongs to both worlds – 'an impressionable creature, who combined modern nerves with primitive feelings'.

Hers is a return-of-the-native situation. Sent away from the woods to
be educated, by a father socially ambitious on her behalf, she finds it
difficult to readjust to life at Little Hintock on her return. Giles's
awkwardness of manner at their reunion in Sherton Abbas jars on her,
and she patronises him a little on the drive back, while he in turn notes
that she can no longer distinguish John-apple trees from bitter-sweets
and has 'fallen from the good old Hintock ways' of frank and intimate
conversation. It is not surprising that she takes a keen interest in the
unexpected presence of Fitzpiers in the woodland: 'It was strange to
her to come back from the world to Little Hintock and find in one of
its nooks, like a tropical plant in a hedgerow, a nucleus of advanced
ideas and practices which had nothing in common with the life around'.
And it is not surprising that, egged on by her class-conscious father, she
should allow Giles to drift away from her on the current of his misfortunes, and give her hand to the superficially more eligible Fitzpiers.
It does not take her long to discover her mistake, but the real turning-
point of the novel comes when to this bitter knowledge is added a new
appreciation of what she has rejected. It is one of the finest scenes in
The Woodlanders – indeed, in all of Hardy's fiction – and merits close
attention.

In Chapter 28 Grace accompanies Fitzpiers to the edge of Hintock
woods to see him off on what is supposedly a professional call, but
which she knows to be another secret assignation with Mrs Charmond,
who is staying at Middleton Abbey, some twelve miles away. Fitzpiers
is weary from several similar excursions, and seems like a man compelled by an obsession to do something from which he expects little
satisfaction. There is poignancy as well as irony in his sincerely affec-
tionate farewell to his wife. Grace mounts to the top of High-Stoy Hill
and watches him traverse White-Hart Vale. It is one of those peculiarly
cinematic scenes – rarer in *The Woodlanders* than in the other Wessex
novels because of the all-enclosing woods – in which Hardy sets a
diminutive human figure in a deep, broad landscape, the contrast on the
visual scale corresponding to a moral or emotional or thematic irony in
the situation. Fitzpiers is travelling east, and the setting sun, reflected
on the white coat of his (or, rather, Grace's) horse, Darling, renders him
visible as he crosses the valley floor, carrying his sterile and destructive
infatuation (an implication enforced by the allusion to Tannhaüser)
through the smiling, fertile autumn landscape. As the white speck is
finally eclipsed by distance, and Grace muses on the irony that her
faithless husband is riding to his mistress on a horse donated to her by
her first, faithful lover, Giles himself appears out of the same valley.
Whereas Fitzpiers's route was betrayed by the reflected light on Darling, Giles's approach is heralded by glancing beams of the same light
reflected from the blades of his cider-making apparatus; and whereas

Fitzpiers had been an alien figure in the landscape Giles seems to personify it:

He looked and smelt like Autumn's very brother, his face being sun-burnt to wheat-colour, his eyes blue as corn-flowers, his sleeves and leggings dyed with fruit-stains, his hands clammy with the sweet juice of apples, his hat sprinkled with pips, and everywhere about him that atmosphere of cider which at its first return each season has such an indescribable fascination for those who have been born and bred among the orchards. Her heart rose from its late sadness like a released bough; her senses revelled in the sudden lapse back to Nature unadorned. The consciousness of having to be genteel because of her husband's profes-sion, the veneer of artificiality which she had acquired at the fashion-able schools, were thrown off, and she became the crude country girl of her latent early instincts.

The lyrical intensity, the Keatsian sensuousness of this passage scarcely needs comment (except perhaps to note that 'like a released bough' was an inspired revision, in the second edition of 1887, of the original 'like a released spring', thus continuing the rhetoric of the first sen-tence, in which the metaphorical language is deliberately drawn from the same source as the literal language); and the dramatic importance of Giles's appearance is equally clear. The encounter is a kind of epiphany for Grace, a moment of truth; and it is not long before she is blaming her discomfited father for having deprived her of the happy life she might have enjoyed with Giles:

'I wish you had never, never thought of educating me. I wish I worked in the woods like Marty South! I hate genteel life, and I want to be no better than she! . . . Cultivation has only brought me inconveniences and troubles . . .'

Grace's 'revolt . . . against social law' and 'passionate desire for primitive life' are, however, only spasmodic impulses. She is not really prepared to follow her instincts in defiance of convention, and her timidity is compounded by Giles's chivalrousness and their continuing mutual inability to communicate effectively. So they abide by the laws which will not allow them to marry, and Giles dies from illness and exposure because he will not compromise Grace by staying in his hut while Grace is using it as a refuge. Her cry of *'Come to me dearest! I don't mind what they say or what they think of us any more'* is uttered too late, and it is only after he is dead that she falsely claims they were lovers.

   After a period of grief, remorse and passionate devotion to Giles's memory, Grace is reconciled to Fitzpiers and goes off to start a new life

with him in the world outside Hintock, while the faithful Marty is
left behind to mourn the man who never knew she loved him.

The ending of *The Woodlanders* upset many contemporary readers,
and is still capable of surprising and disconcerting modern ones. Some
of the latter[5] have supposed that Hardy was cynically fixing up a
'happy ending' for his heroine in accordance with the expectations of
his reading public. But contemporary reviewers were shocked that a cad
like Fitzpiers was rewarded rather than punished for his sins. Hardy's
own recorded comment on the subject suggests that both criticisms are
slightly, though not wholly, beside the point: 'the ending of the story –
hinted rather than stated – is that the heroine is doomed to an unhappy
life with an inconstant husband. I could not accentuate this strongly in
the book, by reason of the conventions of the libraries etc.'[6] Nevertheless, the good characters do seem to come off worse, in the end,
than the less good. What is Hardy trying to tell us by this? Do the good
suffer because of some flaw in themselves, or because of some outside
cause?

As is usually the case with Hardy, there is a bewildering plurality of
possible answers. They are not necessarily mutually exclusive, but we
can discount some, and relegate others to a minor position. For instance, although Grace's false hopes of getting a divorce contribute
significantly to the emotional drama of herself, Giles and her father, it
would be absurd to regard the book as in any important sense a protest against the contemporary law governing marriage. Hardy makes
quite clear in the Preface that this law, and the observance of it, though
open to question outside the novel, are taken for granted within it.
Similarly, the misfortunes of Giles and Grace are not to be attributed to
chance, ill-luck or accident, implying that their lives would have been
happy and fulfilled if this or that event had turned out differently. The
coincidences and mishaps that stud the pages of Hardy's novels are
more often symptoms than causes. A good example is the episode of
the writing on the wall, in Chapter 15. This involves several apparently
fortuitous misunderstandings between Giles, Grace and Marty, and
results in Giles breaking off his engagement to Grace, and her acqui-
escence, against the deepest wishes of both of them. 'From this day . . .
onward', we are told, Giles 'retired into the background . . . Grace,
thinking that Winterborne saw her write, made no further sign, and the
frail barque of fidelity that she had thus timidly launched was stranded
and lost'. The episode, then, seems crucial. On reflection, however, it
is clear that Hardy could have contrived a much simpler, more plausible
and more pointed cause of misunderstanding between Giles and Grace,
and that, given their characters and situations, if their betrothal had not
foundered on this occasion, it would have foundered on another.

Furthermore, since the whole complicated sequence of events is narrated in a couple of pages, it is clearly not designed to arouse suspense. It is another piece of symbolic action, expressing an 'obstructed relationship': people emotionally dependent on each other failing to understand each other or to communicate their real feelings.

One of the most widely shared interpretations of Hardy's fiction as a whole – put forward with particular force by Douglas Brown – is that it is a lament for the passing of a traditional agrarian culture under the impact of 'progress', industrialisation and metropolitan values; that the tragic love-stories Hardy relates are, in a sense, allegories of a wider social tragedy which he lived through and observed at close quarters: land capitalism, enclosure, the decline of English agriculture in the era of free trade, the mechanisation of such agriculture as remained, the migration of workers from the land to the cities, and the gradual decline and disappearance of rural customs, traditions and folklore. *Tess of the d'Urbervilles* is the favourite example for this view of Hardy, but *The Woodlanders* can also be invoked readily enough. Brown's description of the typical Hardy plot is clearly relevant to *The Woodlanders*:

His protagonists are strong-minded countrymen disciplined by the necessities of agricultural life. He brings into relation with them men and women from outside the rural world, better educated, superior in status, yet inferior in human worth.[7]

We have already seen how the evident moral superiority of Giles and Marty is associated with their *rapport* with the natural life of the woodland and their skill in its characteristic forms of work; and we have seen how, correspondingly, the morally dubious characters are sophisticates ill-at-ease in that environment. The moral of the story seems plain enough. Yet it would be a mistake not to recognise the extent to which the woodlanders – especially Giles – are responsible for their own defeat by the outsiders. Does Giles, in the last analysis, deserve Brown's epithet, 'strong-natured'? '*Good*-natured', yes. But there is some fatal streak of weakness in Giles, a vulnerable innocence, and some of that 'listlessness' ('passivity' in the earlier versions) which the narrator remarks is characteristic of rural backwaters like Little Hintock. Hardy makes a point of telling us that Giles's father had never troubled to take the simple legal steps that would have protected his leasehold, and even when Giles discovers this loophole he postpones acting on it ('his scheme could not be carried out in a day') until it is too late. His death itself, however poignant and noble in motive, is strikingly non-heroic, a negative rather than a positive gesture, and arguably a futile one.

My point is that we should not interpret the human story of *The Woodlanders*, and the larger social-historical process it may be held to reflect, in too simple or sentimental a way. Hardy was capable of appreciating the old agricultural order without idealising it, and did not suppose that its passing was something that could be arrested or reversed. Like many thoughtful late Victorians, he was both an evolutionary and a pessimistic thinker: he believed in the inevitability of change without assuming that it would necessarily be change for the better. Fitzpiers survives because he is fitter, not better, than Giles – fitter to survive in a 'modern' age. That is the real significance of the doubtfully 'happy ending': Grace chooses life over death, a man with the future in his bones over a man whose individual death symbolises an old order passing. But the 'life', the 'future', that awaits her is only bourgeois prosperity and respectability, eaten away by the worm of sexual distrust.

The evolutionary pessimism that underlies *The Woodlanders* is most clearly visible in passages of natural description. So far, I have stressed the benign and beautiful aspects of the woodland – the fruitful, health-giving connection established between the woods and the people who live and work in them. But there is another, much darker strain in the presentation of nature, just as there is a neurotic and superstitious side to the sympathy between woodlanders and woods (notably in old South's obsession with the tree – not the first such case in Hintock, we are told). Consider this striking passage of description from Chapter 7, where Giles is following Melbury and Grace:

They went noiselessly over mats of starry moss, rustled through interspersed tracts of leaves, skirted trunks with spreading roots whose mossed rinds made them like hands wearing green gloves; elbowed old elms and ashes with great forks, in which stood pools of water that overflowed on rainy days and ran down their stems in green cascades. On older trees still than these huge lobes of fungi grew like lungs. Here, as everywhere, the Unfulfilled Intention, which makes life what it is, was as obvious as it could be among the depraved crowds of a city slum. The leaf was deformed, the curve was crippled, the taper was interrupted; the lichen ate the vigour of the stalk, and the ivy slowly strangled to death the promising sapling.

Here the authorial voice explicitly denies the conventional pastoral antithesis between town and country and establishes instead an identity of brutal and ruthless evolutionary struggle. Because it works strongly against his reading, Brown seeks to discredit this passage as an unfortunate lapse into 'intrusive commentary',[8] but it is in fact a powerful piece of writing in a strain that has already appeared several times previously in the novel:

. . . the creaking sound of two overcrowded branches in the neighbouring wood, which were rubbing each other into wounds. . .

Owls that had been catching mice in the outhouses, rabbits that had
been eating the winter-greens in the gardens, and stoats that had been
sucking the blood of the rabbits . . .

In the hollow shades of the roof could be seen dangling and etiolated
arms of ivy that had crept through the joints of the tiles and were
groping in vain . . . for want of sunlight; others were pushing in with
such force at the eaves as to lift from their supports the shelves that
were fixed there.

There is, of course, no mystery about where this view of Nature comes
from. In discussing the influence of Charles Darwin on Hardy, Harvey
Curtis Webster quotes a passage from *The Origin of Species* (1859),
about the forests of America, that is strikingly similar to those just
cited from *The Woodlanders:*

What a struggle must have gone on during long centuries between the
several kinds of trees, each annually scattering its seeds by the thousand; what a war between insect and insect – between insects, snails and
other animals with birds and beasts of prey – all striving to increase, all
feeding on each other, or on the trees, their seeds and seedlings, or on
the other plants which first clothed the ground and thus checked the
growth of the trees.
   We behold the face of nature bright with gladness, we often see
superabundance of food. We do not see, or we forget, that the birds
which are idly singing round us live mostly on insects or seeds, and are
thus constantly destroying life; or we forget how largely these song-
sters, or their eggs, or their nestlings, are destroyed by birds and beasts
of prey.[9]

   The intensely written passages of natural description in *The Woodlanders* seem to bear all the hallmarks of the pathetic fallacy, yet this is
not quite an accurate categorisation. The pathetic fallacy Ruskin defined as 'a falseness in our impressions of things' produced by 'violent
feelings'. It is exemplified by Mrs Charmond's projection of her mood
upon the weather – 'Sorrow and bitterness in the sky and floods of
tears beating against the panes' – or Melbury's vision of the winter trees
as 'haggard, grey phantoms whose days of substantiality were past' at
a time when he himself is undergoing a kind of identity crisis. The
evolutionary struggle in nature is not, however, observed by such emotionally disturbed characters, but by the omniscient, reliable narrator;

and it is not a 'falseness' but an empirically verified fact of biological science. In the descriptions of the woods at the time of Giles's final decline and death, this authorial perspective mingles with, and gives authority to, the perceptions of Grace, anxiously penned in the hut – perceptions which otherwise we should characterise as straightforward examples of the pathetic fallacy.

Sometimes a bough from an adjoining tree was swayed so low as to smite the roof in the manner of a gigantic hand smiting the mouth of an adversary, to be followed by a trickle of rain, as blood from the wound. To all this weather Giles must be more or less exposed; how much, she did not know.

From the other window . . . she could see . . . more trees close together, wrestling for existence, their branches disfigured with wounds resulting from their mutual rubbings and blows. It was the struggle between these neighbours that she had heard in the night. Beneath them were the rotting stumps of those of the group that had been vanquished long ago, rising from their mossy setting like black teeth from green gums.

Thus Giles's death takes place to the accompaniment of a crescendo of imagery expressing the ideas of violent struggle, ugly decay and the extinction of obsolete forms of life. The death itself, however, is non-violent, almost peaceful. As Jean Brooks has observed in a very sensitive commentary on this part of the novel, Giles 'dissolves into the wood by imperceptible degrees':

As Giles moves down the evolutionary scale, distinguished at first by a cough that sounds like a squirrel or a bird, then as a 'voice . . . floating upon the weather as though a part of it' and finally indistinguishable as 'an endless monologue, like that we sometimes hear from inanimate nature in deep secret places where water flows, or where ivy leaves flap against stones', the meaning of identity with the natural world, so often sounded as his keynote, comes home with tragic force to the modern reader, developed beyond the primitive, hardly conscious needs answered once by fertility ritual.[10]

With these suggestive words in mind, I should like to return to my earlier suggestion that *The Woodlanders* may be described, generically, as a novelistic adaptation of the pastoral elegy.

In its classical form, as practised by the Greek bucolic poets Theocritus, Moschus and Bion, and imitated by countless poets subsequently, the pastoral elegy is a lament of one shepherd, goatherd or cowherd for another who is dead or dying, often of disappointed love. The convention has been found especially appropriate to expressions of grief for the deaths of poets themselves. But Northrop Frye has observed, in a brilliant essay on Milton's 'Lycidas', that this highly artificial form has deep roots in religion and myth:

In the classical pastoral elegy the subject of the elegy is not treated as an individual but as a representative of a dying spirit of nature. The pastoral elegy seems to have some relation to the ritual of the Adonis lament, and the dead poet Bion, in Moschus' poem, is celebrated with much the same kind of imagery as Bion himself uses in his lament for Adonis. The phrase 'dying god' for such a figure in later pastoral is not an anachronism . . . Milton and his learned contemporaries . . . knew at least as much about the symbolism of the 'dying god' as any modern could get out of *The Golden Bough*, which depends mainly on the same classical sources that were available to them.[11]

Sir James Frazer, who began his researches for *The Golden Bough* at just about the time Hardy was writing *The Woodlanders*, argues in that monumental study that the myth and cult of Adonis derived from primitive religious and magical rites concerned with vegetation and its seasonal variation.[12] According to the myth, the beautiful youth Adonis was beloved by Aphrodite. He was mortally wounded by a boar, but the grief of the goddess was so great that he was released from the Underworld for part of every year. Adonis's death and resurrection was, by a natural symbolism, associated with the seasonal death and restoration of vegetation, and especially with the growth-cycle of corn, which is 'buried' in the earth in winter, and reappears in spring and summer as a new crop. Originally, however, Adonis was probably a tree-spirit. The cult of Adonis was celebrated chiefly by women and girls, who performed extravagant rites of mourning for the death of the god, followed by ritual acts expressing hope of his rebirth. Traces of these pagan practices are to be found in folk-customs up to comparatively recent times, like the Midsummer Night ceremonies of the Little Hintock maidens.

These ceremonies are the most obvious but, because they are so thoroughly demythologised, probably the least significant trace in *The Woodlanders* of the literary and anthropological material summarised above. The rhythm of the seasons, the changes in the vegetation of the woods, are constantly insisted upon throughout the novel, and Giles himself is, as we have seen, closely associated with this vegetation. When he descends from the elm-tree he has been shrouding, it is as if a 'tree-spirit' is detaching itself: 'the tree seemed to shiver, then to heave a sigh: a movement was audible, and Winterborne dropped almost noiselessly to the ground'. Later in the novel this association with nature is given an explicitly divine emphasis: when Grace is recovering from her first illness

He rose upon her memory as the fruit-god and the wood-god in alternation: sometimes leafy and smeared with green lichen, as she had seen him amongst the sappy boughs of the plantations: sometimes cider-stained and starred with apple-pips, as she had met him on his return from cider-making in Blackmoor Vale.

When he dies, and is buried, all nature is described as mourning his death: 'The whole wood seemed to be a house of death, pervaded by loss to its uttermost length and breadth. Winterborne was gone, and the copses seemed to show the want of him'. This is a characteristic sentiment of pastoral elegy. Compare 'Lycidas':

> Thee, shepherd, thee the woods, and desert caves
> With wild thyme and the gadding vine o'ergrown,
> And all their echoes mourn.

or the opening of Moschus's 'Lament for Bion', an English translation of which, by a most intriguing coincidence, appeared in *Macmillan's Magazine* when that periodical was serialising *The Woodlanders*:

> Come weep with me ye Dorian glades and springs,
> Ye Dorian rivers, weep for Bion dead.
> Ye groves, and all ye green and flowering things
> In funeral clusters be your sweetness shed.[13]

This translation appeared in the January 1887 issue of *Macmillan's*, in which Chapters 34–7 of *The Woodlanders* appeared. Hardy would probably have received an advance copy of the issue, and we know that he did not finish the composition of the novel until 4 February 1887.[14] Hardy, who read widely in classical literature, especially Greek, which he taught himself, was undoubtedly well acquainted with the tradition of the pastoral elegy (Theocritus, for instance, is listed among the authors he read in 1887),[15] but it is interesting to speculate that his attention, and his imagination, may have been caught by the appearance of the 'Lament for Bion' in *Macmillan's* just as he was writing, or preparing to write, the closing chapters of *The Woodlanders*, in which the presence of that tradition is most strongly felt.

The religious and ritual undertones of the classical pastoral elegy are also clearly discernible in the last part of *The Woodlanders*. 'I go with Marty to Giles's grave,' Grace tells Fitzpiers. 'I almost *worship* him.

We *swore* we would show him that *devotion*' (my italics). And we are told that

Weeks and months of mourning for Winterborne had been passed by Grace in the soothing monotony of the memorial act to which she and Marty had devoted themselves. Twice a week the pair went in the dusk to Hintock Churchyard, and, like the two mourners in *Cymbeline*, sweetened his sad grave with their flowers and their tears.

Cymbeline, like all of Shakespeare's late plays, is much concerned with the ideas of death and resurrection, with magic, ritual and the literary tradition of pastoral. In the scene to which Hardy alludes, Guiderius and Arviragus, the supposed sons of Bellarius (in fact, the sons of Cymbeline) find their sister Imogen, whom they have befriended in her disguise as a youth called Fidele, apparently dead of 'melancholy'. Arviragus says:

> With fairest flowers
> Whilst summer lasts, and I live here, Fidele,
> I'll sweeten thy sad grave: thou shalt not lack
> The flower that's like thy face, pale primrose; nor
> The azured harebell, like thy veins . . . [Act IV, sc. II]

Primrose and harebell are flowers of spring and early summer, like most of the flowers listed at the end of 'Lycidas' ('And purple all the ground with vernal flowers./Bring the rathe primrose that forsaken dies', etc.), and thus suggestive of the renewal of life. The same symbolism appears in *The Woodlanders* in Grace's 'periodical visit to Winterborne's grave with Marty, which was kept up with pious strictness for the purpose of putting snowdrops, primroses and other vernal flowers thereon as they came'. In *Cymbeline* Imogen comes spectacularly to life after the performance of these rites, for she has been drugged merely; but in Hardy's novel there is and can be no such resurrection. There is, however, a good deal of verbal play on the idea in the exchanges between Grace and Fitzpiers in the closing chapters. 'If you could condescend even only to see me again you would be breathing life into a corpse,' he writes to her, trying by this metaphor to substitute himself for Giles in her affective life. 'Why not give me a very little bit of your heart again?' he pleads at their next meeting. The crash of a felled tree at that moment recalls Giles to Grace, and she answers, 'Don't ask it. My heart is in the grave with Giles.' He accuses her of keeping open the grave. On a later occasion he returns to the same subject: ' "I think you might get your heart out of that grave," said he with playful sadness. "It has been there for a long time".' Eventually Fitzpiers and Grace are reconciled through another variation on the death-and-resurrection theme: finding remnants of her clothing in the man-trap, Fitzpiers jumps to the conclusion that she has been killed and gives vent to passionate grief. This gives Grace proof of his devotion, and brings the issue of their reunion to a swift resolution: 'He clasped his arms completely round her, pressed her to his breast and kissed her passionately. "You are not dead! – you are not hurt! Thank God – thank God!" '

The characteristic emotional curve of a pastoral elegy is an extravagant expression of grief which, having worked itself out, modulates into a mood of resignation, and indeed hope, based on the promise of renewed life in Nature (and in Christian adaptations of the genre, like 'Lycidas', on the promise of eternal life). In *The Woodlanders* this conventional resolution is split into two. Grace and Fitzpiers go off to 'fresh woods, and pastures new' (in a metaphorical sense only, for their destination seems to be a city) with their love at least temporarily revived and renewed, while Marty is left behind in the Hintock woods to nourish the memory of Giles. On the last night covered by the narrative Marty, fully aware that 'Mrs Fitzpiers was by that time in the arms of another man than Giles', returns alone to the churchyard, replaces the withered flowers she and Grace had laid on Giles's grave the previous week with fresh ones, and whispers her final, deeply moving elegy. Although she invokes the cycle of the seasons, it is to guarantee remembrance, not renewal of the life that has been extinguished: 'Whenever I plant the young larches I'll think that none can plant as you planted; and whenever I split a gad, and whenever I turn the cider wring, I'll say none could do it like you.'

The classical pastoral elegy was, we have seen, a formalised literary development from rituals designed to celebrate and promote the seasonal renewal of Nature's fertility; it was also, in later literary tradition, a convenient way of expressing personal grief, and also concern about the state of literature, the Church and the world at large (cf. 'Lycidas', Shelley's 'Adonaïs', Matthew Arnold's 'Thyrsis', etc.). In *The Woodlanders* the conventions of realism, to which Hardy as a nineteenth-century novelist was committed, replace – or, to use Northrop Frye's word, 'displace' – the conventions of pastoral, so that these appear mainly on the periphery of the work, or beneath its surface, in allusion, metaphor and suggestion. But the dual character of the pastoral elegy – its combination of traditionalism and topicality, primitivism and sophistication – persists in Hardy's novel in a most interesting and pointed form. Giles, and the whole action of which he is a part, clearly symbolise the passing of a certain kind of society and way of life – 'Now I've seen the end of the family, which we can ill afford to lose, wi' such a scanty lot of good folk in Hintock as we've got,' moans poor Robert Creedle. Hardy felt, and expressed, the pathos of this process, but his linear and evolutionary view of history compelled him to accept it as inevitable. Correspondingly he expressed, with rare eloquence, the old view of nature as cyclical, harmonious, life-giving, self-renewing, susceptible of magical or intuitive control by suitably endowed persons, while at the same time articulating in many of his most powerful descriptive passages the new evolutionary account of the biological world that was superseding it. It is the delicate, precarious balance which Hardy manages to hold between these conflicting and logically incompatible value-systems and knowledge-systems that makes *The Woodlanders* the powerful, absorbing and haunting work of fiction it is.

7 Thomas Hardy as a Cinematic Novelist

Thomas Hardy's last novel, *Jude the Obscure* (1895), was published well before film had properly evolved as a narrative medium. By calling him a 'cinematic' novelist, therefore, I mean that he anticipated film, not that he was influenced by it. In a general sense this is true of all the great nineteenth-century realistic novelists. As Leon Edel has observed:

Novelists have sought almost from the first to become a camera. And not a static instrument but one possessing the movement through space and time which the motion-picture camera has achieved in our century. We follow Balzac, moving into his subject, from the city into the street, from the street into the house, and we tread hard on his heels as he takes us from room to room. We feel as if that massive 'realist' had a prevision of the cinema . . . Wherever we turn in the nineteenth century we can see novelists cultivating the camera-eye and the camera movement . . .[1]

One way of explaining this affinity between film and classic realistic fiction is to say that both are 'metonymic' forms, in Roman Jakobson's sense of that term.* 'Following the path of contiguous relationships, the realistic author metonymically digresses from the plot to the atmosphere and from the characters to the setting in space and time', says Jakobson (this matches Edel's description of Balzac's technique exactly). 'He is fond of synecdochic detail. In the scene of Anna Karenina's suicide Tolstoy's attention is focused on the heroine's handbag . . .'[2] The handbag is a synecdoche for Anna. It will be remembered that she throws it aside as she jumps beneath the train, and that her first attempt is checked when the bag becomes entangled in her clothing. One could easily imagine a cinematic treatment of the scene in which the camera cuts away from the fatal leap to a close-up shot of the

---

*For an account of Jakobson's distinction between metaphor and metonymy, see above, pp. 10–11 and 21–2.

poignantly abandoned handbag on the platform. Close-up is the filmic equivalent of synecdoche (part standing for whole). Film has its metaphors too, of course (e.g. waves pounding on the shore signifying sexual intercourse in the pre-permissive cinema), but this kind of montage must be used sparingly in narrative film, or disguised as contextual detail, if intelligibility is to be preserved. For the same reasons modernist or symbolist novels in which the metaphorical principle of similarity largely determines the development of the discourse (e.g. Joyce's *Ulysses*) are much more difficult to translate into film than realistic novels.

'Realism' as an aesthetic effect depends upon the suppression of overt reference to the conventions employed, so that the discourse seems to be a transparent window on reality, rather than a code. Avant-garde and experimental movies may draw attention to their own optics, but most narrative films do not. As experienced viewers of films we tend to take the camera eye for granted and to accept the truthfulness of what it shows us. Though its perspective is never that of ordinary human vision, it is close enough to the latter to seem a transparent medium for the rendering of reality rather than an artificial system of signs. Similarly the narrative style of realistic fiction, derived from non-fictional types of discourse such as biography, confession, letters and historiography, bestows upon the fictitious narrative a pseudo-historical authenticity. Both novel and film are able to shift their point of view between an 'omniscient' or impersonal perspective and the perspective of a particular character without sacrificing realistic illusion. Roland Barthes has observed that 'the discourse of the traditional novel alternates the personal and the impersonal very rapidly, often in the same sentence, so as to produce, if we can speak thus, a proprietary consciousness which retains the mastery of what it states without participating in it',[3] and the same may be said of film.

If there is so close an affinity between the classic realistic novel and film, what is the justification for distinguishing Hardy as a 'cinematic novelist'? To answer that question we must emphasise the *differences* between novel and film. Apart from dialogue and monologue (which are available to both) and the use of music for emotive suggestion, film is obliged to tell its story purely in terms of the visible – behaviour, physical appearance, setting – whereas the verbal medium of the novel can describe anything, visible or invisible (notably the thoughts passing through a character's head), and can do so as abstractly as it pleases. A cinematic novelist, then, is one who, as it were, deliberately renounces some of the freedom of representation and report afforded by the verbal medium, who imagines and presents his materials in primarily visual terms, and whose visualisations correspond in some significant respect to the visual effects characteristic of film.

That description, especially description of the natural settings of his stories, plays a crucially important part in Thomas Hardy's fiction is, of course, a commonplace. But I don't think it has been observed how remarkably 'cinematic' he is, both in the way he describes landscape and in the way he deploys his human figures against it. Hardy uses verbal description as a film director uses the lens of his camera – to select, highlight, distort and enhance, creating a visualised world that is both recognisably 'real' and yet more vivid, intense and dramatically charged than our ordinary perception of the real world. The methods he uses can be readily analysed in cinematic terms: long shot, close-up, wide-angle, telephoto, zoom, etc. Indeed, some of Hardy's most original visual effects have since become cinematic clichés. One thinks of his use of mirrors to dramatise encounters in which there is an element of guilt, suspense or deception (e.g. Eustacia in *The Return of the Native* realising that Clym has discovered the truth about her treatment of his mother when she sees his grim face reflected in the mirror of her dressing-table, or Grace in *The Woodlanders* startled to discover in the mirror of Fitzpiers's sitting-room that he is regarding her from his couch, though when she turns round he is apparently asleep);[4] and his use of 'aerial shots' (of Tess on the floor of the valley of the Great Dairies, for instance, or of Wildeve and Eustacia on Egdon Heath at night).[5]

Hardy, like a film-maker, seemed to conceive his fictions, from the beginning, as human actions in a particular setting: the dense woods of *The Woodlanders*, the wild heathland of *The Return of the Native*, the contrasting valleys and heights of *Tess*, are integral to the imaginative unity of those novels. He called them 'novels of character and environment', and it is his ability to make concrete the relationship between character and environment in a way that is both sensuously particular and symbolically suggestive that makes him such a powerful and original novelist, in my opinion, rather than his skill in storytelling, his insight into human motivation or his philosophic wisdom. This emphasis on the visual presentation of experience makes him no less of a *writer* – quite the contrary, since he must do through language what the film-maker can do by moving his camera and adjusting his lens; correspondingly, it is difficult for film adaptation to do justice to Hardy's novels precisely because effects that are unusual in written description are commonplace in film.[6]

To illustrate my argument I will comment in some detail on the opening chapters of *The Return of the Native* (1878). This novel begins, like so many films, with an emotionally loaded, panoramic establishing shot of the *mise-en-scène*, Egdon Heath:

A Saturday afternoon in November was approaching the time of twilight, and the vast tract of unenclosed wild known as Egdon Heath

embrowned itself moment by moment. Overhead the hollow stretch
of whitish cloud shutting out the sky was as a tent which had the
whole heath for its floor.

The emphasis in the first chapter is on the heath's symbolic properties,
especially its consonance with the mood of late nineteenth-century
cosmic pessimism in which this novel is, a little self-indulgently,
steeped. For this purpose the heath is empty (Chapter 2 is headed,
'Humanity appears upon the Scene, Hand in Hand with Trouble') but
it is noteworthy that at several points Hardy postulates an observer as a
kind of descriptive formula: 'Looking upwards, a furze-cutter would
have been inclined to continue work; looking down, he would have
decided to finish his faggot and go home' . . . 'To recline on a stump of
thorn in the central valley of Egdon, between afternoon and night, as
now, where the eye could reach nothing of the world outside the sum-
mits and shoulders of heathland which filled the whole circumference
of its glance' . . . 'On the evening under consideration it would have
been noted that, though the gloom had increased sufficiently to con-
fuse the minor features of the heath, the white surface of the road
remained almost as clear as ever.'

The invocation of a hypothetical or unspecified observer in description is one of the signatures of Hardy's narrative style. His novels are
full of phrases like, 'An observer would have remarked', 'a loiterer in
this place might have speculated', or verbs of perception, often in the
passive voice ('it was seen', 'it was felt', etc.), that are not attached to
any specified subject. Why should a novelist who did not shrink from
exercising the authorial privilege of intrusive philosophical comment
feel compelled to invent surrogates for himself when it came to description? The habit is linked with Hardy's heavy reliance on *specified*
observers in his fiction: there are an extraordinary number of scenes in
which one character observes, spies on or eavesdrops on others. J. Hillis
Miller has plausibly traced this feature of Hardy's novels to the writer's
own unconscious wish 'to escape from the dangers of direct involvement in life and to imagine himself in a position where he could safely
see life as it is without being seen and could report on that seeing'.[7]
But we may also interpret Hardy's reliance on specified and unspecified observers as evidence of the importance he attached to visual perspective – it is as though he is trying to naturalise devices of presentation that would require no such explanation or justification in film.
These observing eyes act like camera lenses – and if there is often something voyeuristic about their observations, this only reminds us that
film is a deeply voyeuristic medium.

To return to the *Native*: the opening paragraph of Chapter 2 introduces an old man, walking along the road whose whiteness was remarked

at the close of Chapter I. The physical appearance of the old man is described, followed by these words: 'One would have said that he had been, in his day, a naval officer of some sort or other.' Again, the unspecified observer: 'One would have said . . .' There is nothing to prevent Hardy from telling us that this is Captain Vye, retired, but he prefers to enact the process by which we interpret purely visual information, thus restricting himself voluntarily to a limitation that is binding on the film-maker. The old man now becomes the 'lens' through which we see. The road stretches before him, 'dry, empty and white. It was quite open to the heath on each side, and bisected that vast dark surface like a parting line on a head of black hair, diminishing and bending away on the furthest horizon.' Then, 'at length he discerned, a long distance in front of him, a moving spot which appeared to be a vehicle . . . It was the single atom of life that the scene contained.' This is a very characteristic, and very cinematic, effect in Hardy's fiction: the little speck of human life in a vast expanse of nature, expressing (though one does not wish to interpret too allegorically) the vulnerability of the individual human life, its relative insignificance in the temporal and spatial scale of the earth and the universe at large.

Gradually Captain Vye overtakes the van, which turns out to be 'ordinary in shape, but singular in colour, this being a lurid red. The driver walked beside it; and like his van, he was completely red.' In a Technicolor film, this would surely be a stunning moment. Indeed, Diggory Venn the reddleman is one of Hardy's most cinematically conceived characters. There is little to him psychologically: he is honest, chivalrous, loyal, a rather dull 'goodie'. The interest and appeal of his character is all in his picturesque appearance and behaviour: his weird pigmentation, his lonely nomadic existence, his dramatic interventions into the action – notably the scene in Chapter 8 of Book III where, like the strong silent hero of a Western, he strides into the circle of lamplight on the heath where Christian has just lost to Wildeve all the money entrusted to him by Mrs Yeobright:

Wildeve stared. Venn looked coolly towards Wildeve, and without a word being spoken, he deliberately sat himself down where Christian had been seated, thrust his hand into his pocket, drew out a sovereign, and laid it on the stone.

'You have been watching us from behind that bush?' said Wildeve.

The reddleman nodded. 'Down with your stake,' he said. 'Or haven't you pluck enough to go on?'

In Chapter 2 of Book I, Diggory, having been presented to us first through the eyes of Captain Vye, himself provides the eyes through which we first glimpse the heroine of the story, Eustacia Vye: a carefully

composed visual sequence that begins with a wide-angle shot of the
heath and then zooms in on the distant barrow where a figure is out-
lined against the sky.

There the form stood, motionless as the hill beneath. Above the plain
rose the hill, above the hill rose the barrow, and above the barrow rose
the figure. Above the figure was nothing that could be mapped elsewhere than on a celestial globe . . . The figure perceptibly gave up its
fixity, shifted a step or two, and turned round. As if alarmed, it descended on the right side of the barrow, with the glide of a water drop
down a bud, and then vanished. The movement had been sufficient to
show more clearly the characteristics of the figure, and that it was a
woman's.
      The reason of her sudden displacement now appeared. With her
dropping out of sight on the right side, a newcomer, bearing a burden,
protruded into the sky on the left side, ascended the tumulus, and
deposited the burden on the top. A second followed, then a third, a
fourth, a fifth, and ultimately the whole barrow was peopled with
burdened figures.
      The only intelligible meaning in this sky-backed pantomime of
silhouettes was that the woman had no relation to the forms who had
taken her place, was sedulously avoiding these, and had come thither
for another object than theirs.

Once again information is conveyed to the reader through visualised
action, made striking and vivid by an unusual perspective, interpreted
by a narrator who could have used his authorial privilege to simply *tell*
us the facts.
      The third chapter begins characteristically: 'Had a looker-on been
posted in the immediate vicinity of the barrow, he would have learned
that these persons were boys and men of the neighbouring hamlets.'
The transition from Diggory's distant viewpoint to the hypothetical
'looker-on' is equivalent to a cinematic 'cut' from a long-distance shot
to a close-up of a given subject. It situates us on the barrow, able to
observe the local rustics as they build their bonfire, and to overhear
their conversation. And now *they* become the observing eyes of the
narrative, surveying the dark expanse of Egdon on which 'Red suns
and tufts of fire one by one began to arise, flecking the whole country
round. They were the bonfires of other parishes . . .'
      To work through the entire novel in this way would be tedious, and
I hope I have indicated clearly enough my grounds for regarding *The
Return of the Native* as a 'cinematic novel' *avant la lettre*. That it is the
product of an intensely *visual* imagination is surely undeniable. The
plot, *qua* plot – considered as a sequence of human actions connected

by cause and effect – has little to recommend it, heavily dependent as it is on melodramatic stereotypes in character and action. Yet we scarcely register these things as flaws because they are overlaid by, or are actually the occasion of, stunning visual effects. The reasons, the circumstances, that cause Eustacia not to open the cottage door to her mother-in-law, thus bringing about the latter's death and eventually her own, matter less than the visual image, perceived by Mrs Yeobright and frequently recalled later, of Eustacia's cold, hostile face at the window. The business of the gold guineas which are won by Wildeve from Christian, and then by Diggory from Wildeve, is not particularly interesting as plot, is, indeed, entirely dispensable on this level, but one would be sorry to lose that memorable and intensely visual scene where the two men gamble on desperately into the night, surrounded by insects and cattle attracted by the light, and then, their candle extinguished by a moth, continue their game by the light of glow-worms. The same is true of the characters. For instance, all Hardy's efforts to dignify Eustacia with classical allusion cannot make her into a complex or morally interesting character. She is essentially a rather shallow-minded, self-dramatising young woman, primarily interesting (like many heroines of the screen) because of her physical beauty, which Hardy evokes very powerfully by close-ups of her lips, throat, eyes and hair ('rich romantic lips' and 'beautiful stormy eyes' are representative phrases), and by posing her picturesquely against the background of the heath.

Subtract all description of the heath from the novel, and you would be left with a rather contrived melodrama of unhappy love, relieved by some amusing comic dialogue from the rustics. The novel as we have it, with the descriptions of Egdon, is powerful and memorable. A line in Chapter 7 of Book IV, 'moving figures began to animate the line between heath and sky', epitomises the characteristic visual motif of the novel, established in its opening chapters: the two masses of heath and sky, one dark and the other lighter, both inscrutable and indifferent to the pathetically small, vulnerable human figures occasionally visible against these backgrounds. Usually the perspective is horizontal, but on at least one occasion Hardy switches to the vertical, when Wildeve and Eustacia are walking back from the country dance:

The moon had now waxed bright and silvery, but the heath was proof against such illumination, and there was to be observed the striking scene of a dark, rayless tract of country under an atmosphere charged from its zenith to its extremities with whitest light. To an eye above them their two faces would have appeared amid the expanse like two pearls on a table of ebony.

This emphasis throughout the novel on the smallness and vulnerability of the human being is conveyed primarily through panoramic views with deep perspective, combined with effects of 'zooming in' on distant figures. But it is worth noting that Hardy's visual imagination is just as active in close-up treatment of small-scale subjects. As blindness encroaches on Clym, for example,

His daily life was of a curious microscopic sort, his whole world being limited to a circuit of a few feet from his person. His familiars were creeping and winged things . . . Bees hummed around his ears with an intimate air, and tugged at the heath and furze-flowers at his side in such numbers as to weigh them down to the sod. The strange amber-coloured butterflies which Egdon produced, and which were never seen elsewhere, quivered in the breath of his lips, alighted upon his bowed back, and sported with the glittering point of his hook as he flourished it up and down. Tribes of emerald-green grasshoppers leaped over his feet, falling awkwardly on their backs, heads or hips, like unskilful acrobats . . . Litters of young rabbits came out from their forms to sun themselves upon hillocks, the hot beams blazing through the delicate tissue of each thin-fleshed ear, and firing it to a blood-red transparency in which the veins could be seen.

This passage has the eye-opening beauty of a good natural history film, and in the treatment of the grasshoppers anticipates the witty anthropomorphism of Disney at his best.

Hardy's most powerful and characteristic descriptive passages are generally 'exteriors'; but it is worth noting that his treatment of interiors is equally cinematic, both in the way he lights them and in his choice of viewpoints from which to observe them. *The Woodlanders* is especially rich in instances of this kind, perhaps because the dense, all-enclosing woods in which the action is mainly set made impossible the broad, panoramic descriptions of scenery at which Hardy excelled. (The notable exception is that remarkable scene in Chapter 28, so like a film Western in effect, when Grace watches Fitzpiers cross White Hart Vale on her horse Darling, the setting sun catching the white coat of the horse and making it visible until it is a mere speck on the opposite ridge.) In Chapter 2, Barber Percomb regards the unsuspecting Marty South through the open door of her cottage as she sits making spars by the light of her fire, which is also dimly and ominously reflected in the scissors protruding from the barber's waistcoat pocket. Here, as so often, Hardy invokes the art of painting to convey the particular visual effect he had in mind, but it is one that the cinema has since made very familiar:

In her present beholder's mind the scene formed by the girlish spar-maker composed itself into an impression-picture of extremest type, wherein the girl's hair alone, as the focus of observation, was depicted with intensity and distinctness, while her face, shoulders, hands, and figure in general were a blurred mass of unimportant detail lost in haze and obscurity.

The situation in which a figure in an illuminated interior is observed from outside, through a door or window, is a recurrent motif in the novel. After bringing Grace back to her home in Chapter 6, Giles, outside the house, wistfully watches through a door the family gathered round the parlour fire, and observes an effect of light on Grace's hair similar to that described in the earlier scene. Later, Giles sees Grace looking at herself in her bedroom mirror by candlelight as she anticipates the next day's visit to Mrs Charmond (Chapter 7). When Giles agrees to keep Fitzpiers company on his nocturnal drive in Chapter 16, the latter identifies Grace when they both catch sight of her drawing the curtains of her bedroom. After summoning Fitzpiers to attend Mrs Charmond following her accident, Giles 'stepped back into the darkness . . . and . . . stood for a few minutes looking at the window which, by its light, revealed the room where Grace was sitting' (Chapter 26). The most bizarre variation on this theme, with the point of observation reversed, comes in Chapter 36 when Mrs Charmond pulls back the shutter of her drawing-room window to reveal on the other side of the pane 'the face of Fitzpiers . . . surrounded with the darkness of the night without, corpse-like in its pallor, and covered with blood' – a moment worthy of Hitchcock.

Hardy's most stunning visual effects are, however, never introduced just 'for effect' (as they are sometimes in Hitchcock); they are invariably part of some larger aesthetic and thematic pattern. The recurrent motif in *The Woodlanders* of the illuminated figure inside, observed by an unobserved observer outside, symbolises the imperfect understanding and defective communication that obtain between the main characters in the novel; just as the diminutive figures on the rim of a huge horizontal landscape in *The Return of the Native* symbolise the vulnerability of human creatures and the indifference of Nature to their agonies and ecstasies. The same kind of patterning of visual effect is observable in the most substantial relic we have of Hardy's first work of fiction, *The Poor Man and the Lady*. Before Hardy destroyed the manuscript of this work, he carved out of it a short serial story, called 'An Indiscretion in the Life of an Heiress', which was published in the *New Quarterly Magazine* in 1878, and recently reprinted in book form.[8] The plot is simple and melodramatic: Egbert Mayne, a gifted but poor young man, falls imprudently in love with Geraldine, the beautiful daughter of the local squire, and she with him. He goes to London to make his fortune, and after a number of years have passed she almost

gives herself in loveless marriage to an aristocratic suitor. After a dramatic meeting on the eve of the wedding the lovers elope and marry. The
strain of attempting a reconciliation with her stern father, however,
proves fatal to Geraldine. The story is certainly among Hardy's less
impressive achievements, as he acknowledged by excluding it from his
collected works, but it demonstrates his ability to give power and
poignancy to commonplace and even stereotyped emotions by artful
effects of lighting and perspective. The opening chapter, set in a parish
church closely modelled on Hardy's own at Stinsford, is representative
in this respect. Afternoon service in winter is in progress. From the
gallery Egbert looks down intently at Geraldine in her pew below, as
the natural light fades from the windows:

The lady was the single person besides the preacher whose face was
turned westwards, the pew that she occupied being the only one in the
church in which the seat ran all around. She reclined in her corner, her
bonnet and dress growing by degrees invisible, and at last only her up-
turned face could be discerned, a solitary white spot against the black
surface of the wainscot. Over her head rose a vast marble monument,
erected to the memory of her ancestors, male and female, for she was
of high standing in that parish. The design consisted of a winged skull
and two cherubim, supporting a pair of tall Corinthian columns, between which spread a broad slab, containing the roll of ancient names,
lineages, and deeds, and surmounted by a pediment, with the crest of
the family at its apex.

   As the youthful schoolmaster gazed, and all these details became
dimmer, her face was modified in his fancy, till it seemed almost to
resemble the carved marble skull immediately above her head.[9]

This intensely visualised scene symbolises the social gap between the
lovers, expresses the effort of will required of Egbert to maintain their
relationship, and hints at its tragic conclusion. All the most important
encounters between the lovers take place in darkness, or the melancholy half-darkness that follows dusk or precedes dawn, fitfully illuminated by candlelight or firelight: their first embrace, their parting when
Egbert leaves for London, their meeting on the eve of the wedding. The
final fatal meeting of Geraldine with her father also takes place at
night, and its melodramatic character is somewhat muted by the fact
that it is not presented directly. Instead, as Geraldine goes into the
house, the narrative stays outside in the dark grounds with the anxious
Egbert. The passage subtly echoes the opening scene in the church:

he watched her crossing the grass and advancing, a mere dot, towards
the mansion. In a short time the appearance of an oblong of light in the

shadowy expanse of wall denoted to him that the door was open: her outline appeared on it; then the door shut her in, and all was shadow as before. (Chapter 7)

Nothing could be more 'cinematic' – the best word, it seems to me, to describe what Hardy himself called his 'idiosyncratic mode of regard'.[10]

8 Pessimism and Fictional Form: *Jude the Obscure*

We can all agree, perhaps, that *Jude the Obscure* is about frustration and failure in two areas of life – sex and education. It is about Jude Fawley's failure to get to the University, and about his disastrous relationships with women. But as soon as we ask what is the meaning of these themes as presented in the narrative, doubt and disagreement commence.

Some readers interpret the novel as an indictment of the society that made it impossible for a working man to obtain higher education and that punished any deviation from conventional norms of sexual behaviour. And there is some justification in the text for such a reading, which sees Jude and Sue as martyrs in the cause of progress and en-lightenment. 'Our ideas were fifty years too soon to be any good to us', says Jude at the end. But is it true that he and Sue would have been happier in the age of the Open University and the Permissive Society? Hardly. If we look closely at the narrative we see that Jude's failure to get to the University is largely the result of his own character and his involvement with Arabella and Sue. There *were* very real social and economic forces working against a man in his position and with his aspirations, but they are only portrayed in the margins, so to speak, of the story; and Jude never puts them seriously to the test. When he realises the hopelessness of his academic ambitions, this realisation is presented in terms of awakening from a delusive dream and perceiving his own folly and impracticality. 'Well, all that was clear to him amounted to this, that the whole scheme had burst up, like an irides-cent soap-bubble, under the touch of a reasoned enquiry' (II, VI). Jude then recognises that his destiny lies among the ordinary working people of Christminster, and there is some suggestion that this could be a valu-able and fulfilling life – more so than the lives of scholars and students. 'He began to see that the town life was a book of humanity infinitely more palpitating, varied, and compendious than the gown life.' This sounds hopeful, yet one could scarcely say that it is confirmed by the rest of the novel. In so far as the ordinary people of Christminster are presented – and it is not very far – they are a rather unpleasant and

106

unsympathetic group, whose lives seem mean, narrow and monotonous rather than 'palpitating, varied, and compendious'. There is, in fact, no fulfilling community available to Jude.

If we turn to the sexual theme, we find the same ambiguity and negativity. In its own day the novel was seen as an attack on the institution of marriage, but again this is a very marginal implication. Neither Jude nor Sue finds much difficulty in obtaining the dissolution of their ill-advised marriages, but divorce does not solve their problems. Social disapproval of their irregular union is not the most important of these problems. Sue is, in fact, incapable of making Jude happy either inside or outside marriage because of her sexual frigidity and because (as we are frequently reminded) they are cousins in a family with a sombre history of marital problems. The story confirms this suggestion of a hereditary weakness where matrimony is concerned. Sue's marriage and remarriage to Phillotson are contracted in obedience to her own peculiar neurotic drives, just as, in marrying and remarrying Arabella, Jude is essentially a dupe and victim, a Samson to her Delilah (a picture of this Biblical couple ominously decorates the wall of an inn they visit during their courtship).

In short, there is no suggestion, in the novel, that the protagonists could have achieved happy and fulfilled lives. Their ideals and aspirations prove to be vain, impracticable illusions, and when they try alternative courses of action these, too, prove to be disappointing, or worse. Jude and Sue are trapped in a maze of unhappiness, from which there is no escape – except death. The last words of the novel, spoken by Arabella about Sue after Jude's death, are: 'She's never found peace since she left his arms, and never will again till she's as he is now!' This saying, as Michael Millgate has observed,[1] echoes a sentiment from one of Hardy's favourite texts, the *Oedipus Rex* of Sophocles: 'Call no man happy ere he shall have crossed the boundary of life, the sufferer of nought painful.' Perhaps more significantly, it agrees with an authorial comment very early in the novel about the boy Jude's abnormal sensitivity. This is a typical sentence of Hardy's in that it is full of small surprises or shocks; it keeps going on after you expect it to stop, becoming more and more daunting: 'This weakness of character, as it may be called, suggested that he was the sort of man who was born to ache a good deal before the fall of the curtain upon his unnecessary life should signify that all was well with him again' (I, II).

Jude the Obscure is, by general agreement, Thomas Hardy's bleakest, most pessimistic, most depressing novel. What I want to examine in the rest of this essay is the way the form of *Jude* works to articulate and reinforce the pessimism of its vision of life. I use the word *form* in its widest sense to include all the means of literary presentation from the largest to the smallest in scope: the design of the plot, the point of view of the narration, the tone of the narrator, symbolic action, figurative language, right down to the construction of the simplest sentences. In one sense everything in a novel is form, since it is only by virtue of having form that a novel communicates at all. But we become conscious of form, as readers, through the perception of recurrence and repetition (and the negative kind of repetition which is contrast) in the stream of apparently random or historically 'given' particularity that, in the realistic novel tradition to which Hardy belonged, creates the illusion of life. In practice, Hardy was often prepared to risk breaking realistic illusion for the sake of an expressive effect. In this respect he had a kinship with American rather than European novelists of the nineteenth century, such as Hawthorne and Melville. But *Jude*, his last work of fiction, is a highly patterned novel which rarely strains the reader's credulity, with the exception perhaps of the murder of the children and some of the dialogue that is put into the characters' mouths. On the whole *Jude* combines a Sophoclean sense of tragic fate with the scrupulous verisimilitude of nineteenth-century realism and naturalism. No wonder it makes uncomfortable reading.

In a famous passage of Proust's *À la recherche du temps perdu*, Marcel, putting forward the theory that every novelist's work has a secret signature which makes it unmistakably *his* creation, refers to what he calls the 'stone-mason's geometry' which gives Hardy's novels their special character.[2] By this phrase he means the elaborate concern for parallelism and symmetry with which Hardy constructed his novels – a trait that Marcel attributes to Hardy's training and professional experience as an architect. The idea seems particularly illuminating with regard to *Jude the Obscure*, and not merely because the hero is himself a stone-mason by trade. The plot, for instance, considered in its bare outline as a design or structure, is strikingly symmetrical: the two marriages, the two divorces, the two remarriages. As Jude changes from religious belief to scepticism, so Sue changes from scepticism to religious belief. As Arabella changes from worldliness to religiosity and back to worldliness, so Phillotson changes from conventionality to unconventionality and back again to conventionality. This intricate pattern of shifting relationships between the two couples, which leaves them all, in the end, as they began, trapped with uncongenial and incompatible partners, embodies the idea which I find central to *Jude* – that life is a closed system of disappointment from which only death offers an escape.

Such a permutation of relationships between two couples could, of course, have provided the basis for a comedy. It doesn't, in this case, because the human consequences are tragic and painful, because the tone of the narrative is grave, and for several other obvious reasons. In the form of a novel, all the components are interdependent. Its effect is cumulative, and every word makes its contribution. I can best illustrate the point, however, by talking about larger units of meaning than words and sentences – by talking about scenes, or incidents or gestures. Most of the incidents in the novel belong to a series or 'set', all the items of which are related to each other either by similarity or by contrast. Indeed most incidents can be placed in more than one such series, and it is this complexity and multiplicity of cross-reference that prevents the elaborate patterning of *Jude* from seeming too obviously willed by the novelist. We have, rather, the sense of an inevitable destiny underlying the apparently gratuitous particularity of the stream of experience.

Let us first look at a specific example – the famous, or notorious, scene in which Jude first meets Arabella. The young Jude is walking along a country road, meditating enthusiastically upon his academic ambitions, oblivious to the provocative cry of 'Hoity-toity' from Arabella and her two companions, who are washing chitterlings in a stream behind the hedge.

' . . . I can work hard. I have staying power in abundance, thank God! and it is that which tells . . . Yes, Christminster shall be my Alma Mater; and I'll be her beloved son, in whom she shall be well pleased.'

In his deep concentration on these transactions of the future Jude's walk had slackened, and he was now standing quite still, looking at the ground as though the future were thrown thereon by a magic lantern. On a sudden something smacked him sharply in the ear, and he became aware that a soft cold substance had been flung at him, and had fallen at his feet.

A glance told him what it was – a piece of flesh, the characteristic part of a barrow-pig, which the countrymen used for greasing their boots, as it was useless for any other purpose. Pigs were rather plentiful hereabouts, being bred and fattened in large numbers in certain parts of North Wessex. (I, VI)

The symbolic and prophetic function of this incident need not be laboured. The seduction of Jude by the coarsely sexual Arabella is to be the first major check to Jude's academic ambitions, and this could scarcely be more vividly foreshadowed than by making her hit him on the ear with the sexual organ of a pig[3] at the moment when he is rapt in his dream of scholarly achievement. What may not be so obvious is that this particular incident, vivid and expressive in its own place, also has parallels before and after in the narrative.

To being with, it belongs to a series of moments of disillusionment, or 'rude awakening', which in their constant recurrence make up the primary rhythm of Jude's life. I have already referred to one such moment: when Jude's scheme to study at Christminster 'burst up, like an iridescent soap-bubble, under the touch of a reasoned enquiry'. The shock of Arabella's missile is clearly a premonition of that later rude awakening, for the simile of the soap-bubble, applied to Jude's plans, is matched by the image of the magic lantern in the earlier passage. It is important to recognise that the throwing of the pig's pizzle does not only reflect upon the thrower – it also represents the reality principle breaking in upon illusion.

A more obvious parallel appears in the second chapter of the novel, when Jude, in a mood of sympathetic identification with the rooks whom he is being paid to frighten away, encourages them to eat the corn, and suddenly receives a smart blow on the buttocks from the irate farmer. Other moments of disillusionment and deflation include: Physician Vilbert's failure to remember his promise to supply Jude with Latin and Greek grammars; Jude's bitter disappointment on discovering that there is no quick method of learning those languages; Phillotson's failure to recognise Jude when the latter seeks him out in the spirit of a disciple visiting his old master; the crass materialism of the composer of the hymn that had moved Jude so deeply that he made a pilgrimage to meet him; Jude's discovery on his wedding night that Arabella wears false hair; and his realisation, when Sue leaves Phillotson and elopes with him, that she does not want to consummate their love. One could multiply examples.

Going back to the first encounter of Arabella and Jude, it is worth noting that she throws the pig's pizzle in order to attract his attention, because she is separated and concealed from him by a hedge and a stream. As the scene proceeds they exchange a few words, then Jude breaks through the hedge and he and Arabella walk along the two opposite banks of the stream until they reach a small footbridge where they can meet. The scene thus belongs to another series which runs through the whole of Hardy's fiction, but which is particularly marked in *Jude the Obscure*. J. Hillis Miller has described them as scenes 'which . . . dramatise some form of obstructed relationship',[4] because in them communication takes place across window-sills, through doors, across streams, or by letter. It is an indication of Sue's neurotic sensibility that she actually prefers obstructed or oblique communication to a direct encounter. One remembers the extraordinary exchange of notes between herself and Phillotson in their school in which she begs to be released from their marriage. And when Jude visits her shortly before that episode at Shaston, she dismisses him, and then, as he is going through the garden, opens the window and calls him back. 'I can talk to you better like this than when you were inside', she says; and the narrator, or Jude, observes: 'Now that the high window-sill was between them, so that he could not get at her, she seemed not to mind indulging in a frankness she had feared at close quarters' (IV, I). Arabella, in contrast, always seeks the direct encounter, in which she can bring her physical presence into play. When Jude discovers her serving in the Christminster pub, they talk across the bar for a while, but she insists on meeting outside, where she immediately takes his arm and, by the end of the evening, she sleeps with him; just as at their first meeting she talked to him across the stream, but exerted her sexual allure upon him at close quarters on the footbridge.

That there is something coarse, degrading and, to a fastidious sensibility, disgusting about Arabella's sexuality, is suggested by her close association with, of all animals, pigs. It is with a pig's sexual organ that Arabella first attracts Jude's attention; it is with the botched killing of a pig that their marriage reaches its crisis and breakdown; and it is in the living quarters behind a squalid pork-butcher's shop that she finally succeeds in recapturing him.

In trying to account for the peculiarly bleak and depressing effect of *Jude the Obscure*, we can reasonably point to the fact that it is the least pastoral, most urban of the Wessex novels. Much of the action takes place in towns and cities, in railway trains,[5] on streets and pavements, or indoors; and these settings are described on the whole perfunctorily and reductively. The interiors are mostly dingy and uncomfortable, and the exteriors of buildings, even the colleges of Christminster, are grimy, decayed and forbidding. But the lowering effect of these drab urban and domestic settings is intensified by the fact that the country, in so far as it is described at all, is equally *dreary*, to use a word that frequently appears in *Jude*. The very first chapter describes Marygreen, where Jude grows up, as a village totally lacking in charm or character, swathed in an oppressive clammy mist; and in the following chapter the ploughed field in which Jude is working calls from him the murmured observation, 'How ugly it is here!' Readers of *Jude the Obscure* are made to feel that there is not much to choose between town and country as environments, that they are both equally drab and unattractive. Again we encounter the peculiarly negative quality of this novel – the cancelling out of alternatives which makes the pursuit of happiness by the protagonists seem a vain endeavour. It is clearly part of Hardy's deliberate avoidance of anything approaching the quality of pastoral idyll, in *Jude*, that the only rural activity to be portrayed in any detail is the rearing of pigs. It makes *Jude* the antithesis of a novel like *Far from the Madding Crowd*, with its loving, lyrical descriptions of the seasonal tasks of the land, and a considerably bleaker novel than *Tess of the d'Urbervilles*, which has the beauty of the valley of the Great Dairies to balance the harshness of Flintcombe-Ash. Instead of milking, sheep-shearing, haymaking and harvesting, we have in *Jude* the painfully convincing scene in which Jude kills the pig, 'a dismal, sordid,

ugly spectacle' as it is justly described by the narrator – who adds, however, the qualification: 'to those who saw it as other than an ordinary
obtaining of meat' (I, X).

    This ambiguous rider is characteristic of Hardy. Is Jude admired, or
mocked, for his distress over the pig's death? The episode certainly
belongs to another set or series in the novel, concerned with animals
and human attitudes towards them: there are the rooks which the
young Jude fails to frighten away, the earthworms which he takes care
not to tread on, the trapped rabbit which he mercifully kills, and the
pigeons which Sue impulsively frees after they have been sold to a
poulterer at an auction of her and Jude's effects. 'Why should Nature's
law be mutual butchery!' (V, VI) Sue complains on this occasion;
while Jude earlier perceived from his experience with Farmer Trout-
ham, 'the flaw in the terrestrial scheme, by which what was good for
God's birds was bad for God's gardener' (I, II). Again we encounter
what might be called the heads-you-win-tails-I-lose syndrome in *Jude
the Obscure.* There is, it appears, no morally irreproachable attitude
towards the butchering of a pig.

    To perceive how Arabella's throwing of the pig's offal belongs to the
same set as the pig-killing scene, which itself recalls Jude's tenderness
towards the rooks, which in turn is connected, through the parallel of
the blow on the buttocks and the blow on the ear, with the pig's offal
scene – to perceive these cross-references is to get some idea of the intri-
cacy of Hardy's 'stone-mason's geometry' in *Jude the Obscure.* And we
have far from exhausted the ramifications of the passage with which we
started. Jude's last recorded thought just before he is hit on the ear is:
'Yes, Christminster shall be my Alma Mater; and I'll be her beloved son,
in whom she shall be well pleased.' This, of course is an allusion to the
baptism of Christ by John the Baptist in the New Testament, when a
voice from heaven was heard to pronounce these words of approval and
a dove descended upon the head of the Saviour. That Jude is standing
beside a stream at this point strengthens the parallel, though what
descends upon him out of the sky is not a dove but a pig's pizzle. This
ironic, almost blasphemous religious allusion again belongs to a series
which runs through the whole novel. It was presumably not fortuitous
that Hardy chose to call Jude's childhood home *Mary*green, and Oxford
*Christ*minster. Certainly, Jude's ill-fated return to the city in Part VI is
heavy with scriptural allusion, especially to Christ's Passion. Seeing
Phillotson in the crowd waiting for the Remembrance Day procession
to pass, Sue remarks: 'He is evidently come up to Jerusalem to see the
festival like the rest of us.' A little later she says that 'leaving Kennet-
bridge for this place is like coming from Caiaphas to Pilate' (VI, I).
Jude's speech to the waiting crowd – a 'sermon' as it is called by one of
the auditors – and his scathing comments on the ill-treatment of the

cab-horse, which brings down upon him the disapproval of authority in the person of a policeman, may be said to recall Christ's preaching in Jerusalem immediately before his Passion, as recorded in Matthew, Chapters 22–5. Jude's own passion is the horrific death of his children and the estrangement this causes between himself and Sue. 'Then let the veil of our temple be rent in two from this hour!' (VI, III), he says when she refuses to sleep with him. In this context Jude's casual exclamation to Sue at the time of their elopement, 'There, dear; don't mind. Crucify me if you will!' (IV, V) seems ominously prophetic.

It is clear that by identifying Jude with Christ, Hardy did not mean to confer on his hero's suffering any aura of redemptiveness or transcendence. Rather, the parallels are reductive and ironic, underlining the futility of Jude's sufferings, and the irrelevance of the Christian myth and its consolations to his plight. Whatever its sources in Hardy's personal experience, *Jude the Obscure* is, in its profound pessimism, very much a novel of its time – the period of *fin de siècle*. God is dead, and according to the doctor who attends the murdered children, there is a 'coming universal wish not to live'. 'All is trouble, adversity and suffering', Sue tells Little Father Time. As readers of *Jude the Obscure* we cannot avoid the challenge of Hardy's pessimism because of the form of the novel, in which every incident is not merely revealing and expressive in its own place, but also reinforces the meaning of innumerable other incidents, all carrying the same general implication. For the reader, as for Jude and Sue, there is no escape.

Part III

Aspects of Waugh

9 Evelyn Waugh: Habits of a Lifetime

Although literary biography appears to be exceedingly popular with the educated reading public, there is a dearth of theory behind this form of writing, and a good deal of uncertainty, therefore, about the appropriate criteria to apply to any particular specimen of it, such as Christopher Sykes's *Evelyn Waugh* (1975). But I suppose most people would agree that literary biography ought to do at least some of the following things: (1) enable us to understand and appreciate better the work of the subject, (2) throw light on the creative process, (3) satisfy our curiosity about the writer as a man, (4) provide a chronologically ordered critical account of the writer's *oeuvre*, (5) show how the writer related to literature considered as an institution, covering such matters as his attitude to tradition, his status with his peers, the critical reception of his work, the financial rewards of his writing, and so on.

The first of these desiderata would seem at first glance to be the most weighty and important justification of literary biography, but in modern times it has been subjected to hostile scrutiny. The Anglo-American New Critics, inspired by Eliot's theory of impersonality ('the more perfect the artist, the more completely separate in him will be the man who suffers and the man who creates'), looked with suspicion upon biographical criticism as a dangerous distraction from the 'words on the page'; and more recently the *nouvelle critique* has poured scorn on the idea that the author as an individual human being is a legitimate object of literary study. 'We should recognise the Author, who is a concept, as the creation of his work, not as its creator', says John Sturrock, paraphrasing Roland Barthes (*New Review*, Vol. 1, No. 2, p. 21). This Gallic paradox can be converted into a form more acceptable to Anglo-Saxon common sense if we suggest that the writer's life, on which his imagination feeds, is itself conditioned by the fact that he is a writer and sees all experience as potential material for art. 'Still all this will make a funny novel so it isn't wasted', Evelyn Waugh wrote to his wife-to-be in a letter describing the tribulations of a war correspondent covering the Italian-Abyssinian war (and how right he was – *Scoop* is one of the funniest novels in the language).

When he sought employment as a regimental soldier in the Second
World War he was no doubt partly motivated by patriotism, but his
diary entry for 27 August 1939 reveals how his literary vocation was
uppermost in his mind: 'I have to consider 30 years of novel writing
ahead of me. Nothing would be more likely than work in a Government
Office to finish me as a writer, nothing more likely to stimulate me
than a complete change of habit.' The only part of a writer's life that
may be said to have an unconditioned effect on his art are his early
years, before the artistic vocation is fully formed, and as Angus Wilson
observed in reviewing this book in the *Times Literary Supplement*,
Christopher Sykes has neglected the opportunity of recovering anything
from the 'lost childhood' of Evelyn Waugh by relying on the writer's
own volume of autobiography *A Little Learning*, in which the child's
experience is very carefully filtered and framed by the adult writer.
This neglect will be regretted by many readers, but it is fully consistent
with Mr Sykes's general abstention throughout his biography from
speculative psychologising.

The critical suspicion of literary biography derives from the fear that
it imposes an oversimplified cause-and-effect model on the process of
literary creation. If the author is seen as the Cause and his work as the
Effect, there is an obvious danger that the former may come to seem
more important than the latter, and that the biographer, equipped with
special knowledge about the author, may claim proprietorial rights in
the interpretation of the work. Is our appreciation/understanding of
Shakespeare's plays as art impaired because we know relatively little
about his life? Would it be enhanced if we knew more? The answer
would seem to be negative in both cases. The next stage is to argue that
since biographical information is clearly not *essential* to criticism, we
are better off without it; and in the more extreme New or *nouvelle*
criticism biographical information is treated as something to be purged
(like heresy) or indulged covertly (like pornography). It is, however,
unnecessary to go to such lengths to avoid error. There is a very simple
and obvious way in which literary biography helps us to understand and
appreciate a writer's work without necessarily imposing a narrowly
genetic approach to it, and that is by giving us some sense of the context – human, cultural, social, historical – in which that work was
originally produced and consumed. While it is true that we can never
recover that context in its entirety, we cannot read a work of literature
meaningfully without some attempt to reconstruct it, and literary biography can play a valuable part in making us aware of all the unspoken,
unformulated assumptions and values that underlie a writer's relationship to his audience at any particular moment, and that fade with the
passing of time.

As well as being an authorised biographer, with full access to his subject's papers, Christopher Sykes has the advantage of having been a close friend of Evelyn Waugh for most of the latter's adult life, and of belonging to the same social milieu – where the spheres of the landed gentry and aristocracy, High Society, London clubs, and the arts intersect and overlap. Evelyn Waugh did not (like his biographer) belong naturally to this milieu – he was elected into it by his success as a novelist and he secured his place in it by the money he earned from writing. His desperate anxiety to succeed in this way explains a good deal of the manic-depressive behaviour of his youth. The diaries reveal that he contemplated suicide while still at school and in one of several farewell letters which he drafted he commented: 'I have no really definite cause for killing myself. I suppose it is really a fear of failure.'

At Oxford, Mr Sykes reports, he was discovered noisily drunk outside the gates of Balliol by Cyril Connolly. ' "Why do you have to make such a noise wherever you are?" angrily asked Cyril. "I have to make a noise," came the astonishing reply, "because I'm poor." ' *Decline and Fall* proved a more effective way of calling attention to himself. 'I had never heard from . . . anyone . . . at Oxford the name of Evelyn Waugh until the publication of *Decline and Fall* in 1928', Sykes records. 'Then everyone remembered him.'

Sykes, then, knows the adult world of Evelyn Waugh well and from inside, but he does not on that account claim privileged status as an interpreter of the novels. There is a good deal of criticism (more of this in a moment) but it is not essentially biographical in orientation. The general lines of connection between Waugh's life and work were, in any case, pretty well known already. His autobiography *A Little Learning* touches on the school-mastering background to *Decline and Fall*; his travel books contain much of the source material used in *Black Mischief, Scoop* and the South American section of *A Handful of Dust*; the breakdown of his first marriage has been traced by several critics in the theme of marital infidelity that recurs in most of his novels, and there has been a spate of memoirs in recent years which have thrown considerable light on the experience behind *Brideshead Revisited, Gilbert Pinfold* and the *Sword of Honour* trilogy.

Mr Sykes has no real surprises or revelations to offer on this level, but he has gathered a lot of interesting detail with which to fill out the general picture. For example, his discussion of the Lygon family makes much more explicit than Lady Dorothy Lygon's guarded memoir in David Pryce-Jones's *Evelyn Waugh and His World* (1973) the extent to which that family's recent history inspired *Brideshead Revisited*; and he is a confident, apparently reliable guide to the identity of the real people who served as models for such immortals as Mrs Stitch and Basil

Seal (asked whether he did not expect some resentment from Peter
Rodd on account of the latter characterisation, Waugh replied characteristically: 'You can draw any character as near to life as you want, and
no offence will be taken provided you say that he is attractive to
women').

   We touch here upon a curious paradox of literary biography, that it
seems to risk destroying the very thing it sets out to celebrate – the
creative imagination – by discovering factual equivalents for fictional
creations. Presumably that is one reason why writers so often request
that no biography of them shall ever be written. Evelyn Waugh made no
such request, but he was significantly unwilling to admit that his
characters were often modelled on real people. Mr Sykes seems to have
made quite a sport of trying to trap him into such admissions, often
successfully. Undoubtedly it is true, as he claims, that there is a *roman-
à-clef* element in most of Evelyn Waugh's novels, but their interest on
this level is obviously limited to a fairly small audience. More remarkable is the extraordinarily wide appeal of these novels to readers who
have little or no personal acquaintance with the society they depict.

Undoubtedly the principal claim of this biography on our attention,
and the main reason why it will be eagerly read, comes under my third
head – satisfying curiosity about Evelyn Waugh the man. In his case this
curiosity is rather more than a simple tribute to the interest and value
of his books. There was always something of the dandy about Evelyn
Waugh,[1] and the dandy is a man who makes his own behaviour and
life style into a work of art. We turn to a biography of Evelyn Waugh,
therefore, with the anticipation that anecdote about him will have some
of the comic quality of his novels. We are not disappointed. Mr Sykes's
biography is full of funny stories and droll observations, especially from
Evelyn Waugh's letters. But let me quote a passage where Mr Sykes
himself has been inspired by his subject to considerable comic achievement. It happens to turn upon the matter of dress – the most obvious,
though not only way, in which the dandy tends to express himself:

One day soon after the War looking through my half-forgotten ward-
robe I came across a rather dandyish piece, a grey bowler hat. With a
dark grey suit I found this rather becoming, and thus clad I went to
White's. Sitting on the leather-seated fender, glaring at every member
who came in, was Evelyn. He leapt to his feet on my entrance, his
eyes blazing and haggard with that concentrated look of jealousy that
I remembered from Tatton Park. 'Give me that hat!' he cried.
   I refused, saying it was a hat I valued and loved.
   'Where did you get it?'
   I told him that it came from Lock's in St James's Street. The same
day Evelyn went to Lock's shop who in due time sent him from the

stores 'one white coke hat'. This he wore frequently from then on, not only in summer for which such hats are designed, but at all seasons.

A grey bowler hat worn with the right sort of clothes can have dignity, but not when worn with the sort of suit Evelyn ordered shortly after. There is a cloth exclusively woven for Officers of the Household Cavalry, used in the making of travelling and sporting overcoats and now usually for country caps. Never in history had this cloth been used for the making of a suit. On a light reddish-brown background it has a bright red check about three inches square. Evelyn made tailoring history by ordering a suit in this cloth. The result surpassed the wildest extravagances of an old-fashioned music-hall comedian. A weird touch of obscenity was added, as the tailor cut the cloth in such a way that a bright red line from the checks ran down the fly buttons. The ensemble of this suit and one white coke hat sensibly diminished any resemblance Evelyn might have had to the Old English Squire. He enjoyed the farce of all this, especially as it increased the sourness of his critics.

Several of Evelyn Waugh's Oxford friends and acquaintances, such as Harold Acton and Brian Howard, were dandies directly descended from the Decadence, as was Ronald Firbank whose fiction he so much admired, and many of his pranks and *bons mots* in younger days were in this 'high camp' tradition. In later life he perfected a kind of reactionary, parodic dandyism that was peculiarly his own: the choleric, bulging-eyed, ear-trumpet-wielding, tweed-clad scourge of modernity in life, art and religion. *The Ordeal of Gilbert Pinfold* relates fascinatingly how this mask or persona began to develop an autonomous life of its own, leading Waugh to the brink of schizophrenia. Yet there can be little doubt that the mask was itself an attempt to conceal from the world's inquisitive gaze the dark, destructive side of his own psyche – or if not to conceal it, to control it, to give it a degree of stylisation that would make it acceptable as a kind of joke or fantasy.

Unfortunately the joke often misfired in the sense that Waugh caused pain and distress on many occasions by his rude and bullying manner towards friends and casual acquaintances. Perhaps, rather sadly and certainly unintentionally, this is the dominating thread in Sykes's biography – certainly it is the aspect that has attracted most attention. That Evelyn Waugh could make himself ferociously unpleasant in company has always been well known, but the extent and frequency of such behaviour is documented here on a somewhat daunting scale. I was particularly struck by the account of Waugh's unpopularity with his fellow-soldiers of all ranks, during the war, which reached such a pitch that his friend and commander Bob Laycock had to tell him that he had become 'unemployable'. Of course, there was an anarchic disregard for military protocol in Waugh's conduct which on occasion one can only applaud (as when he told a general who

complained of his being mildly drunk in the evenings, 'I could not
change the habit of a lifetime for a whim of his'), but it is sobering
to learn that Laycock was sufficiently alarmed by the dislike Waugh
generated among the men he commanded as to have his sleeping quarters covertly guarded. Of his social brutality here is a typical instance
reported by Mr Sykes:

Mary Lygon has told me of an unhappy occasion when she invited him
to a dinner party to meet some admirers who included a well-known
American theatrical producer and his wife. The last-mentioned addressed
him thus: 'Oh Mr Waugh, I have just been reading your new book
Brideshead Revisited, and I think it's one of the best books I have
ever read.' To which Evelyn replied: 'I thought it was good myself, but
now that I know that a vulgar, common American woman like yourself admires it, I am not so sure.'

Christopher Sykes does not attempt to excuse such behaviour; on the
contrary he condemns it forthrightly, but balances against it Waugh's
kindness and charity to friends down on their luck (for example Alfred
Duggan, whom Evelyn Waugh helped to recover from alcoholism and
to establish himself as a writer). To the question how Waugh reconciled
his rudeness with his subscription to the Christian faith, he quotes the
answer Waugh gave to Nancy Mitford when she challenged him with it:
'You have no idea how much nastier I would be if I were not a Catholic. Without supernatural aid I would hardly be a human being.' Certainly we are not concerned, here, with ordinary spitefulness of character. There is a kind of insane recklessness about Waugh's treatment of
the hapless theatrical producer's wife, exactly equivalent to the pointless courage he displayed under fire in the war (for example, during an
air attack in Yugoslavia when his comrades, commanded by Randolph
Churchill, were prudently taking cover in a ditch, he persisted against
orders in walking up and down in a very visible white sheepskin coat,
thus endangering not only his own life but theirs too).

Most of us, perhaps, are nice to each other partly because we want
to be thought nice, because we want to be liked. Only someone totally
indifferent to his own feelings as well as the feelings of others could
deliver such a shattering insult and sit on at the dinner table in the
resulting atmosphere of odium and embarrassment. This is not to say
that Evelyn Waugh never repented of his offences – he did, and said
once that he could no longer afford to come to London because of all
the flowers he had to send to people he insulted in his cups. But Christopher Sykes is surely on the right track when he says that there was a
strong element of self-hatred in Evelyn Waugh. He makes the point in
connection with the diaries, which he regards as factually unreliable,

containing a strong element of self-hating fantasy; but it applies equally
well to his indifference to physical danger and his gratuitous insults.

Perhaps it explains, too, the character of his allegiance to Roman
Catholicism. A Protestant type of piety was impossible for him, for
how could a man who hated himself experience assurance of his personal salvation? The Catholic faith that Evelyn Waugh was received into
in 1930 explained his unhappiness (intensified at that time by the
breakdown of his first marriage) by reference to the doctrine of original
sin (the sense of mankind as exiled from a lost paradise permeates all
his work) and offered the comfort and protection of an institution
under providential guidance. It asked, not for an emotional conversion,
but for an act of will, an intellectual assent to a doctrine of salvation
which was quite objective and impersonal. The truth of this doctrine
was guaranteed by the life of Christ in which God, uniquely, intervened
in History (hence Evelyn Waugh's extremely literal-minded devotion to
the Holy Places, and relics of the True Cross). But the revelation was
not itself historically or culturally conditioned: it was eternal, absolute,
supernatural. The more difficult it was to believe, the more obviously
true it was. This was roughly Evelyn Waugh's faith. To outsiders, and to
many Catholics, it often looked like a parody (as his tweeds were a
parody of the country squire), but there is plenty of evidence that he
took it absolutely seriously. No wonder he feared and detested the
revolutions in Catholic theology, biblical scholarship and liturgy which
swept it all away in the wake of Vatican II, for it was his only bulwark
against despair.

There is therefore, in contemplation, something of the archetypal
tragic comedian about Evelyn Waugh: the despairing heart behind the
comic mask. In the first chapter of *Gilbert Pinfold*, 'Portrait of the
Artist in Middle Age', we read: 'There was a phrase in the thirties: "It
is later than you think." which was designed to cause uneasiness. It was
never later than Mr. Pinfold thought.' In context, these lines point in
two directions. We can refer them back to Mr Pinfold's distaste for
'everything . . . that had happened in his own lifetime', and infer the
meaning: no one could possibly think that human civilisation had
reached a later stage of decadence than did Mr Pinfold-Waugh. And
this is a valid meaning. The 'myth of decline', the idea that civilisation
is in a constant and accelerating state of decay, is one that informs all
Evelyn Waugh's work from his very first novel – significantly entitled
Decline and Fall – and accounts for the inclusive and impartial irony of
his comic imagination. For when culture is seen as a process of continual decline, no secular institution or value is invulnerable: the
modern is ridiculed by contrasting it with the traditional, but attempts
to maintain or restore the traditional in the face of change are also seen

as ridiculous, and in any case the traditional itself also turns out to be, on close scrutiny, in some way false or compromised, already infected by decay. This is essentially the vision of T. S. Eliot's *The Waste Land* (from which Waugh took the title of *A Handful of Dust*) and it is one of the reasons why Waugh's work belongs to the history of modern literature rather than, like P. G. Wodehouse's novels, the history of modern entertainment.

But, 'It was never later than Mr. Pinfold thought' also refers, in its context, to the slowness with which time passed for Mr Pinfold himself, to his boredom with life and impatience for death. This note is struck so lightly and fleetingly that we scarcely realise its significance, but it is *very* significant for the interpretation of Mr Waugh, if not of Mr Pinfold.

'He was the only person I have ever known', Frances Donaldson records, 'who seemed sincerely to long for death.'[2] 'When Evelyn Waugh died suddenly . . .' Douglas Woodruff wrote in his obituary, 'it was a merciful dispensation at the end. He had been unwell for a long time, much troubled by insomnia, and a great depression of spirits.'[3] It is something of a shock to realise that the man of whom these and similar things were said was only sixty-two when he died. One has the same reaction to Evelyn Waugh's presentation of himself in the last decade of his life. In his travel book *Tourist in Africa* he refers to himself as a 'seedy old man' and the passage of his train through Paris calls forth the following sad reflection: 'Paris at the cocktail hour. How gaily I used to jump into a taxi and visit the bars while the train crawled round the *ceinture*. Nowadays, hard of hearing and stiff in the joints, I sit glumly in my compartment.' At the time of this trip, Evelyn Waugh was only fifty-six. It almost seems as if the myth of universal decline rebounded upon its author as a physical affliction, accelerating the ordinary processes of physical decay: if so, Evelyn Waugh nourished rather than resisted the visitation, exaggerating his slight deafness, for instance, by affecting an old-fashioned ear-trumpet, which he would sometimes put aside as a silent but crushing indication that he was bored.

And boredom, rather than aches and pains and deafness, was Evelyn Waugh's great affliction. Not the common-or-garden boredom generated by idleness or frustration, but a deep, permanent, almost metaphysical boredom, something comparable to the existentialist *angst* or nihilistic sense of the void that he affected to despise in other modern writers. 'From early manhood', Douglas Woodruff wrote, with a proper appreciation of this aspect of Waugh's character, 'he had suffered from ennui, an affliction which ought to be classed among the major ills to which suffering humanity is exposed, something on a par with blindness or deafness.' Woodruff recalled in this context an occasion 'when he had ordered champagne in the afternoon at White's and when it came he gazed sadly at it and said: "One thinks it will be enjoyable, and then when it comes, it isn't." ' What makes this little anecdote so poignant is, I think, that drinking champagne in the afternoon itself seems a last-ditch defence against boredom.

'He was joyous as a young man,' Father Martin D'Arcy, S.J., who received Evelyn Waugh into the Church, recalled after his death. 'But he grew rather embittered.'[4] 'Joyous' is a word made resonant by its rarity in modern English. Evelyn himself used it in a wry comment on a group of Anglican nuns with whom he found himself travelling in *Tourist in Africa:* 'They did not seem notably joyous. But who am I, of all people, to complain about that?'

One of the most vivid accounts of Evelyn Waugh in his youthful and joyous days is that of his friend of the twenties, Harold Acton, writing in 1948: 'Though others assure me he has changed past all recognition, I still see him as a prancing faun, thinly disguised by conventional apparel . . . So demure, yet so wild! A faun half-tamed by the Middle Ages, who would hide in some suburban retreat, and then burst upon the town with capricious caperings.'[5] Interestingly, Acton used the same word, 'embittered,' as Fr D'Arcy to describe his later character: 'Evelyn had to set out on his travels again, embittered but not, as his writings prove, dispirited altogether. It was an arduous journey, for he had been wounded. His bitterness was a source of anxiety to his friends, for it made a most lovable person cantankerous. After many trials and errors his wound was healed by the Catholic Church.'[6] The event to which Acton refers here was the breakdown of Waugh's first marriage (later dissolved by Rome) after only a year's duration; and certainly, if we are looking for a simple, single explanation of the pessimistic, melancholic strain in his character, we need look no further, so insistent is the theme of sexual betrayal in nearly every one of his novels. But while still a schoolboy Waugh had felt sufficiently disillusioned with life to contemplate suicide, and, as a young bachelor, he actually attempted it. The story of that episode – of how he left his clothes and a suitable Greek quotation on a Welsh beach one summer night, and swam out to sea intent on drowning himself, only to be driven back by stinging jellyfish – is the carefully chosen conclusion to his volume of autobiography, *A Little Learning.* It suggests that there was always within Evelyn Waugh a bitter spring of negation and despair which experience was bound to release, whatever his particular fortunes might be. His conversion to Catholicism ensured, perhaps, that this negative current in his character would never again be suicidal, but it grew stronger with the years. It was, I believe, to insulate himself from this negativity, and to conceal it from the world's inquisitive gaze, that he adopted Pinfold's compound mask of 'testy colonel and eccentric don'.

Mr Sykes sensibly assumes that anyone reading his biography will already be familiar with Evelyn Waugh's fiction, and does not bore us with tedious paraphrases. He does, however, offer critical evaluations of all the novels. Auberon Waugh, writing in *Books and Bookmen* (October 1975), took some exception to this vein in the biography, and although his filial loyalty has a notorious hair-trigger, one can understand why he finds Mr Sykes's book a somewhat grudging tribute to Evelyn Waugh the artist. 'I am as aware of his glaring literary errors as I am of his striking literary virtues', says Mr Sykes in his Preface. This rather implies that the errors are about as obvious and extensive as the virtues, which is difficult to reconcile with the view shared by many judges (and it would seem by Mr Sykes himself) that Evelyn Waugh was one of the finest (if not *the* finest) English novelists of his generation.

The same impression is left, and the same problem raised, by Mr Sykes's critiques of individual novels, where again he talks a great deal about 'errors', 'blemishes' and 'flaws'. His critical method is indeed one of conscientious weighing of pros and cons, a totting up of debits and credits. But is this how we read? Is it how we read Evelyn Waugh? It seems to me that there comes a point in every reading of a novel when the writer either commands our assent or he does not – and if he does, then the holes or flaws in his work become less perceptible because our attention is fully occupied in the collaborative task of extracting the maximum amount of delight from what he *does* give us. In Waugh's novels that point is reached very soon, particularly in the pre-war period. It seems churlish to make any complaint about the sequence from *Decline and Fall* to *Scoop*. *Brideshead Revisited* is admittedly a deeply flawed and ultimately unsatisfactory work, as no one realised better than its author. But the war trilogy seems to me to be a more triumphant achievement as a whole than Mr Sykes will allow. He considers *Unconditional Surrender* to be Waugh's 'best book', but has no time at all for *Men at Arms*. Are these judgments mutually compatible? Is it adequate to say *Men at Arms* fails because Guy Crouchback is 'ineffectual . . . Paul Pennyfeather cast for the principal role in an enormous tragedy'? I think not.

One of the most perceptive critical points made by Mr Sykes is with regard to the cinematic cross-cutting technique of the early comic novels, and it is fascinating to learn that Waugh was consciously experimenting with cinematic form in one of his earliest publications, a story (never reprinted) called 'The Balance' which Arthur Waugh included in an anthology of prose he edited in 1926. 'I have quite suddenly received inspiration about my book', he writes in a diary entry evidently referring to this work. 'I am making the first chapter a Cinema film and have been working furiously ever since'. Glimpses like this into the laboratory of the artist's mind are tantalisingly few and far between. Perhaps Waugh, unlike James or Virginia Woolf, did not in later life confide his thoughts on work in progress to his diaries – we shall see when they are published in full. But we might reasonably have expected in this biography more detailed documentation of his professional life, such as sales figures for the various books, quotations from contemporary reviews, correspondence with publishers and agents on technical matters, and his comments on the work of contemporaries.

Mr Sykes's biography has many negative virtues and some positive ones. It is not dogmatic or over-ingenious in interpretation, it is not sensationalist, it is not overprotective towards its subject, and it is not overburdened with trivial detail. It is clearly written, brisk in pace, and succeeds admirably in disentangling complicated contextual matters such as the Yugoslavian political situation in 1945. It is dignified without being dull. As a *literary* biography, however, for reasons I have suggested, it is a little disappointing.

10 The Fugitive Art of Letters

In *A Little Learning* (1964), Evelyn Waugh described his father as 'a Man of Letters . . . a category, like the maiden aunt, that is now almost extinct'.[1] Evelyn himself was certainly never a Man of Letters in the ripe, fully resonant sense of the term, but he began his literary career in circumstances not unlike those of his father at the same age, and occasional journalistic writing was always a part of that career.

Arthur Waugh came down from Oxford in 1890 with a disappointing third-class degree, and took his chance in the world of London publishing and literary journalism. An opportune biography of Tennyson published a few weeks after the Laureate's death, and, later, an essay on 'Reticence in Literature' which attracted considerable attention by appearing incongruously but (it seemed to many) appositely in the first issue of the *Yellow Book*, brought him regular employment as a reviewer. He calculated that he noticed approximately six thousand books in the course of his life, mostly in his spare time as Managing Director of Chapman & Hall. 'Some of my earliest memories are of book-reviewing', Evelyn wrote in 1953:

> My father wrote a weekly literary article for the *Daily Telegraph* . . . He greatly enjoyed this work, would read the book under review attentively and discuss it at table. Then on Saturday mornings a hush fell on the house while he wrote his article. My own first regular literary employment was reviewing for the *Observer* in the late '20s. I too enjoyed it . . . Since then, off and on, I have done a good deal of such work, always with pleasure.[2]

Evelyn, too, came down from Oxford with a disappointing Third,[3] and after several false starts adopted the profession of letters: 'I realised that there was nothing for it but to write books; an occupation which I regarded as exacting but in which I felt fairly confident of my skill.'[4] In his autobiography *One Man's Road* (1931), Arthur Waugh observed, 'When young men consult me . . . upon the best way of starting life as a reviewer or literary journalist, I can only give them the advice that comes of my own experience, and exhort them to write a book, and get their name upon a title page. It is extraordinary what faith an editor, or even a publisher, seems to put in the judgment of someone other than himself.'⁵ This seems to have been his son's experience also. The reviewing for the *Observer* in the late 1920s, mainly of art books, followed the publication of his own first book, *Rossetti: His Life and Works* (1928). His Mediterranean travel book *Labels*, his reporting of the coronation of Haile Selassie for *The Times* and the resulting book *Remote People* qualified him as a regular reviewer of travel books for the *Spectator* in the 1930s. And the success of *Decline and Fall* made him a fashionable commentator on the 'Younger Generation' – a phrase much in use at the time. 'The War and the Younger Generation' appeared in the *Spectator* of 13 April 1929. A little earlier, the *Evening Standard* printed a more racily titled piece, 'The Claim of Youth, or Too Young at Forty; Youth Calls to Peter Pans of Middle Age Who Block the Way'.⁶

The theme of the *Spectator* article overlaps the last chapter of Arthur Waugh's autobiography, which begins, 'The end of the War was the end of our generation. We did not realise it at the time, but it was the end all the same.' That whole chapter is a rueful, rather poignant attempt to come to terms with the violent upheaval in traditional values caused by the war, and with the particular strain thus laid upon parent–child relationships. The young Evelyn Waugh shared his father's view, but expressed it more coldly:

In the social subsidence that resulted from the War a double cleft appeared in the life of Europe, dividing it into three perfectly distinct classes between whom none but the most superficial sympathy can ever exist. There is (a) the wistful generation who grew up and formed their opinions before the War and who were too old for military service; (b) the stunted and mutilated generation who fought; and (c) the younger generation.

Especially interesting is the severity with which the author dissociates himself from 'this latter generation – the undiscriminating and ineffectual people we lament today'. The continuity of tone and attitude with the later Waugh is remarkable. When we read, 'Everything was a "substitute" for something else and there was barely enough even of that. The consequence is a generation . . . lacking in any sense of qualitative value', we may easily imagine that it is the children of the second war who are being referred to. When we read, 'the restraint of a traditional culture tempers and directs creative impulses. Freedom produces sterility', we might be listening to Scott-King or Gilbert Pinfold.

'There was nothing left for the younger generation to rebel against', the article continues, 'except the widest conceptions of mere decency.

Accordingly it was against these that it turned. The result in many cases is the perverse and aimless dissipation chronicled daily by the gossip-writers of the press'. One is not surprised to work out that Waugh must at this time have been preparing to write *Vile Bodies* (in which 'the topic of the Younger Generation spread like a yawn through the company' at Anchorage House), though the novel has a humour and compassion which the article lacks. It is worth noting that Waugh's disillusionment with contemporary society and 'Society' was emphatically stated before the break-up of his first marriage and his conversion to Catholicism. He seems already to have identified himself, in the spring of 1929, with 'a small group of young men and women [who] are breaking away from their generation and striving to regain the sense of values that should have been instinctive to them'.

At about the same time Waugh published 'Ronald Firbank',[7] in my opinion his best essay in 'pure' literary criticism, and a very useful key to an understanding of his own art. Everybody knows, of course, that Firbank 'influenced' Waugh, but the nature of the influence has not been analysed very deeply, perhaps because few critics have been prepared to take Firbank seriously, as Waugh did, as a technical innovator. His innovations, Waugh argued, were the result of a very specialised sense of humour seeking a means of expression, but they opened up possibilities for artists as different from Firbank in their values and aims as Ernest Hemingway.

He is the first quite modern writer to achieve . . . a new, balanced inter-relation of subject and form. Nineteenth-century novelists achieved a balance only by a complete submission to the idea of the succession of events in an arbitrarily limited period of time . . . [Firbank's] later novels are almost wholly devoid of any attributions of cause to effect; there is the barest minimum of direct description; his compositions are built up, intricately and with a balanced alternation of the wildest extravagance and the most austere economy, with conversational *nuances* . . . His art is purely selective. From the fashionable chatter of his period, vapid and interminable, he has plucked, like tiny brilliant feathers from the breast of a bird, the particles of his design . . . The talk goes on, delicate, chic, exquisitely humorous, and seemingly without point or plan. Then, quite gradually, the reader is aware that a casual reference on page one links up with some particular inflexion of phrase on another until there emerges a plot; usually a plot so outrageous that he distrusts his own inferences.

The examples Waugh gives show clearly how much the chronicler of the unlucky little Lord Tangent owed to the creator of Cardinal Pirelli. But he learned more than particular devices: Firbank offered the model of a kind of fiction that could be distinctively 'modern' in form and mood, quite liberated from the conventions of nineteenth-century fiction, without surrendering the classical literary virtues which Waugh valued or sacrificing the power to please. 'Other solutions are offered of the same problem, but in them the author has been forced into a subjective attitude to his material; Firbank remained objective and emphasised the fact which his contemporaries were neglecting, that the novel should be directed for entertainment. That is the debt which the present generation owes to him.'

Few of Waugh's essays and reviews of the 1930s, almost all of which were published in the *Spectator*, are as interesting or revealing as those two pieces of 1929. Really important books seldom seemed to come his way, and many that did, especially the travel books, were often very bad. On the whole, Waugh seems to have been a tolerant reviewer, more interested in praising merit than in punishing failure – or perhaps he had a lower motive for being kind: 'I used to have a rule when I reviewed books as a young man', he recalled in an interview late in life, 'never to give an unfavourable notice to a book I hadn't read. I find even this simple rule is flagrantly broken now.'[8] He began a review of a book called *White, Brown and Black* with the ominous words, 'Very occasionally it is worth while noticing a bad book at some length, if only to give hitherto reputable publishers a reminder that they must not be insolent in what they try and put over on a public already stupefied by literary over-production.'[9] This particular authoress was unfortunate enough to have recorded her impressions of a country Waugh knew well, Abyssinia:

She claims to have seen a slave caravan and describes it with all the stereotyped details of chinking chains, goads and whips and kicks, expressionless masks of faces, sockets of eyes, gaping mouths. This procession, she says, passed quite near her bed; she even saw one of the slave-drivers 'bury the point of his lance' in the back of one of the captives. I wonder how common these caravans are; I imagine they are pretty rare; she was in luck to run across one. Chain gangs of convicts are much more common in every part of Africa; she was clever to know the difference.

Waugh was always quick to pounce on any sign of pretentiousness. Sacheverell Sitwell, whom he respected, was gently rebuked for melodramatically comparing the inhabitants of Fez to 'Dante's damned souls'.

Those serene old men whom he saw jogging along the streets become extremely optimistic over their dinner; they are much richer than

Mr Sitwell or me, and they have the jolliest ideas of how to employ
their leisure; they can outface any race in the world in commercial
negotiation; every year or so they travel down to Tangier, change into
bowler hats and black suits and embark on a profitable but slightly
lugubrious journey to Manchester; they return with their business com-
pleted and eagerly change back into their white robes; at home a
shabby, scarcely noticeable door in a high white wall opens into a
courtyard of light tiles and running water, and beyond it, in a cool
drawing-room furnished with brass bedsteads and cuckoo-clocks,
they can forget the inferno of Western life of which they have had a
glimpse.[10]

Undoubtedly the best travel-book Waugh had for review was Graham
Greene's *The Lawless Roads*, a work in which he acknowledged a
special interest because 'It so happens that I arrived in Mexico last summer with ulterior literary motives a few weeks after Mr Greene had
left with his notebooks full'.[11] Mingled with Waugh's sincere admiration for Greene's 'heroic' journey and vivid reporting there is a certain,
sly humour:

There is a great deal to be said for travelling poor . . . the chief dis-
advantage is that the physical exhaustion incurred in merely getting
from place to place often makes one abnormally unresponsive to their
interest. Mr Greene, particularly, suffered from this. He makes no
disguise of the fact that Mexico disgusted him. In fairness it must be
added that England disgusts him too.

This review was, I think, Waugh's first public comment on the work
of Graham Greene, with whose name his own was to be so often
coupled as a 'Catholic novelist'; and he must have been one of the
earliest critics to remark the Jansenist flavour of Greene's Catholicism:

Mr Greene is, I think, an Augustinian Christian, a believer of the dark
age of Mediterranean decadence when the barbarians were pressing
along the frontiers and the City of God seemed yearly more remote and
unattainable . . . Contemplation of the horrible ways in which men
exercise their right of choice leads him into something very near a
hatred of free-will.

Though their lives ran parallel at many points,[12] the attitudes and
values of the two men were, of course, very different. Reviewing
Greene's illustrated book *British Dramatists* in 1942, Waugh complained that Greene was excluded from sympathy with the larger part

of his subject because of his subscription to 'the popular belief in "the People" . . . the new, complicated and stark crazy theory that only the poor are real and important and that the only live art is the art of the People'.[13] In this review, Waugh for the first time struck full and clear the militantly anti-democratic note for which he was to become increasingly notorious, quoting disdainfully the Henry Wallace phrase, 'the century of the Common Man', that recurs with almost obsessive frequency in his later journalism. But he describes Greene as 'a writer of outstanding imaginative power' and the ideological differences between the two men never prevented Waugh from expressing his admiration for Greene's fiction. He wrote, much later, appreciative and perceptive reviews of *The Heart of the Matter*[14] and *The End of the Affair*,[15] praising the latter, characteristically, for 'the variety and precision of the craftsmanship'.

Evelyn Waugh always had a great respect for literary craftsmanship, perhaps deriving from his early interest in graphics and his brief but enjoyable period as a student-carpenter (cabinet-making was the last vocation he tried before adopting that of letters). He was always happiest, as a critic, with writers whose technical skill and control were highly developed, whose individual and innovatory effects were obtained by a subtle modification rather than a radical readjustment of traditional forms. Firbank, Wodehouse, Belloc, Beerbohm, Knox – these were the writers, 'minor' by the standards of orthodox literary criticism, whom he delighted to praise.[16]

Style always obsessed him. 'Properly understood, style is not a seductive decoration added to a functional structure; it is of the essence of a work of art', he wrote. 'The necessary elements of style are lucidity, elegance and individuality; these three qualities combine to form a preservative which ensures the nearest approximation to permanence in the fugitive art of letters.'[17] This was said in a late essay, but he was applying the same criteria in his early reviews. 'The phrases are involved and slovenly, the metaphors mixed, the sentences in gross defiance of analysis', is a typical reproof of a travel-writer.[18] Malcolm Muggeridge, on the other hand, is praised for the correctness of his English:

It is a pleasure to welcome him into that very small company of writers whose work would escape the red ink of the Victorian governess. His new book gives the reader hope that no two words mean exactly the same to him; the punctuation, though not always orthodox . . . is usually consistent; with the exception of three painful conjunctival uses of 'like' there are no barbarities of grammar; there is an abundance of literary allusion and concealed quotation to flatter the reader's knowledge. It is, in fact, a highly unusual and welcome piece of workmanship.[19]

Christopher Isherwood earned similar praise for his contribution to *Journey to a War:* 'Not only does he seldom use a cliché, he never seems consciously to avoid one; a distinction due to a correct habit of thought.'[20]

Isherwood was the only one of the Left-wing writers of the 1930s for whom Waugh had any respect. The same review is curtly dismissive of Auden, and one of the most savage reviews he ever wrote was of Stephen Spender's volume of autobiography, *World Within World* (1951). His resentment at the way in which these writers 'ganged up and captured the decade' had by no means exhausted itself in the portrayal of Parsnip and Pimpernell in *Put Out More Flags:*

What made them unlike any writers in English history except the early pre-Raphaelites was their chumminess. They clung together. They collaborated. It seemed always to take at least two of them to generate any literary work however modest. They praised one another tirelessly and an unfavourable review anywhere raised a babble of protest from the author's young friends . . . but the nuisance is past. At the first squeak of an air-raid warning the gang dispersed.[21]

The air-raid sirens of World War II reduced Waugh's own output of occasional journalism to a thin trickle, but he found time in 1941 to write (perhaps with official encouragement) an article for the American mass-circulation magazine, *Life*, about the British Commandos with whom he himself was then serving. 'Commando Raid on Bardia',[22] thrillingly subtitled, 'Specially Trained British Bands Stealthily Attack Axis Strongholds in Libya at Night', and liberally illustrated with grainy monochrome photographs of British commandos in training – leaping out of landing barges, lighting smokeless fires and queasily watching a demonstration of how to kill, dress and cook wild game – makes it fascinating reading for anyone acquainted with the *Sword of Honour* trilogy. The source material is common, but the difference in tone may be indicated by comparing the military journalist's first impressions of the commandos –

. . . the officers' mess was at a seaside hotel. I had come from the austerity and formality of the Royal Marines. I found a young troop leader wearing a military tunic and corduroy trousers. He was reclining in a comfortable chair, a large cigar in his mouth. Then I noticed above the pocket of his coat the ribbon of the Military Cross and later when I saw him with his troop I realised that his men would follow him anywhere

– with Guy Crouchback's arrival on the island of Mugg:

He was directed from the quay to the hotel. At three o'clock he found it empty except for a Captain of the Blues who reclined upon a sofa, his head enveloped in a turban of lint, his feet shod in narrow velvet slippers embroidered in gold thread with his monogram. He was nursing a white pekinese; beside him stood a glass of white liqueur . . . Guy recognized Ivor Claire, a young show jumper of repute . . .

(Claire, so far from inspiring his men with his leadership, deserts them at Crete.)

It is not surprising that the note of mock heroic travesty and disillusionment that permeates the war trilogy is entirely absent from the *Life* article. The latter was published at a politically critical time when America was edging nearer and nearer to involvement in the war, and it was no doubt designed to interest the American public in the Allied cause. What is difficult to determine is Waugh's own attitude to the facts presented. The raid on Bardia is narrated in a completely straight, patriotic style – very much, indeed, in the 'Truslove spirit' so exquisitely parodied in *Men at Arms*. Did Waugh suppress his sense of humour in the interest of propaganda, or was he still in the honeymoon stage of his military service? And, in either case, how inspiring did he suppose his story was? The raid is described throughout as though it was a dangerous and successful mission, but to the dispassionate reader it seems to have had much in common with the fiasco at Dakar in *Men at Arms* and Trimmer's inglorious invasion of occupied France in *Officers and Gentlemen*. After a tense description of the assault party's climb up the escarpment from the beach, fearful of discovery at every moment, comes the anti-climactic revelation that the garrison at Bardia is completely deserted. The commandos proceed to blow up various installations and at last the enemy appears in the form of two motorcyclists. 'Everyone near had a shot at them with Tommy guns and grenades but they somehow got through. They were not an easy target. It was lucky really that they did escape for it was through them that the enemy learned, as we particularly wanted them to learn, that a raid was taking place.'

The withdrawal was no more impressive than the marksmanship. The ramp of Waugh's landing-craft got jammed and it floated helplessly in the bay for half an hour until it was freed, so it was fortunate that the garrison was undefended. They caught up with the mother-ship only just in time; another landing craft missed the rendezvous completely and sailed back to Tobruch under its own steam; and a third boatload of men returned to the wrong beach and were apparently abandoned to death or captivity. Somehow, one doubts that this article was very reassuring to American supporters of the Allied cause, or that it struck much terror into the German High Command. Yet Waugh never indicates by so much as a flicker of an eyelid that he regarded the raid on Bardia with anything less than pride.

After the war, he wrote quite frequently for American magazines, attracted, no doubt, by the comparatively large financial rewards of such work, and rendered eligible for it by the popular success of *Brideshead Revisited* (1945) in the United States. His second article for *Life*, 'Fan-fare', was, in fact, a droll open letter to the many American readers, mostly female, who had written to him about that novel.

In a civilized age this unexpected moment of popularity would have endowed me with a competency for life. But perhaps in a civilized age I should not be so popular. As it is the politicians confiscate my earnings and I am left with the correspondence. This is something new to me, for English women do not write letters to men they do not know . . . I have momentarily become an object of curiosity to Americans and I find that they believe that my friendship and confidence are included in the price of my book. My father taught me that it was flagitious to leave a letter of any kind unanswered. (Indeed his courtesy was somewhat extravagant. He would write and thank people who wrote to thank him for wedding presents and when he encountered anyone as punctilious as himself the correspondence ended only with death.) I therefore eagerly accept this chance of answering collectively all the cordial enquiries I have received.[23]

Like many an English writer before and after him, Evelyn Waugh found the differences and incongruities of American mores opened up fresh fields for satiric observation and gave a new zest to his own role-playing.

In the following spring, he visited Hollywood in connection with a projected film of *Brideshead*. He recorded his disenchantment in a cool but penetrating essay called 'Hollywood is a Term of Disparagement:'[24] 'Each of the books purchased [by the studios] has had some individual quality, good or bad, that has made it remarkable. It is the work of a staff of "writers" to distinguish this quality, separate it and obliterate it.'

Waugh's last article for *Life* was 'The American Epoch in the Catholic Church',[25] a somewhat dull and circumspect piece in which even the commercialisation of devotional objects – 'a "rosary aid" which records each "Ave" on a dial with a sharp click, and a plastic crucifix which, I was assured, had the advantage that you could "throw it on the ground and stamp on it" ' – provoke only the mildest satire. Waugh contemplated with surprising calm the possibility that American Catholicism might come to dominate the Universal Church. 'It may well be that Catholics of today, in their lifetime, may have to make enormous adjustment in their conception of the temporal nature of the Church.' But when Vatican II asked him to accept doctrinal and liturgical change, Waugh jibbed.

In 1949, he had contributed to a symposium of Catholic converts a short piece entitled 'Come Inside' describing his loss of Christian faith as a schoolboy and his subsequent reception into the Church of Rome.[26] The appeal of Catholicism for him was, he suggests, historical in a way that an American might find difficult to understand. The spirit of *aggiornamento* released by the second Vatican Council, which most 'ghetto-Catholics' found liberating, seemed to Waugh to threaten the foundations of the Church's historic role and the grounds of his own faith.[27]

The core of that faith was, I feel, his sense of mankind exiled from a state of pre-lapsarian happiness, needing some providential guidance and institutional order. He has an eloquent passage praising Ronald Knox's rendering of the patriarchs of the Old Testament: 'They are precisely what they should be, men and women living in a fallen and un-redeemed world, haunted by ancestral memories of a lost Eden, taught by hints and portents, punished by frightful dooms, people half lost waiting for something to happen.'[28] The theme recurs frequently in his writing, and if he went to religion for a saving idea of order, he often turned to literature for a fleeting recovery of lost innocence. In a lyrical celebration of Aldous Huxley's *Antic Hay*, a book that exhilarated his youth, he says, 'It is Henry James' London possessed by carnival. A chain of brilliant young people linked and interlaced winds past the burnished front doors in pursuit of happiness. Happiness is growing wild for anyone to pick . . .'[29] And his enthusiasm for P. G. Wodehouse becomes easier to understand when we read in 'An Act of Homage and Reparation': 'For Mr Wodehouse there has been no fall of Man . . . the gardens of Blandings Castle are that original garden from which we are all exiled.'[30]

There is much more variety in Evelyn Waugh's occasional writing after the war than before it, in both content and places of publication. He renewed his association with the *Spectator*, but also wrote for *Time and Tide*, for the Catholic weekly the *Tablet* and for the Jesuit periodical the *Month*; towards the end of his life he reviewed occasionally for the *Sunday Times*. In America, *Life*, *Esquire*, the *Atlantic*, *Commonweal* and even *Playboy*[31] published his work. Over the same period, he indulged in polemics of various kinds, not only in his frequent letters to the Press, but sometimes in full-length articles. One of the earliest of these was 'Palinurus in Never-never-land',[32] an effective satire on a Utopian manifesto printed in *Horizon* by Cyril Connolly, in which we may detect the germ of *Love Among the Ruins*. In 1953, he was given the opportunity, in a *Spectator* series, to review the reviewers of that story, but his only serious complaint was of the treatment he had received in the Beaverbrook Press.[33] He continued this feud in 1955 with 'Awake my Soul! It is a Lord!'[34] the ironical account of an unsolicited and successfully repelled visit to his home by Nancy Spain of the *Daily Express* and Lord Noel-Buxton – an unchivalrous but effective broadside, which provoked some amusing correspondence in the *Spectator*.

In 1956, Waugh leaped to the defence of P. G. Wodehouse against an allegedly 'caddish' and ill-informed review by John Wain, who was made to stand for a new, university nurtured, cultural barbarism which was to be the subject of frequent complaint thereafter.[35] In the same year appeared his celebrated 'Open Letter to the Honble Mrs Peter Rodd (Nancy Mitford) on A Very Serious Subject',[36] a witty intervention into a rather laboured current debate about U (Upper-class) and Non-U speech and behaviour. Waugh argued brilliantly that 'there are no classes in England; there is only precedence . . . There is a single line extending from Windsor to Wormwood Scrubs, of individuals all justly and precisely graded (no one knows this order of precedence: it is a Platonic idea)!' This letter is a very characteristic piece of late Waugh, full of outrageously provocative anti-democratic sentiment ('Mr Butler in his Education Act . . . provided for the free distribution of university degrees to the deserving poor') and at the same time subtly subversive of upper-class pride and prejudice.

Of the occasional prose which Evelyn Waugh published in the last years of his life, two pieces of 1962 stand out for their high literary quality and autobiographical interest. The first of these is 'Sloth', commissioned by the *Sunday Times* for a series on the Seven Deadly Sins.[37] Waugh begins by quoting St Thomas Aquinas's definition, *'tristitia de bono spirituali*, sadness in the face of spiritual good. Man is made for joy in the love of God, a love which he expresses in service. If he deliberately turns away from that joy, he is denying the purpose of his existence'. No one who has read *The Ordeal of Gilbert Pinfold*, or the memoirs of Waugh's friends, can doubt that this was the sin that tempted him in later years – as indeed he all but openly confesses in his conclusion: 'It is in that last undesired decade, when passion is cold, appetites feeble, curiosity dulled, and experience has begotten cynicism, that *accidia* lies in wait as the final temptation to destruction.' In between these sombre passages, Waugh forcefully examines the deleterious effect of secular sloth upon civilisation, especially in his own field of literature.

The second essay is 'My Father', also commissioned for a series in a Sunday newspaper.[38] Though the same ground is covered in *A Little Learning*, the article is quite distinct, and in some ways is more revealing. What it reveals above all is the profound and painful alienation of father and son, which was aggravated by Evelyn's apparent aimlessness and irresponsibility as a young man, and healed only by his successful start as a writer. 'Immediately the whole relationship with my father was changed. Here at last I was engaged in an activity he fully understood. Moreover he was himself the publisher of my novels, so that he had a double satisfaction in my prosperity. He read my reviews with keener interest than I felt myself. The cheques bearing his signature were now sent with a light heart.' But it was too late for a total reconciliation. 'We were never intimate in the sense of my coming to him with confidences or seeking advice. Our relationship was rather that of host and guest.' It is poignant to set these words beside Arthur Waugh's, thirty years earlier:

Perhaps . . . the greatest mistake our own generation made lay in its effort to keep on equal terms with its successor, to be brother and sister to its boys and girls . . . We saw the limitation of the Victorian home . . . the lack of confidence between father and son . . . We would be young with the young . . . It cannot be done. It never has been done and it never will . . . Youth and age can never keep on terms together.[39]

My survey, which began by juxtaposing one of Evelyn Waugh's earliest pieces, on the Generation Gap, with his father's autobiography has thus come full circle, or should one say, cycle? 'My Father' ends:

I am now the father of three sons, two at school, the eldest already embarked on the family trade of writing. I have very little knowledge, or curiosity, about what they think of me. They are always polite. I have tried to fulfil the same duties to them and provide the same amusements as my father did to me. I lack his gift of reading poetry and his liveliness. I think I am less good company to them than he was to me, but I think I am kinder than my grandfather. Perhaps host and guest is really the happiest relation for father and son.

Part IV

Fiction and the Reading Public

11 Ambiguously Ever After: Problematical Endings in English Fiction

What first provoked me to give any extended thought to this subject was the experience of reading John Fowles's fascinating novel *The French Lieutenant's Woman* (1969). It is set in England about one hundred years ago, and chiefly concerns three people: the hero, Charles, a respectable, well-connected young man of moderately advanced opinions; his fiancée, the charming and rich, but conventional Ernestina, and the beautiful, mysterious, tragic Sarah – known to the community of Lyme Regis, where the story opens, as 'The French Lieutenant's Woman', because of some romantic and morally ambiguous episode in her past. Against all the dictates of prudence, common sense and honour, Charles is irresistibly attracted to Sarah. A familiar novelistic situation, then: the eternal triangle. But the story has three endings as well as three principal characters.

Sarah runs away from Lyme Regis, then sends Charles her address, in the city of Exeter: an address without a message. In chapter 43, Charles, travelling through Exeter, faces a critical choice: to seek out Sarah, and accept the consequences (the collapse of his plans for a comfortable, respectable life), or to drive on and forget her. He drives on, and in the next chapter is reconciled to Ernestina. The authorial voice narrating the story comments:

And so ends the story. What happened to Sarah I do not know – whatever it was she never troubled Charles again in person, however long she may have lingered in his memory.

We then get what Victorian novelists and their publishers called 'the wind-up' – a brief résumé of the subsequent lives of the principal characters. But since it is palpably obvious to the reader that there are another hundred pages still to go, it is not surprising to discover in the next chapter that this ending is a false one – it is the future that Charles predicted for himself if he abandoned Sarah, a future which he then rejected. Charles, in fact, seeks out Sarah, makes love to her, and after some hours of anguished introspection decides to marry her. While he

143

is painfully breaking off his engagement to Ernestina, however, Sarah disappears once again, evidently misunderstanding his intentions. The remainder of the novel is concerned with Charles's quest for her.

At the point where Charles begins this quest, Fowles introduces himself as author into the narrative, whimsically disguised as a staring stranger in Charles's railway compartment, and proceeds to share with his reader his hesitations and doubts about the direction the story should take. Not for the first time: he has already, in chapter 13, explained that, though he is writing the book in the intrusive authorial style favoured by Victorian novelists, he himself subscribes to a modern, existentialist philosophy of life which obliges him to leave his characters free to behave in unpredictable ways. 'The novelist is still a god, since he creates,' he says, 'but no longer the God of the Victorian Age, omniscient and decreeing.' In chapter 55, contemplating his hero asleep in the railway carriage, the author wonders what the devil he is going to do with him.

I have already thought of ending Charles's career here and now: of leaving him for all eternity on his way to London. But the conventions of Victorian fiction allow, allowed, no place for the open, the inconclusive ending: and I preached earlier of the freedom characters must be given. My problem is simple? What Charles wants is clear? It is indeed. But what [Sarah] wants is not so clear; and I am not at all sure where she is at the moment . . .

Fowles then proceeds to discuss the art of fiction in terms of professional boxing, using the analogy of 'fixing' a fight:

Fiction usually pretends to conform to reality: the writer puts . . . conflicting wants into the ring and then describes the fight, letting that want he himself favours win. And we judge writers of fiction both by the skill they show in fixing the fights (in other words persuading us that they were not fixed) and by the kind of character they fix in favour of: the good one, the tragic one, the evil one, the funny one, and so on.

Fowles goes on to say that 'the chief argument for fight-fixing is to show one's readers what one thinks of the world around one, whether one is a pessimist, an optimist, what you will'. But, he protests, he does not want to fix his story in favour of one character or one world-view. He will, therefore, give two different resolutions of Charles's quest, one that will satisfy his desire, and the other that will satisfy Sarah's. This, he observes, 'leaves me with only one problem. I cannot give both versions at once, yet, whichever is the second will seem, so strong is the tyranny of the last chapter, the final, the "real" version'.

Accordingly he, as author, pretends to toss a coin to decide which of the two alternative endings of the story will be given first. Naturally he does not tell us the result, or what the endings will be. To satisfy our curiosity, we must read on.

Now John Fowles represents his dilemma as that of a modern novelist trying to write a Victorian novel – modern artistic assumptions being irreconcilable with the conventions of Victorian fiction. But there is plenty of evidence that Victorian novelists themselves had difficulty on occasion with the endings of their stories, especially with regard to the union of heroes and heroines. Perhaps the best-known example is that of Dickens's *Great Expectations*. In the last chapter of that novel the narrator, Pip, returns, eleven years after the conclusion of the main action, to the site of Miss Havisham's house, now demolished; and there in the dusk he meets his old love Estella. She, who once cruelly spurned him, has learned humility through her unhappy marriage to Bentley Drummond, now dead, and the reconciliation of the lovers is plainly hinted in the closing words of the novel:

I took her hand in mine, and we went out of the ruined place; and, as the morning mists had risen long ago when I first left the forge, so the evening mists were rising now, and in all the broad expanse of tranquil light they showed to me, I saw no shadow of another parting from her.

Originally, however, Dickens had intended a less happy ending, as his friend and biographer John Forster was the first to reveal in his *Life* of Dickens. In the cancelled conclusion, now often printed as an appendix to the novel, Pip hears that Estella has married a second time. One day he is walking along Piccadilly with his nephew, little Pip,

. . . when a servant came running after me to ask would I step back to a lady in a carriage who wished to speak to me. It was a little pony carriage, which the lady was driving; and the lady and I looked sadly enough on one another. 'I am greatly changed, I know. but I thought you would like to shake hands with Estella, too, Pip. Lift up that pretty child and let me kiss it.' (She supposed the child, I think, to be my child.) I was very glad afterwards to have had the interview; for in her face and in her voice, and in her touch, she gave me the assurance that her suffering had been stronger than Miss Havisham's teaching, and had given her a heart to understand what my heart used to be.

It was the popular novelist Bulwer Lytton who, having followed *Great Expectations* with immense admiration as it appeared serially in Dickens's *All the Year Round*, and having read the original conclusion in proof, persuaded Dickens to change it for a happier ending. 'I have put in as pretty a piece of writing as I could,' Dickens told Forster, perhaps a little defensively. 'And I have no doubt that the story will be more acceptable through the alteration.' Forster drily comments: 'this turned out to be the case; but the first ending nevertheless seems more consistent with the drift, as well as the natural working out of the tale . . .' Most modern critics have agreed with Forster. Estella was, after all, the sexual symbol of all the false values on which Pip based his early life, and to reward him for his renunciation of these values with marriage to her is a kind of contradiction. It also compromises the novel's sober recognition that not all the damage we do to ourselves and to others is reparable. In the original version, Pip, having realised belatedly that Estella is incapable of love, turns too late to the loving Biddy, and, twice disappointed, accepts his single, childless state as in a sense his just deserts (hence the irony, in the cancelled conclusion, of Estella's assumption that little Pip is his own child).

When novels were published in serial form, or in volumes published separately over a longish period, there was continual feedback from the audience during the process of composition, and the author was always likely to come under pressure from his friends, his publishers and the reading public at large to provide an ending that conformed to their desires. Dickens first experienced this pressure on a major scale as he approached the end of *The Old Curiosity Shop*, where he described himself as 'inundated with imploring letters recommending poor little Nell to mercy'. But it was not a peculiarly Victorian phenomenon. It happened in the eighteenth century to one of the first English novelists, Samuel Richardson. He recorded in a postscript to his great novel *Clarissa*, 'The foregoing work having been published at three different periods of time, the author, in the course of its publication, was favoured with many anonymous letters in which the writers differently expressed their wishes with regard to the apprehended catastrophe. Most of those directed to him by the gentle sex turned in favour of what they called a *fortunate ending*.' One of these ladies was a Lady Bradsheigh, who wrote to Richardson under an assumed name, asking him to confirm or deny the rumours that *Clarissa* was to end tragically by placing a small ad. in the *Whitehall Evening Post*. When Richardson complied, a lengthy correspondence ensued in which the lady begged that the rake Lovelace should reform in time to be honourably married to the heroine whom he had ravished. Richardson, though clearly relishing every moment of the highly sentimental correspondence that ensued, stuck to his principles and his tragic ending.

By the time of Victoria, the reading public, and the publishers and editors who served that public, had become more tyrannical. Some novelists adjusted more easily than others. Trollope, as Henry James observed, was successful precisely because he shared his readers' tastes and prejudices, including what James called their 'love of a comfortable ending'. Trollope actually breaks off the narrative of *Barchester Towers* to reassure his readers that the heroine is not going to marry any of her more disagreeable suitors. 'But let the gentle-hearted reader be under no apprehension whatsoever,' he says. 'It is not destined that Eleanor shall marry Mr Slope or Bertie Stanhope.' Here Trollope, by drawing his readers' attention to his own authorial control over the narrative, plays riskily with the illusion of reality he has painstakingly built up; and, surprisingly, comes closer to the metafictional experiments of a modern novelist like John Fowles than Henry James, who deplored 'these little slaps at credulity' and never overtly betrayed the fictitiousness of his own narratives. James was more 'modern' than Trollope in other respects, of course, notably in his repudiation of the 'comfortable ending' that Trollope, like most Victorian novelists, was always ready to give his readers – 'a distribution at the last', as Henry James scathingly describes it, 'of prizes, pensions, husbands, wives, babies, millions, appended paragraphs and cheerful remarks'.

Cheerful remarks were never very much in Thomas Hardy's line, but he was frequently forced to temper his essentially tragic vision of life in deference to the forces of the fiction market, in those days largely controlled by the circulating libraries and serial-publishing magazines. His novel *The Return of the Native* offers one of the most interesting – and blatant – examples of a Victorian novelist's hesitation over the ending of a story. It concerns not the principal characters, but two important subsidiary ones – Thomasin, the sister of the hero Clym Yeobright, and her faithful lover Diggory Venn, the reddleman. When the tragedy centring on the heroine, Eustacia Vye, is played out, and Thomasin is widowed in consequence, Diggory Venn woos her again, and is accepted. Their wedding invests the end of this sombre novel with a certain cheerfulness. In a footnote to a later edition, however, Hardy repudiated this ending without actually changing it, by inserting a footnote into the text:

The writer may state here that the original conception of the story did not design a marriage between Thomasin and Venn. He was to have retained his isolated and weird character to the last, and to have disappeared mysteriously from the heath, nobody knowing whither – Thomasin remaining a widow. But certain circumstances of serial publication led to a change of intent. Readers can therefore choose between the endings, and those with an austere artistic code can assume the more consistent conclusion to be the true one.

This is asking rather a lot of the reader! In fact, there is nothing self-evidently inconsistent about the way the novel ends in the text, and a strong argument could be made out for preferring it to the one Hardy originally envisaged.

Charlotte Brontë showed rather more subtlety, and determination, in tackling a similar problem at the end of *Villette*, that remarkable study of a plain English girl who goes to Brussels to work as a teacher in a girls' school and falls in love successively with two very different men. Her publishers were unhappy about the way the heroine's affections shifted, in the latter part of the narrative, from the conventionally eligible hero, Dr John Graham, to the odd, unprepossessing little teacher, Monsieur Paul Emanuel; and they were dismayed when it appeared that even this second love would not be happily consummated. The formidable figure of Charlotte Brontë's father added his pressure. According to her biographer, Mrs Gaskell,

Mr Brontë was anxious that her new tale should end well, as he disliked novels which left a melancholy impression on the mind; he requested her to make hero and heroine (like the heroes and heroines in fairy tale) 'marry and live happily ever after.' But the idea of M. Paul Emanuel's death at sea was stamped on her imagination. All she could do in compliance with her father's wish was so to veil the fate in oracular words, as to leave it to the character and discernment of her readers to interpret her meaning.

Having set up Lucy as mistress of her own school, M. Paul has to leave her for three years while he attends to business in the West Indies. As Lucy awaits the return of her affianced lover, there is a storm in the Atlantic, described in Charlotte Brontë's most apocalyptic vein. There are references to the wreckage of ships strewn on many shores, to the anguish of people waiting for news of their loved ones at sea. Then the narrator – Lucy Snowe herself – breaks off. Almost the last words of the novel are these:

Here pause – pause at once. There is enough said. Trouble no quiet, kind heart; leave sunny imaginations hope. Let it be theirs to conceive the delight of joy born again out of great terror, the rapture of rescue from peril, the wondrous reprieve from dread, the fruition of return. Let them picture union and a happy succeeding life.

It would be a somewhat insensitive reader, however, who could follow this injunction with an easy conscience.

Villette has, very understandably, attracted a good deal of attention in recent years from feminist critics. Kate Millett was one of the first to present Lucy Snowe and her creator as early evangelists for women's liberation, and she interprets the ambiguity of the ending in this light:

Charlotte Brontë is hard-minded enough to know that there was no man in Lucy's society with whom she could have lived and still been free . . . As there is no remedy for sexual politics in marriage, Lucy very logically doesn't marry. But it is almost impossible for a Victorian novel to recommend a woman *not* to marry. So Paul suffers a quiet sea-burial.[1]

One must quibble with the word 'quiet' – the storm, we are told, 'roared frenzied for seven days'. But there are more important reasons for dissenting from Ms Millett's reading of the conclusion. It is clear from both internal and external evidence that Charlotte Brontë's avoidance of the conventional happy ending expressed her contempt for – not the institution of marriage – but the false comforts of sentimental romance. The death of M. Paul is aesthetically fitting because *Villette* is the story of a sensitive person painfully coming to terms with the fact that she is not going to enjoy the ordinary satisfactions of life for which she yearns, and achieving an impressive maturity and integrity in the process.

All the examples I have discussed involve a hesitation between – to put it simply – a happy and an unhappy ending, expressed in terms of a love relationship which is or is not sealed in marriage. The marriage knot is the primary symbol of happiness, of the optimistic idea that the nice and the good are one and shall inherit the earth. Conversely, the novelist's refusal to tie the marriage knot between hero and heroine expresses a bleaker and more pessimistic view that life rarely conforms to our desires, or our notions of justice.

I touch here on the thesis of Frank Kermode's brilliant and stimulating study, *The Sense of an Ending*, where he argues that the history of fiction is the history of a continuous dialogue or dialectic between credulity – our wish to believe – and scepticism – our wish to be told the truth. On the one hand we enjoy the reassurance that stories provide, the reassurance that there is a meaningful order in reality, especially if it is one that conforms to our hopes and desires. On the other hand we know that the patterns of narrative are generally false to experience – that, for instance, bride and groom do not live 'happily ever after'. The aim of most writers of realistic narrative – which is to say, the aim of most novelists – has been to satisfy the reader's credulity while appeasing his scepticism; to provide patterns, order, meaning, but to make it seem that the patterns, the order, the meaning are derived from life itself, rather than from literature and its conventions. If we can recognise a pattern in narrative, if we can predict the way a particular story is going to end by reference to earlier models, we are less likely to feel that it is 'true to life'. Hence, one of the oldest devices of narrative art is the reversal or peripeteia discussed by Aristotle in the *Poetics*, which is both unexpected and yet the completion of a pattern. Peripeteia is, then, a concession to the reader's scepticism. 'The more daring the peripeteia, the more we feel that the work respects our sense of reality,' says Professor Kermode.[2] But peripeteia itself can easily become a recognisable – and predictable – device of literary patterning, and it is then avoided by writers anxious to maintain an 'illusion of life'. Even ending a story at all – ending in the sense of tying up all the loose ends of plot, settling the destinies of all the characters – even this comes to seem like a falsification of reality. This seems to have been felt with special force by literary intellectuals in the late nineteenth and early twentieth centuries, a period of declining belief in orthodox Christianity, which had structured history as a complex plot in which everything would eventually be explained and accounted for in the last chapter, the bad would be punished and the good would live happily ever after. In the more thoughtful mid- and late-Victorian novelists, therefore, we see a tendency towards more and more open, less and less cheerful endings, as the Christian metaphysic loses its authority. When George Eliot wrote to her publisher John Blackwood in 1857, at the very outset of her literary career, 'Conclusions are the weak point of most authors, but some of the fault lies in the very nature of a conclusion, which is at best a negation', she was expressing reservations about the conventional ending of Victorian fiction that surely stemmed from her own loss of Christian faith.

The cases I have discussed so far suggest that the fiction-reading public is invariably a conservative force, craving the comforts of stereotyped endings that authors feel, with more or less conviction and courage, would compromise their vision of reality. This was certainly the case in the high Victorian age, when the novel was a popular medium, comparable to series television drama today. In the twentieth century the audience for prose fiction becomes fragmented and specialised, and the more artistically ambitious novelists write for a minority whose assumptions are as sophisticated and sceptical as their own. Henry James was a writer of the transition between these two periods and Joseph Conrad, who was another, remarked on the significant inconclusiveness of James's endings, his fondness for ending a book on a note of renunciation or rejection which leaves the destiny of the hero or heroine bleakly uncertain. This is what Conrad says:

It is obvious that a solution by rejection must always present a certain lack of finality, especially startling when contrasted with the usual methods of solution by rewards and punishments, by crowned love, by fortune, by a broken leg or a sudden death. Why the reading public which, as a body has never laid upon a story-teller the command to be an artist, should demand from him this sham of Divine Omnipotence, is utterly incomprehensible. But so it is; and these solutions are legitimate inasmuch as they satisfy the desire for finality, for which our hearts yearn, with a longing greater than the longing for the loaves and fishes of this earth. Perhaps the only true desire of mankind . . . is to be set at rest. One is never set at rest by Mr Henry James's novels. You remain with the sense of life going on. It is eminently satisfying, but it is not final.[3]

How true that is. Consider, for example, the ending of *The Wings of the Dove*, when Kate Croy and Merton Densher confront each other over the fact that their cynical plot to marry on the proceeds of Merton's courtship of the dying heiress Milly Theale has become repugnant to both of them at the very moment of its success.

Then he only said: 'I'll marry you, mind you, in an hour.'
    'As we were?'
    'As we were.'
    But she turned to the door and her headshake was now the end. 'We shall never be again as we were.'

End of novel. Or think of the rather similar ending of *The Ambassadors*, where Lambert Strether is resisting the temptation to marry the attractive and well-off Maria Gostrey, whom he likes and who has very clearly hinted her availability – Strether insisting that he must return to America and face the consequences of the failure of his mission in order to be 'right':

So then she had to take it, though still with her defeated protest.
'It isn't so much your *being* "right" – it's your horrible sharp eye for what makes you so.'
    'Oh, but you're just as bad yourself. You can't resist me when I point that out.'
    She sighed it at last all comically, all tragically, away. 'I can't indeed resist you.'
    'Then there we are!' said Strether.

End of novel. Both books, it is worth noting, end on a line of direct speech, in the middle of a dialogue. This is a very modern way of ending a novel: the author, as narrator, deliberately declines to have the last word, and leaves us with the characters in mid-conversation, their futures and fortunes uncertain. James, indeed, by the oxymoron 'all comically, all tragically', artfully alludes to the two traditional types of closed ending, happy and unhappy, which he has rejected.

Most of the great modern novels end in the same sort of way, 'with the sense of life going on': *Ulysses, Women in Love, Mrs Dalloway, A Passage to India* and many others. With the increasing acceptance of the open rather than the closed ending, the issue of whether or not to conclude a story with a happy union of lovers scarcely arises for the modern novelist as it did so frequently for the Victorians. But I can think of two modern instances comparable to the case of *Great Expectations*, i.e. where we can compare two different endings to the same story. The first is Evelyn Waugh's *A Handful of Dust* (1934). In the standard text, the disillusioned hero, Tony Last, who has gone abroad after being deceived by his wife, meets a gruesome living death in the Brazilian jungle, condemned to read aloud the works of Dickens to a mad, homicidal settler. The American magazine that published the novel in serial form, however, found the last chapter too macabre, and asked for a less disturbing conclusion. With a readiness more characteristic of a Victorian than of a modern novelist, Waugh obliged, and even reprinted the alternative ending later in a volume of his own short stories. In this version, Tony Last returns from an uneventful visit to Brazil, is reconciled to his now penitent wife, and quietly plots to deceive her as she deceived him. Not exactly a happy ending, but one that has more old-fashioned poetic justice about it than the original, in which Tony Last seems to suffer out of all proportion to his sins.

In the 1930s, it would appear, the American reading public was rather more squeamish than the British (*A Handful of Dust* was serialised in the British *Vogue* with the original ending). But times have changed, as the case of Anthony Burgess's *A Clockwork Orange* illustrates. *A Clockwork Orange* is a futuristic fantasy narrated by a teenage hoodlum called Alex who is guilty of appalling acts of violence. When he is convicted and sent to prison, he is offered his freedom on condition that he accepts Pavlovian aversion therapy. This cures him of his violent urges, but it also dehumanises him. By an accident, the effects of his therapy are lost, and he reverts to his evil but vital character. Burgess seems to be offering us a stark choice between accepting the evil consequences of freedom or the tyranny of a totalitarian law-and-order state. In the form in which most readers know the novel, there does not seem much to choose between them in terms of human happiness. But in the first edition of the novel there was a final chapter which ended the story more hopefully, with a hint of real regeneration for Alex. Burgess explained in an interview:

When I wrote it, originally, I put in a chapter at the end where Alex was maturing. He was growing up and seeing violence as part of adolescence.

He wanted to be a married man and have children. He sees the world going round and round like an orange. But when they were going to publish it in America, they said, 'We're tougher over here,' and thought the ending too soft for their readers. If it was me, now, faced with the decision, I'd say no. I still believe in my ending.[4]

It is surprising, in view of this latter statement, that the British paperback edition of *A Clockwork Orange*, published by Penguin, follows the American hardback edition, as does the celebrated film of the novel made by Stanley Kubrick. The vast majority of the audience for *A Clockwork Orange* know it, therefore, in a far more pessimistic form than its author intended.[5]

Jonathan Culler has recently suggested[6] that every narrative operates according to 'a double logic', namely a logic of events, according to which a novel pretends to unfold a sequence of events that have already happened, revealing a chain of cause and effect, and a logic of coherence, according to which the characters and their actions confirm or complete a certain pattern of meanings. In George Eliot's novel *Daniel Deronda*, for instance, the hero's growing self-identification with Jewish culture and values is explained, according to the logic of events, by the revelation, at the end of the story, that unknown to himself Daniel Deronda was born of a Jewish mother; on the other hand, it is clear to the reader that the development of the story positively requires that Daniel Deronda should in the end turn out to be Jewish; so that according to the logic of coherence, it is true to say that his revealed origin is not the cause but the effect of his commitment to Jewish culture.

These two logics (which in a sense correspond to Kermode's 'scepticism' and 'credulity', respectively) are, Culler maintains, essentially contradictory, and not reconcilable by some kind of compromise formulation. This contradiction I would prefer to call a paradox, one that is at the heart of all mimetic art – namely, that we attribute value and significance to representations which are neither verifiable nor falsifiable. Lady Bradsheigh, who begged Richardson to write a happy ending for *Clarissa*, enacted this paradox in a very transparent form, for by the very act of making the request she simultaneously reacted to events and characters as if they were real and acknowledged that they were *not* real, but fabrications at the disposition of the author. Her involvement with Clarissa's and Lovelace's destiny derived from her reaction to the logic of events in the novel; her request for a happy ending was based on a correct intuition that the logic of coherence demanded a tragic conclusion.

In realistic fiction, the illusion of life is created principally according to the logic of events, and the task of the writer is, therefore, to construct as perfect a 'fit' as possible between the logic of events and the logic of coherence, or to disguise the latter under the appearance of the former. That is why the suggestion or revelation of alternative endings in the classic realistic novel, such as *Great Expectations* or *Villette*, imparts a *frisson* of shock or scandal to the reader. The ending of a novel is the very point at which every reader, however naïve, must recognise that it is not reality but an imitation of it, not a slice of life but a statement about it; and this recognition is made relatively easy and reassuring if there is a perfect fit between the two logics, like the seam between a glove and its lining. The well-made classic novel, like a glove, can be turned inside out and back again by the interpreting reader, changing its aspect, but still retaining the same shape. Problematical endings are like gaping seams: they indicate the stress points in the manufactured article.

Cases like *A Clockwork Orange* and *A Handful of Dust* are anecdotally interesting, but they are, I think, less significant as regards what they tell us about the literary situation at large than the Victorian examples of alternative or ambiguous endings. With the acceptance of the open ending in modern fiction, the ending which is satisfying but not final, the recognition of ambiguity or uncertainty in experience is institutionalised as form. Even this kind of ending, however, can seem too comfortable or consoling in its endorsement of the commonplace that life, somehow or another, goes on; and insufficiently self-conscious about its own conventionality. The open ending, like the closed ending, still, after all, asserts the existence of *an* order, rather than a plurality of orders, or an absence of order; and it still makes a claim for the fiction's realism, verisimilitude, or 'truth to life'. These claims have been strongly challenged by many contemporary novelists sometimes designated postmodernist. Instead of the closed ending or the open ending, we get from them the multiple ending, the false ending, the mock ending or the parody ending. *The French Lieutenant's Woman* belongs to this category.[7]

And what happens at the end of *The French Lieutenant's Woman*? After two years, Charles traces Sarah to a house in London, which turns out to be the house of the Rossettis. When he presents himself he is dismayed by Sarah's coldness. It seems that she has been deceiving him about her true feelings from the beginning. He reproaches her bitterly for having ruined his life, and is about to leave the house when she detains him and produces a child that, unknown to Charles, was the result of their single sexual encounter. Her coldness was, it appears, merely some kind of test. Now she looks at him, her eyes melting with tears. It is one of those moments, the narrator says, 'when we know in the resolution of profound need that the rock of ages can never be anything else but love . . .' A happy ending, in fact, with all the stops out. But enter the novelist, once again, to turn back the clock fifteen minutes, and this time Charles leaves the house, bitter, baffled and alone.

In the passage I quoted earlier, Fowles, as author, suggested that the choice he wished to avoid was fixing the fight in favour of either Charles or Sarah. This is not quite the case. We never see inside Sarah, we never know what she desires, and I rather doubt whether Fowles himself knows. Charles is the only fully realised character, the one whose consciousness is presented with full interiority. The issue of the endings, therefore, is whether his quest for Sarah will end happily or unhappily for him, and – since he is the character we inevitably identify with – for us, as readers. Fowles does not, of course, avoid the onus of decision by giving both endings. The second ending disqualifies the first, and not only because it comes second. The happy, closed ending is Victorian; the unhappy, open ending, which leaves Charles walking grimly along the deserted Embankment, beside a Thames figured symbolically as 'the river of life, of mysterious laws and mysterious choice' – this is modern, and commands our assent. More plausible than either, perhaps, by empirical criteria, is the first discarded ending, where Charles decides to let Sarah go, and settles for a safe, respectable, married life with Ernestina. But not even a modern existentialist novel can afford to have an ending as banal, as anticlimactic, as that.

12 Turning Unhappiness into Money: Fiction and the Market

'Critics and historians of the novel generally pay too little attention to the consumer and to the conditions prevailing in the market.' wrote Mr Ronald Hayman in 1976, concluding his survey of contemporary British fiction, *The Novel Today 1967–75*. As if in response to this complaint, two books appeared not very long afterwards which attempt a serious and properly researched study of contemporary writing, especially prose fiction, in its socio-economic context – as something that is produced, bought and sold: Per Gedin's *Literature in the Market Place* (1977) and J. A. Sutherland's *Fiction and the Fiction Industry* (1978). The first of these authors is a Swedish publisher, and the second Reader in English at University College, London. They thus offer an interesting combination of perspectives on the subject – commercial and academic, British and European.

The writers share two assumptions. The first is that the character of prose fiction at any given time is to a considerable extent determined by the prevailing methods of production, distribution and consumption, and by the patterns of financial reward for publishers, booksellers and authors. To some extent this must be true of any cultural product in the modern world, but the novel differs from poetry and drama and most other arts in that its emergence as a distinct literary form was more or less contemporaneous with the rise of industrial capitalism and the development of the first machine for mass-production, the printing-press. Its fortunes have been inextricably involved with economics and technology ever since. Unlike a poem, a novel cannot conveniently be circulated in manuscript; unlike a play, it cannot be given the trial run of a cheap amateur production. To achieve even a minimal public existence, a novel needs to be printed and bound, and this has always been a relatively expensive business, with unpredictable returns on investment. Hence the emergence of the printer-bookseller (later to split into two distinct trades) as a supplier of the necessary risk capital.

As Per Gedin points out, novels have always had a special attraction for publishers, not only because they are culturally glamorous and prestigious, but because of their relatively quick return on investment,

156

simplicity of production and capacity to guarantee an audience for subsequent works by the same author. Fiction has, therefore, been a staple of the publishing business for the last two centuries and, during most of that time, the largest single category of trade books. This brings me to the second assumption common to Gedin and Sutherland, namely, that there was a publishing 'crisis' in the early 1970s which particularly affected the novel, the main symptoms of which were: a staggering rise in costs (between 30 per cent and 40 per cent per year), a general reduction in the number of titles published, a much more drastic reduction in the number of copies sold, the increasing Americanisation of European publishing practice, and widespread expressions of gloom and pessimism within the trade about the future of the literary novel. On this much, our two authors are agreed, but they differ considerably in their diagnoses of the underlying causes of the crisis and the gravity of its cultural implications. Paradoxically, Gedin, the publisher, is the more concerned with values, and more pessimistic about the future, while Sutherland, the academic, is more pragmatic, hardnosed and cautiously optimistic about the capacity of literary art to survive in a harsher economic climate.

Gedin's argument will be familiar to students of the 'cultural debate' that extends from Coleridge and Carlyle to the Leavises, Hoggart, Williams and Steiner. Within this frame of reference he occupies a conservative or elitist position, unashamedly committed to 'bourgeois' values. The rise of the novel, he correctly observes, coincided with the rise of the bourgeoisie, its triumph (in the literature of the nineteenth century) with the triumph of the bourgeoisie, and he greatly fears it will disappear with the bourgeoisie. For the graduated class structure of industrial society, in which the bourgeoisie exerted powerful influence as arbiters of taste and value, and conspicuously consumed the products of high culture even when these were critical of themselves, has been superseded by a mass or 'service' society, a post-industrial society in which culture is homogenised and packaged for mass consumption, in which the better educated have much the same debased standards and tastes as the less educated, in which people have less and less time or inclination for reading, so occupied are they with travelling, watching television or practising divers expensive, mechanised hobbies. Thus arises a literary situation in which the market for fiction is polarised between, on the one hand, a few 'best sellers' designed simply as entertainment, promoted by ruthless advertising, saturation merchandising and pre-selection through book clubs, and, on the other hand, fiction of serious literary pretension that loses money for its publishers and brings meagre rewards to its authors – or, in the more concise words of a contemporary American publisher, a situation where 'fiction is either big or dead'.

There is obviously more than a grain of truth in this analysis. But the fact that it has been expounded before suggests that it cannot entirely account for the publishing crisis of the 1970s. Gedin quotes a German publisher, S. Fischer, writing in remarkably similar terms in 1926:

It is . . . symbolic that the book now is an object that can be most easily dispensed with in our daily life. We indulge in sports, dance, spend our evenings by the radio or at the cinema; after the day's work is done we are all too busy and have no time to read books . . . The lost war and the American wave of culture have transformed our way of life, changed our tastes . . . It would seem that the bourgeois class that remained after the cataclysm and which before the war comprised the cultural and economic leadership of the country, is in a state of disintegration.

Gedin calls these words 'prophetic', but Fischer was evidently describing the situation as he saw it. And as Dr Sutherland observes, in a Postscript to his book that takes specific issue with Gedin's, 'the same gloomily terminal views have been delivered authoritatively any time these last 100 years (by Ruskin, Henry James and Q. D. Leavis among others)'. One could go back further still, to the diatribes of the Romantic poets against Gothic fiction and of Pope against Grub Street. The fact is that, ever since art entered the age of mechanical reproduction (to use Walter Benjamin's phrase), which began with the printing press and has now reached the stage of electronics and micro-processors, humanist intellectuals have been filled with terror and nausea at the obscene ease with which texts, images and musical compositions can be replicated and multiplied without regard to their value, and have tended to construct myths of cultural decline out of their own dismay. Ironically, the printed book, which in earlier versions of the myth was seen as an agent of cultural decline, is now revered as a cultural totem.

To classify Gedin's argument in this way is not to suggest that his decent anxiety about the future of the literary novel is unfounded; and the publishing crisis of the early 1970s was far from being a myth. Gedin has hard figures to show how the readership for serious fiction has declined, at the same time that the 'break-even' point for sales has risen. In Sweden, a crucial factor would seem to have been the escalation of publishers' overheads which by 1974, in Gedin's own firm, had reached the staggering proportion of 160 per cent of production costs. This was clearly the consequence of the rapid evolution of post-war Sweden into a high-wage, egalitarian society. But Gedin sees the root of the problem as being cultural rather than economic. Dr Sutherland's emphasis is quite the reverse. He shows that the British publishing crisis of the early 1970s was part of a much more general economic panic which gripped the country as a result of the 1973 oil crisis, with consequent cuts in public spending. Here we come to a peculiar feature of the economics of fiction publishing in this country – its heavy dependence upon the public library system.

The situation may be baldly summarised as follows: in the post-war period, with the disappearance of commercial libraries and the growth of the paperback revolution, public libraries became the main purchasers of new, hardback fiction. In one perspective this could be seen as a state hand-out to novel readers at the expense of novelists, and thus led to the campaign for the Public Lending Right. In another perspective it provided a reasonable prospect of break-even sales for novels of merit but minority appeal. What happened in the post-1973 'freeze' was that public libraries all over the country drastically curtailed and in some cases suspended their purchasing of new novels. Publishers thus found themselves deprived overnight of their most reliable customers. In 1977 Tom Rosenthal of Secker & Warburg estimated that 'the safe library sale' of 'a good literary first or second novel' had sunk from 1,500 to 300 or 400 copies. Publishers responded to the crisis by reducing the proportion of fiction titles they published, and by printing fewer copies. One gathers that the print run of a first novel nowadays is often as low as 1,200 copies: unless the paperback rights are sold, this will hardly break even for the publisher and will bring the author a derisory sum in royalties. Even highly successful novelists are selling, apparently, fewer copies than formerly. In 1973, before the crisis was fully felt, the late Tony Godwin of Weidenfeld & Nicolson was complaining that his best-selling novelists, such as Margaret Drabble, Edna O'Brien and Eric Ambler, were selling only 15,000 copies, whereas fifteen years earlier writers of comparable status would have sold twice that quantity. Meanwhile the *real* bestsellers – the Alistair Macleans, the Frederick Forsyths, the Peter Benchleys – had never had it so good.

In the last sentence of *Literature in the Market Place*, Per Gedin asserts: 'An immediate and sizeable contribution by society is needed in order to preserve and continue to develop the literary book – as much for the sake of society itself as for the book.' Dr Sutherland, however, is not wholly convinced that the novel is 'intrinsically humane and culturally necessary', and is sceptical about the various ways in which society has tried or might try to guarantee the survival of the literary novel. His verdict on PLR is that it has been 'a tragedy of procrastination'. 'What could have been done in 1966 painlessly could not be done in 1976 [in 1976 the PLR bill was filibustered by a trio of populist backbenchers named, unbelievably, Moate, Sproate and English] and what was done after 1976 would necessarily be too little and too late.' PLR is still worth pursuing as a matter of principle[1] but, apart from the fact that libraries are buying much less fiction anyway, it seems unlikely that any government will ever provide enough money to make an individual writer's income from this source significant. The financial commitment of the government to the 1976 bill was only £1 million, of which £400,000 would have been spent on administration,[2] and there are an estimated 113,000 authors eligible. It is the last figure that is perhaps the most daunting. In their heroic campaign for PLR, the Writers' Action Group has often cited the success of organised action by authors in Denmark and Sweden (oddly, Per Gedin makes no mention of this in his book) in establishing and improving the terms of their PLR, but the literary communities of those countries are tiny by comparison with ours. And there is an obvious incentive for the government of any non-Anglophone nation to invest in its own literary language in the face of the steady development of English as an international language.

The main source of public subsidy for the literary novel in Britain is the Arts Council, which gives bursaries and endows fellowships, subsidises literary magazines, and underwrites the New Fiction Society, a kind of non-profit-making book club offering quality fiction by new and established authors at a 20–30 per cent discount. Sutherland's account of this latter enterprise makes particularly melancholy reading. In spite of an extensive advertising campaign, the NFS never added more than 600 copies to the sale of any one novel. Between October 1974 and January 1977 it sold only 13,000 books at a cost of £60,500 to the Arts Council (i.e. £4.65 per volume of public money). As Sutherland remarks, 'it would have been cheaper to buy the novels at full price from a bookshop and give them away to passers-by in Piccadilly'. As for the other Arts Council subventions of literature, Sutherland makes the obvious points that its budget is pitifully inadequate and that there is no way of giving hand-outs to individual authors that will be seen to be fair by all concerned, including unlucky applicants.

Another option he considers is a system of academic patronage of writers on the American model, through the development of creative writing courses in universities. This he thinks is unlikely to happen, because of an ingrained British prejudice (which he seems to share) against such courses, and because there is at present no money to spare for new initiatives in British higher education. My own view is somewhat different: there is a real demand on the part of students for such courses, and since higher education is a buyers' market these days, they are likely to become increasingly common. However, in the form in which they are educationally defensible they are not necessarily best taught by professional writers, and to do a lot of such teaching can certainly have a deleterious effect on the writer's own creativity.

Other ways of keeping the serious novel afloat considered by Sutherland include: self-publishing, publishing collectives, literary prizes, writing consciously for an international market (e.g. Anthony Burgess, Muriel Spark), writing for television (e.g. Frederick Raphael's *The Glittering Prizes*, a series of plays later published as a novel). None of these seems to offer a general panacea. Indeed, the only success story in the book world of recent years seems to have been Melvyn Bragg's television programme *Read All About It* (now conducted by Ronald Harwood), which, whatever reservations one may have about its show-biz style, has demonstrated that there is a large reading public interested in information and comment about new books. But they are, of course, paperback books – and that is where the paying audience for fiction, for any kind of fiction, really is these days. The NFS failed, I would guess, because the discount it offered was not enough to compete with paperback prices. Many of the 15,000 'missing' readers who should, according to Tony Godwin, have been buying Margaret Drabble's or Edna O'Brien's latest novels, were presumably waiting for the paperback to appear. There are few novels, after all, that one 'cannot wait' to read, and the paperback bookshelves are distractingly full of novels that one always meant to read. There is no scarcity of good fiction in Britain (unlike certain East European countries, where any novel whatsoever sells out as a matter of course). But the cheapness of paperbacks entails long print runs, short shelf-life, and a highly selective list of titles. This is why the fiction industry does not 'go paperback', as it is often urged to do by laymen: to do so would entail killing the seedcorn – the promising young writer who gets his chance with a first printing of 1,200–1,600 copies. But the end result is a strangely artificial literary market place, in which all the action and excitement (the reviews, the promotional publicity, the prizes, etc.) seem to be going on at the hardback end, but most of the actual buying and selling is going on at the other, paperback, end. The future of the novel as we know it probably depends in large part upon the success of the publishing industry and the book trade in bringing these two spheres of activity into a more logical and mutually advantageous relationship with each other.

The portents are not particularly encouraging. Sutherland's analysis suggests that the British book market will inevitably follow the pattern set by America, where, according to Richard Kostelanetz, 'as far as commercial publishing is concerned, the *end* has come and gone; that world has passed beyond hell'. It is a world in which books can be made into multi-million-dollar best-sellers before they have even been published, in which paperbacks have a shelf-life of two weeks and 50 per cent of them are returned and pulped as a matter of course, in which the sale of 3,500 copies of a hardback means an inevitable loss for the publisher of $7,000–10,000 'on condition one hasn't paid out too much for advertising'.

It is not clear whether Dr Sutherland thinks this prospect is a disaster which must be avoided at all costs, or a disagreeable fact of modern economic life to which the genteel and (until recently) protected world of British publishing will have to adjust sooner or later. As I have already implied, the main disappointment of his lively and informative book is its curious evasiveness about literary values. He has, for example, a fascinating chapter on the publication history of Edward Doctorow's *Ragtime* – the initial promotional 'hype', the orchestrated rapturous reception in America, the sensational early sales and subsidiary rights figures, the defensive hostility of the British reviews, the second thoughts in America, and so on – but the crucial core of this analysis, the question whether *Ragtime* is really any good or not, is curiously absent. (My own opinion is that it is a work of genuine, though not outstanding, literary merit.) Although he assumes that his readers will be concerned about the survival of the literary novel, it is by no means certain that he himself is, or that he would lose much sleep if the world never heard another word from the likes of Margaret Drabble and Edna O'Brien, Anthony Burgess and Muriel Spark – or the 'campus novelists' to whom he devotes half a chapter, and amongst whom I was amused to discover myself portrayed in 'a kind of guarded, retreated pose'.

In conclusion, I shall drop my guard and lead with my chin. I have already indicated the dependence of the novel as a material object on industrial methods of manufacture; and it has always seemed to me that as a mode of *literary* production novel-writing conforms closely to the model of primitive capitalism. 'Writing', the novelist J. P. Donleavy once remarked, 'is a way of turning the unhappiest moments of one's life into money.' The joke conceals a profound truth.

The novelist risks his 'capital' – his experience, his imagination, his verbal skill, his time (a lot of that), his nervous energy, his psychological privacy and his self-esteem in the construction of an artefact, a fictional text which he takes to the market place, hoping someone will pay him for the right to reproduce and sell it, and that others will, at a second remove, pay him for the privilege of reading it. Nobody has asked him to write it. No one is born into or brought up to novel-writing as a trade or calling. Writing a novel is a gratuitous act, like Robinson Crusoe running away from his comfortable home to make his fortune. It is an intensely individualistic and competitive activity, which is why attempts at co-operative publishing ventures nearly always fail. The New York Fiction Collective, Dr Sutherland touchingly records, held 'consciousness-raising sessions designed to eliminate the counterproductive addiction to "success." ' Vain endeavour! Novelists are driven by the dream of personal success (why else would they persist in such a difficult, laborious, psychologically taxing activity?) and their relationships with their peers usually include strong feelings of rivalry. They compare jealously advances, sales, terms of contract. They deeply resent – even socialist novelists deeply resent – paying income tax on their writing earnings, and often get into serious difficulties on this account. I do not mean to imply that novelists are a peculiarly mercenary group of writers. It is simply that they recognise (in a way which I suspect is not true of poets) that their fortune in the market – the readiness of strangers to risk or expend money on their creative work – is a significant criterion of achievement. Not the only one, of course – we also want to be loved, respected, praised by the discerning (we are insatiable) -- but an essential one, because an objective one. Indeed I believe most novelists, even 'literary' ones, would, forced to choose, prefer to be judged by the market (assuming it is free from censorship) than by any other institution. One reason, after all, why novelists are so ill-rewarded, on the whole, for their labours, is that there are too many of us, too many manuscripts for publishers to choose from, too many titles for bookshops and literary editors to cope with, too many novels for customers to buy. The situation could be drastically altered in favour of novelists by controlling their numbers by means of a union and a closed shop (as is the practice in most communist countries). But who would willingly yield up his absolute right to publish the products of his imagination? Who would confidently undertake to discriminate between competing applicants for that right? All attempts to tinker with the free play of the market by grants, subsidies, bursaries, etc., are open to similar objections, in a milder form. It is highly significant that the only form of state subsidy that has won the broad support of novelists themselves in this country is a form of PLR scrupulously related to the individual writer's success in the library 'market';[3] unfortunately a scheme that is so fair cannot, it seems, benefit anybody very significantly.

The literary market, then, has functioned historically not merely as a means of material production and distribution of prose fiction, but a as a kind of sounding board for the novelist's own sense of his literary identity and achievement. But the literary market can fulfil that function only as long as it is accessible to all works of merit. It may produce a great deal of rubbish, but it must not exclude the good. There must be a general faith that, sooner or later, any novel of real value will find a publisher. I personally believe that this is still true of the British publishing world. But it may not be true of America, and, if present trends continue, it may one day no longer be the case here. *That* will be the real crisis for publishing and for the novel.

Part V

Contemporary Culture

13 *Crow* and the Cartoons

> Man's and woman's bodies lay without souls,
> Dully gaping, foolishly staring, inert
> On the flowers of Eden.
> God pondered.

> The problem was so great, it dragged him asleep.

> Crow laughed.

What kind of a work is Ted Hughes's *Crow: From the Life and Songs of the Crow*? It is an attempt to create a new mythology; or, more precisely, to revise an old one – the old one being primarily that of Christianity. On its much smaller scale, *Crow* imitates the scope of the Bible, covering the history of the world from beginning to end, from Genesis to Apocalypse, and taking in on the way the universal human themes: birth, copulation and death; language, art, science; love and war; nature and the city. Stylistically, *Crow* often echoes the Bible and associated Christian liturgical forms – genealogies:

> In the beginning was Scream
> Who begat Blood
> Who begat eye . . .

catechism:

> Who owns these scrawny little feet? Death.
> Who owns this bristly scorched-looking face?
> Death . . .

litanies and chants:

> When God hammered Crow
> He made gold

> When God roasted Crow in the sun
> He made diamond . . .

Some of the most striking poems are those in which Crow is introduced
into certain well-established Biblical contexts – the Garden of Eden or
Calvary – and the familiar stories are given a startling and sometimes
shocking new twist. 'A Childish Prank', with which I began, is a good
example. In this poem, man's helplessness before the power of his own
sexual instincts is traced back, not to the Fall, but to Crow, getting up
to mischief while God is dozing. His work of creation half done. Crow
bites the Worm in two:

> He stuffed into man the tail half
> With the wounded end hanging out.
>
> He stuffed the head half headfirst into woman
> And it crept in deeper and up
> to peer out through her eyes
> Calling its tail-half to join up quickly, quickly
> Because O it was painful.
>
> Man awoke being dragged across the grass.
> Woman awoke to see him coming.
> Neither knew what had happened.
>
> God went on sleeping.
>
> Crow went on laughing.

Ted Hughes himself has described Crow as 'created by God's nightmare'. This seems to imply that Crow is a bad dream from which God –
and the reader – will eventually awake, and to the extent that *Crow* is a
fiction, this is true. But the Bible – certainly Genesis – is also a kind of
fiction, or if you prefer, a myth. 'A Childish Prank', therefore, com-
petes with Genesis as an imaginative explanation of the origins of
human sexuality. The general assumption underlying the whole cycle of
poems is, I think, that the Crow myth is a more plausible explanation
of the world as we know it (or as Hughes finds it) than the myth of
orthodox Christianity.

There is, of course, nothing particularly novel about the attempt to
create a new mythology, or to re-invent an old one. This has been a
persistent endeavour of poets from the Romantic period onwards,
usually attributed to the de-mythologizing effect of science and ration-
alism upon the traditional explanations of the universe provided by

religion and poetry. *Paradise Lost* is the last great poem in the English language based on a more or less orthodox belief in the Bible. The Romantics either (like Wordsworth) tried to do without mythology or (like Keats and Shelley) tried to adapt classical mythology to their own purposes or (like Blake) concocted a heterodox mythology of their own.

If we look for a poetic precedent for *Crow*, perhaps Blake would be the first name to present itself: not so much the Blake of the turgid and obscure Prophetic Books, as the Blake of *Songs of Experience* and the poems and fragments of the Rossetti Manuscript, the Nobodaddy poems and the Proverbs of Hell. There is, for example, a certain similarity of poetic function between Blake's Tyger and Hughes's Crow: both creatures symbolize some kind of non-ethical energy or principle in the universe which is not satisfactorily accounted for by orthodox religion. Well one might ask of Crow, 'Did He who made the Lamb make thee?' (The question is in fact raised in many of the poems, but is ambiguously answered.) Compared with Blake's Tyger, however, Crow is a much less conventionally 'poetic' creature, with no fearful symmetry – no beauty, dignity or nobility of any kind. He has 'scrawny little feet', a 'bristly, scorched-looking face' and 'unspeakable guts'. In a poem called 'Crow and the Birds', while the rest of the ornithological creation is putting on a spectacular flying display, Crow is revealed in the last line:

> . . . spraddled head-down in the beach-garbage,
> guzzling a dropped ice-cream.

It is impossible, I think, not to visualize this pose without seeing Crow's backside cocked vulgarly and derisively towards the sky where the other birds are going through their paces.

Crow, in short, is the beast of a very modern apocalypse, one in which images of global disaster and individual violence take absurd and grotesque and debased forms that derive quite as much from contemporary mass culture as from literary tradition:

> Cars collide and erupt luggage and babies
> In laughter
> The steamer upends and goes under saluting like a stuntman
> In laughter

And Crow himself, it seems to me, is conceived and handled in ways which invite comparison with a popular art form peculiar to the twentieth century: the animated cartoon, and its printed relative, the strip cartoon.

The original impetus for the Crow poems, we are told, came from the American artist Leonard Baskin, and one of Baskin's drawings decorates the dust jacket of Hughes's book. It depicts a crow, drawn more or less naturalistically as to the head and wings, but supported by two brawny, muscular legs of human appearance and hung with human male genitals. It is a striking drawing, but it is not how I visualize Crow from the poems. The Crow I see there is a much more stylized creature: half human not because he has some human organs, but because he caricatures certain human traits and is involved in parodic versions of familiar human situations. Does this not relate Crow to the anthropomorphic animals and birds of Walt Disney and his imitators: Donald Duck, Mickey Mouse, Tom and Jerry, Bugs Bunny, Woody Woodpecker, the Pink Panther and all the rest? Consciously or unconsciously, Hughes seems to be dropping a hint to this effect in the poem called 'The Battle of Osfrontalis':

> Words came with warrants to conscript him –
> Crow feigned mad.
> Words came with blank cheques –
> He drew Minnie Mice on them.

If you draw Minnie Mouse in a slightly different attitude on each page of a cheque book and make the leaves spring open in rapid succession from under your thumb, you will produce the effect of an animated cartoon. A recent, not very good novel satirizing the contemporary arts scene, William Cooper's *You Want the Right Frame of Reference*, has a rather striking dust jacket on which the brightly coloured stylized figure of Donald Duck is superimposed upon a reproduction of the Mona Lisa; and this to me is a much closer visual equivalent for the emotive effect of *Crow* than Baskin's fine drawing.

The world of the animated cartoon, particularly in its harsher, post-Disney phase, is one in which animals and birds, drawn in such a way as to caricature both their species and certain human types, are involved in knockabout comic situations in which there is a strong element of sado-masochistic fantasy. The narratives are usually simple and stereotyped: usually there is some kind of conflict situation, which is developed in a series of short, parallel episodes in the course of which one or more of the characters are subjected to extreme and grotesque forms of physical violence. They are propelled through walls with such force that they leave holes corresponding to their own shapes. They walk over precipices and fall chin-first to the ground, in which they impale themselves. They are shot out of gun barrels, or flattened by steamrollers, then peeled off the ground only to be blown up with high explosives or frozen into blocks of ice or encased in concrete. They are battered, burned, stretched and squashed and always, quite incredibly, they survive.

Crow often reminds me of such cartoon films. Or, to put it another way, the films help me to make sense of the poems. Where else can one find a precedent for a series of short narratives which present a quasi-human bird, both comic and sinister, popping up in all kinds of situations – now in the Garden of Eden, now charging through space, now guzzling ice-cream on a modern beach, now wrestling with the Old Man of the Sea . . . sometimes coming off best, sometimes coming off worst, but always surviving? In a poem called 'Truth Kills Everybody', admittedly, Crow is 'blasted to nothing' in the last line; but he re-appears in the very next poem, where he is significantly described as 'he who has never been killed'. 'Truth Kills Everybody' contains one image straight out of the cartoon world:

> It was a naked powerline, 2000 volts –
> He stood aside watching his body go blue
> As he held it and held it

'It' here is Proteus, the Old Man of the Sea who changes his shape to evade capture. There are several poems on this theme of metamorphosis – 'Crow goes Hunting', for instance, and 'Magical Dangers' – which is a theme especially associated with classical poetry. But the *Crow* poems could hardly deviate more sharply from classical standards of poetic decorum. Crow's Proteus turns first into 'the famous bulging Achilles' – which is classical enough; but then into a shark – a 'wreath of lashing mambas' – the powerline – a screeching woman – the steering wheel of a runaway car – a trunk of jewels – 'the ankle of a rising, fiery angel' – 'Christ's hot pounding heart' – and finally the earth 'shrunk to the size of a hand-grenade', which then explodes: evidently an allusion to the contraction and explosion of matter in space. There is no logical or emotional consistency in this sequence of transformations. It is 'a mish-mash of scripture and physics', to use a memorable phrase from another poem. Indecorum reigns, as it does in the cartoons.

I don't mean to *equate* Ted Hughes's poems with cartoons, the vast majority of which are of minimal interest and value as art. I am merely pointing to a certain similarity of style and convention: the caricatured, quasi-human bird reappearing in a series of heterogeneous but familiar contexts; the mixture of comedy and violence; the stark, hard-edged quality of the visual images; the construction of narrative in a series of parallel episodes, or statements, climaxed by some unexpected twist or deflating pay-off line; the sudden transformations, mutations, mutilations, reversals and recoveries, which defy all the laws of logic, physics and good taste; above all, perhaps, the very direct, rapid, economic, simple manner of delivery. For there is nothing *subtle* about the technique of these poems: there are no nuances, no tentative evocations, no haunting cadences.

Such a description of the poems could, of course, be turned against them, and indeed the reviewer* in the *Times Literary Supplement* (8 January 1971) has already done so. In his opinion, the techniques of *Crow* 'grant total licence to the poet's freewheeling inventiveness' which he uses, or rather abuses, to unload his obsessions with blood and destruction onto the defenceless reader. Of Crow himself this writer says: 'his human stance – tough, sardonic, blood-soaked, I've-seen-it-all-before-but-I'm-still-here – is so deliberately (and fashionably) cartoon-like for it to seem soppy to complain that it is wholly superficial.'

Obviously I have to agree that such a complaint *is* soppy. Cartoon art (it is not clear whether animated or strip cartoons are being referred to, but it does not greatly affect the issue) is, for the most part, superficial, but Hughes's adaptation of it is not. Cartoon conventions and motifs are combined with literary conventions and motifs to very powerful effect – an effect that is neither superficial nor sublime, but generated by the tension between these two aesthetic poles. Furthermore, it is precisely the cartoon-like, non-realistic, non-poetic characteristics of *Crow* which prevent the admittedly horrific and sensational matter of many of the poems from spilling over into mere self-indulgence or disgust. Consider, for example, 'Crow and Mama', the structure of which is very clearly analogous to the scenario of a cartoon film:

> When Crow cried his mother's ear
> Scorched to a stump.
>
> When he laughed she wept
> Blood her breasts her palms her brow all wept blood
>
> He tried a step, then a step, and again a step –
> Every one scarred her face for ever.
>
> When he burst out in rage
> She fell back with an awful gash and a fearful cry.
>
> When he stopped she closed on him like a book
> On a bookmark, he had to get going.
>
> He jumped into the car the towrope
> Was around her neck he jumped out.

*Subsequently revealed as Ian Hamilton. See his *A Poetry Chronicle* (1973), pp. 165–70.

He jumped into the plane but her body was jammed in the jet –

There was a great row, the flight was cancelled.

He jumped into the rocket and its trajectory
Drilled clean through her heart he kept on . . .

Crow serves Hughes as Sweeney served Eliot, or Crazy Jane served
Yeats. The adapted cartoon-style conventionalizes the experience,
frames it ironically, puts it at a distance and thus makes it manage-
able. Major innovations in the arts are often carried forward by such
collaboration between high and low art – 'both ends against the middle',
in Leslie Fiedler's phrase.

Not the least achievement of *Crow*, to my mind, is that it resolves
(or by-passes) an argument which has generated more heat than light
in the world of contemporary poetry. I mean the argument between
those who regard poetry as written communication and those who regard it as oral communication; between the academic poets and the pop
poets; between the defenders of regular form and the apostles of free
form; between (to caricature both schools of thought) the poem as
crossword puzzle and the poem as cry.

Crow, it seems to me, combines most of the strengths and avoids
most of the weaknesses of both kinds. As the BBC readings demonstrated, the verse lends itself very readily to the speaking voice, especially Hughes's own; and the avoidance, in most cases, of syntactical
subordination means that the verse can be taken in very easily through
the ear. The language has a vernacular robustness, often making effective use of colloquialism and slang. But the poems do not, like so much
modern 'oral poetry', wither and fade on the page. *Crow* is a book to
read, and read again; and one of the rare cases where punctuation and
typographical layout are really functional, guiding and controlling the
reader's inner voice. There are few rhymes, and no regularity of line
length in most of the poems, yet Hughes rarely falls into the slackness
this invites. The poems are strong-lined, packed, purposeful. They
sound as if they came off the top of the poet's head – they have the air
of rapid improvisation – but they are stunningly effective, and when
you examine them it is difficult to see how they could be improved.
One suspects that if they were composed in quick, spontaneous bursts,
with little revision, it was only after the poet had thoroughly mastered
his style by long practice and many failures. And the language, as well
as having a contemporary, idiomatic ring, also echoes ancient and traditional forms of discourse, such as the Old Testament, Anglo-Saxon
poetry, Milton and Marvell. Themes and images from the Bible and
classical mythology mingle with sharply topical allusions to motor-car
accidents, pollution, mechanized war and nuclear devastation.

Crow meets T. S. Eliot's definition of poetic originality in that it is both continuous with and modifies the poetic tradition, and that tradition now, of course, includes Eliot himself. The mixture of the mythical and topical, the sacred and the profane, poetic resonance and brittle colloquialism in *Crow* is indeed reminiscent of *The Waste Land*, yet the effect is quite different. Part of the difference, I suggest, derives from Hughes's assimilation of cartoon techniques. Take a line like:

Crow stropped his beak and started in on the two thieves

The full effect can only be appreciated in context ('Crow's Song of Himself'); but even out of context it's a pretty arresting formulation of post-Christian sentiment. The image is complex, paradoxical, violently indecorous and therefore shocking – but it is not in the least vague or mysteriously suggestive in the symbolist manner. On the contrary, it is starkly graphic, brutally explicit. I cannot think of anything quite like this line elsewhere in modern poetry, and I cannot conceive of its being written before the advent of Walt Disney – much as the connection would have appalled that God-fearing entertainer of the masses.

14 Tom Wolfe and the New Journalism

The New Journalism, an anthology edited by Tom Wolfe and E. W. Johnson, was first published in the United States in 1973, but did not appear in Britain until 1975. Being issued in a paperback edition only (under the Pan Picador imprint) it received relatively slight attention in the review columns of British journals. This neglect was unfortunate and undeserved. Apart from the fact that most of the anthology's contents are entertaining and/or instructive in their own right, Tom Wolfe's long, polemical introduction is a thought-provoking contribution to current debate about modern narrative writing, all the more welcome for coming from a quarter not generally given to aesthetic pronouncements and technical self-scrutiny.

In an essay entitled 'The Novelist at the Crossroads' first published in 1969,[1] starting from the premise established by Robert Scholes and Robert Kellogg[2] that the realistic novel is a synthesis of fictional and historical modes, I argued that as contemporary writers have, for a variety of reasons, lost confidence in the validity of this synthesis, they have tended to cultivate one of its components at the expense of the other; committing themselves either to History, in various forms of 'nonfiction novel', or to Fiction in various forms of what Scholes calls 'Fabulation',[3] where the procedures of allegory, romance and myth are allowed full rein. Some writers may oscillate between the two extremes (e.g. Mailer in *Why Are We In Vietnam?* and *The Armies of the Night*) and others may introduce both modes into the same book and play them off against each other (e.g. Vonnegut's *Slaughterhouse 5* and Julian Mitchell's *The Undiscovered Country*) but such variations do not invalidate – rather, they confirm – the general thesis that for many writers of our time verisimilitude and inventiveness, the demands of historical authenticity and imaginative authenticity, no longer seem easily reconcilable.

The lines of the debate have been drawn rather differently, and more clearly, in America compared with England. Traditional realistic fiction has deeper roots in our literary culture and is therefore more likely to go on reproducing itself. Many of our most admired novelists give no

175

sign that they regard the creation of fictional worlds painstakingly endowed with a pseudo-historical plausibility as a problematical or paradoxical activity. Thus in England propagandists for the non-fiction novel (like the late B. S. Johnson) and for Fabulation (like Brigid Brophy) have tended to merge into the same avant-garde, which sees itself as a minority beating in vain against the bastions of entrenched British literary conservatism. In America, however, Fabulation in various forms has dominated the literary scene in the 1960s and 1970s. Barth, Brautigan, Barthelme, Burroughs, Coover, Hawkes, Pynchon, Sontag, Vonnegut, have been the names to conjure with; and they have also dominated discussion about whither prose narrative is or should be going, either in their own pronouncements (for most of them are highly articulate and self-conscious writers with at least one foot in the campus) or through the considerable body of academic criticism which has accumulated about their work.

And this is where Tom Wolfe comes in. Brash, arrogant and often naïve as it is, his introduction to *The New Journalism* is at least refreshing in putting forward a case for empirical narrative and against Fabulation. 'Fiction writers, currently, are busy running backward, skipping and screaming, into a begonia patch that I call Neo-Fabulism', Wolfe declares; and then: 'The most important literature being written in America today is in nonfiction, in the form that has been tagged, however ungracefully, the New Journalism.' It is not necessary to accept this extravagant claim to take some interest in the reasoning behind it, as a way of both understanding more fully our literary situation, and giving the new journalists their due for their modest but genuine achievements.

According to Wolfe, the New Journalism has taken over the central business of the novel – the recording of social reality – because novelists, chasing false grails of myth, symbolism, 'art', the absurd or whatever, have neglected their duty. The argument therefore turns on that endlessly problematical yet indispensable concept, realism. 'This reality business is very difficult', John Hawkes remarked in a recent interview.[4] 'The questions are: what is it? And where is it?' Other fabulators are less tentative. John Barth has remarked that God was not too bad a novelist except that he was a realist, and declared his own intention of reinventing the world in his books. 'Reality isn't realistic any more', says a blocked writer in one of Norman Mailer's stories. These writers are, of course, only repeating in a more extreme form what the great modernists practised or preached before them (e.g. Virginia Woolf: 'Mr Arnold Bennett says it is only if the characters are real that the novel has any chance of surviving . . . But, I ask myself, what is reality? and who are the judges of reality?') and both the modernists and the postmodernists of our own time have had the approval of approval of the most influential schools of modern criticism. The New Criticism, when it finally got around to grappling with prose fiction, tended to underwrite the techniques of the modernists and to read the classics in their light; later critical stars like Northrop Frye and Leslie Fiedler have obviously given encouragement directly or indirectly to Fabulation; and in France the *nouvelle critique* has been busily promoting modernism and the *nouveau roman* at the expense of traditional realism. Roland Barthes's brilliant analysis of Balzac's 'Sarrasine' in *S/Z* is punctuated with stern reminders that this kind of writing is no longer possible. Realism is a literary mode that encourages the bourgeoisie's illusion that their culture is natural. Balzac could believe this in good faith, but we cannot.

This formidable consensus of opinion might be summed up in the words of the editor of *Partisan Review*, William Phillips: 'realism is just another formal device, not a permanent method for dealing with experience'. Quoting this remark, Tom Wolfe says:

I suspect that precisely the opposite is true . . . the introduction of realism into literature by people like Richardson, Fielding and Smollett was like the introduction of electricity into machine technology. It was *not* just another device. It raised the state of the art to a new magnitude. The effect of realism on the emotions was something that had never been conceived of before . . . for writers to give up this unique power in the quest for a more sophisticated kind of fiction – it is as if an engineer were to set out to develop a more sophisticated machine technology by first of all discarding the principle of electricity.

The analogy drawn here between art and technology is highly misleading, since art does not progress in the sense of getting better and better but merely changes. However, I would agree that realism is not quite like other literary devices. The conventions of fairy story, say, or pastoral poetry, are wholly artificial and understood as such by author and audience. The basic convention of realism is that it observes the laws of time, place, causality, etc., by which we order and make intelligible our non-literary experience. The observance of these laws makes possible (though it does not ensure) the intense emotional involvement of readers and their thrills of recognition for which Wolfe values realistic narrative. This does perhaps give 'realism' a special status in our culture; but it does not, of course, mean that it is indispensable, or that its procedures may not become stale, tired and mechanical, requiring from time to time the challenge of alternative modes in order to renew itself. Such a challenge has been delivered at least twice in our century – first, by the modernists of the early decades and, second, by the postmodernists; and if this has had a more obvious effect on American than

on English writing it is probably because one side of the American
literary imagination has always had a strong tendency towards allegorical, mythical and symbolic narrative forms with transcendental over-
tones – though you wouldn't think so listening to Mr Wolfe. 'The
European "mythic" vogue did not come into American literature until
after the Second World War', he blithely asserts, as if Poe, Hawthorne
and Melville had never written.

Mr Wolfe, in fact, belongs on the other side of a split that runs
right through the history of American literature, which Philip Rahv
once described as a war between Palefaces and Redskins (Jews and
Blacks may join either team, though they tend to divide in predictable
ways). 'Palefaces' are writers who draw on the cultural tradition of
Europe, especially England (and often emigrate there), e.g. Henry
James, or T. S. Eliot. 'Redskins' are writers who celebrate the vitality
of what is indigenous, democratic and of the frontier, e.g. Mark Twain
and Walt Whitman. Tom Wolfe's first book of essays, *The Kandy-
Kolored, Tangerine-Flake Streamline Baby*, was the exultant war-cry
of a modern, urbanised Redskin taking possession of rich territory
scorned by the Palefaces. He records the moment vividly in the introduction to *The New Journalism*:

When I reached New York in the early Sixties, I couldn't believe the
scene I saw spread out before me. New York was pandemonium with a
big grin on. Among people with money – and they seemed to be multi-
plying like shad – it was the wildest, looniest time since the 1920s . . . a
universe of creamy forty-five-year-old fatties with walnut-shell eyes out
on the giblet slab wearing the hip-huggers and the minis and the Little
Egypt eyes and the sideburns and the boots and the bells and the love
beads, doing the Watusi and the Funky Broadway and jiggling and
grinning and sweating and sweating and grinning and jiggling until the
onset of dawn or saline depletion, which ever came first . . . It was a
hulking carnival. But what really amazed me was that as a writer I had
it all practically to myself . . . I just knew that some enterprising novelist was going to come along and *do* this whole marvellous scene with
one gigantic daring bold stroke. It was so ready, so *ripe*, beckoning . . .
but it never happened . . . To my even greater amazement I had the
same experience when I came upon 1960's California. This was the very
incubator of new styles of living, and these styles were right there for
all to see, ricocheting off every eyeball – and again a few amazed
journalists working in the new form had it all to themselves . . . had the
whole crazed obscene uproarious Mammon-faced drug-soaked mau-mau
lust-oozing Sixties in America all to themselves.

A slight exaggeration, of course. What Wolfe means is that the novelists
either treated this material in various forms of fantasy or, if dealing

with it more or less realistically, subjected it to serious moral scrutiny and expressed dismay at what they saw. Saul Bellow's *Mr Sammler's Planet*, for instance, took such a look at New York life in the 1960s and it's significant that Tom Wolfe goes out of his way to abuse that book. For it is essential to the Redskin pose that you give a resounding Yea to experience, however alarming it may be, if it is authentically American (just as it is part of the reporter's professional code to report without moralising). Wolfe's prose, full of long catalogues, jumbled idioms and loose paratactic syntax, is typical Redskin writing (cf. *A Song of Myself*).

However, let us move on to the next part of the argument:

The novelists had been kind enough to leave behind for our boys quite a nice little body of material: the whole of American society, in fact. It only remained to be seen if magazine writers could master the techniques, in nonfiction, that had given the novel of social realism such power.

Wolfe lists four devices of realistic fiction which the New Journalists borrowed (or rediscovered for themselves) and applied to the art of reporting: (1) 'scene-by-scene construction, telling the story by moving from scene to scene and resorting as little as possible to historical narrative', (2) the use of dialogue – direct speech rather than reported speech or summary, (3) the use of 'third-person point of view' – i.e. narrating events from the angle of a participant, 'giving the reader the feeling of being inside the character's mind and experiencing the emotional reality of the scene as he experiences it', (4) 'the recording of everyday gestures, habits, manners, customs, styles of furniture, clothing, decoration, styles of travelling, eating, keeping house, modes of behaving toward children, servants, superiors, inferiors, peers, plus the various looks, glances, poses, styles of walking and other symbolic details that might exist within a scene . . . Symbolic, generally, of people's *status life*, using that term in the broad sense of the entire pattern of behaviour and possessions through which people express their position in the world or what they think it is or what they hope it to be.'

Such details are, strictly speaking, indices rather than symbols of status, but Wolfe is quite right to see their notation as one of the staple devices of realistic fiction, and a distinctive feature of such early masters of realism in literature as Defoe and Balzac. Obviously this is an area in which reporting and novel-writing overlap, for the use of such detail depends for novelist and reporter alike on careful observation, memorising, note-taking, recall, or research, or a combination of all these. The details, being products of culture, are already full of signification. The writer adds his own by the manner of his selection, but since he must select anyway, this procedure can easily be made to look quite innocent of authorial intent, a neutral record of what was there. Apart from the proper names, there is nothing in this opening paragraph of Barbara L. Goldsmith's 'La Dolce Vita' that distinguishes it stylistically from a work of realistic fiction (this text, and all others cited subsequently, are reprinted, in whole or in part, in *The New Journalism*):

In Andy Warhol's new loft studio 'The Factory', Viva leaned against the whitewashed plaster wall, her cotton-candy hair bright blonde under the spotlights. Her fine-boned face and attenuated body were reminiscent of sepia-tinted photographs, found in an attic trunk, of actresses of the early 1930s. She was wearing an Edwardian velvet coat, a white matelassé blouse and tapered black slacks. 'Do I look OK?' she asked Paul Morrissey, Warhol's technical director. 'Like a star,' he replied grandly.

Rhetorically, as Roman Jakobson has pointed out, such detail is a form of metonymy or synecdoche, whereby an attribute of a thing is made to stand for the thing itself, or a part for the whole. The studio in this passage is evoked for us by the whitewashed plaster wall, Viva by the salient features of her physical appearance – fluffy hair, fine-boned face, thin body – and the principal items of her clothing: just a few of the innumerable details present in the actual event. Realistic writing is, however, rarely content *just* to select. Usually the selected details are heightened, or 'defamiliarised', by metaphor or simile, extending their range of connotations: hence the 'cotton-candy' and 'sepia-tinted photographs' in the above quotation. Tom Wolfe himself is very fond of playing metaphorically with metonymic detail, generating that sense of excited discovery, of the extraordinariness that is before-your-very-eyes, which is characteristic of his writing, and a major source of its considerable comic power. Here he is describing the city room of the *New York Herald Tribune* as it first struck him:

The place looked like the receiving bin at the Good Will . . . a promiscuous heap of junk . . . Wreckage and exhaustion everywhere . . . If somebody such as the city editor had a swivel chair, the universal joint would be broken, so that everytime he got up, the seat would keel over as if stricken with a lateral stroke. All the intestines of the building were left showing in diverticultic loops and lines – electrical conduits, water pipes, steam pipes, effluvium ducts, sprinkler systems, all of it dangling and grunting from the ceiling, the walls, the columns. The whole mess, from top to bottom, was painted over in an industrial sludge, Lead Grey, Subway Green, or that unbelievable dead red, that grim distemper of pigment and filth, that they paint the floor with in the tool and die works. On the ceiling were scalding banks of fluorescent lights, turning the atmosphere radium blue and burning bald spots in the crowns of the copy readers, who never moved.

It is quite Dickensian in the way a demonic vitality is attributed to inanimate objects, and one may feel, as one often feels with Dickens, that another step in this direction would take Wolfe out of the realm of realism altogether and into fantasy. But he does not cross that boundary: note that his analogies and allusions, however extravagantly phrased, are always taken from the same world of empirical observation as the things to which they are applied. He is a tremendously *knowing* writer, bristling with inside knowledge and technical terms, intimating that he has been around and missed nothing.

If the exploitation of detail is a natural extension of the 'historical' dimension of realistic fiction, the other three devices are more obviously fictional, or literary. Scenic construction tampers with historical continuity by the very gaps it creates between scenes, and this is particularly obvious when the narrative deviates from strict chronological order – a favourite device of the New Journalism:

Thursday, Williams, the gentle Florida periscope operator, achieved immortality of sorts: he really saw a communist, large as life and twice as spunky, an experience that no other trooper in M's alert battalion was to enjoy throughout this Operation. This special communist was staring at Williams from a bush no farther than the other side of a ping-pong table, staring at him down the gray barrel of a rifle, in fact. '*Ho!*' Williams shouted in consternation: but to begin at the beginning. [from *M* by John Sack]

Scenic construction depends for its effectiveness on the second device listed by Wolfe: the extensive presentation of dialogue in direct speech. This has not been a feature of orthodox reporting partly because, aside from certain specialised and artificial speech situations – law courts, parliamentary assemblies, interviews – it has been difficult or impossible for reporters to make a verbatim record of what was said on any particular occasion. The invention of tape recorders has made some difference, though Tom Wolfe points out their limitations and says that his own *tour de force* in this kind of reporting, the account of the Leonard Bernsteins' party for the Black Panthers in *Radical Chic*, was 'achieved in the oldest and most orthodox manner possible: I came to the Bernsteins' party for no other reason than to write about it, arrived with a notebook and ballpoint pen in plain view and took notes in the centre of the living room throughout the action described'. The real achievement was perhaps Wolfe's nerve in doing this without having been invited. He is quite candid about the brashness, ruthlessness, and at times courage, required of the New Journalist (it all goes with the Redskin image) who must be ready to intrude where he is not wanted, to ask impertinent questions, to live with his subject for long, possibly boring periods, to risk rebuffs, threats and worse (e.g. Hunter Thompson, who ran with the Hell's Angels for eighteen months to write *The Hell's Angels: a Strange and Terrible Saga* and was beaten half to death for his pains), to ensure, in short, that when the revealing moment comes he is there to observe and record it.

More important than the development of the tape recorder, in this respect, is perhaps the curious surrender of personal privacy that seems to be a feature of modern mass society: the surprising willingness of people, in all walks of life, to have their most intimate life reported on (or photographed, or filmed or televised), though experience shows that this is invariably damaging to the subject. Without this deference to the demands of the media, such devastating exposés as the late Nicholas Tomalin's 'The General Goes Zapping Charlie Cong' or John Gregory Dunne's *The Studio* or Joe McGinnis's *The Selling of the President*, would not have been possible. These three texts all use the technique of allowing the persons reported on to condemn themselves out of their own mouths.

Tomalin's gun-toting General watches a napalm strike on the Vietnamese forest from the open door of his hovering helicopter:

'Aaaaah,' cries the General. 'Nice, nice. Very neat. Come in low, let's see who's left down there.'
    'How do you know for sure the Viet Cong snipers were in that strip you burned?'
    'We don't. The smoke position was a guess. That's why we zapp the whole forest.'

The Studio is mainly about the making of the eighteen-million-dollar film of *Dr Doolittle* by Twentieth Century Fox. The extract printed by Wolfe describes an expensive trip of a party of executives and production staff to see a sneak preview of the film in Minneapolis. It is obvious from the response of the cinema audience that the film is going to be an eighteen-million-dollar flop. The studio people and their associates all know this but cannot bring themselves to admit it.

Ted Ashley, the president of Ashley-Famous Artists, Rex Harrison's agents, came up and clapped Jacobs on the back. 'Arthur, you've got yourself a picture here,' Ashley said. Jacobs waited for him to say something else, but Ashley just slapped him on the back again and went over to talk to Zanuck.

'The audience was kind of quiet,' Zanuck said.

Ten Mann, the theatre owner, a large blocky man at one of whose theatres *Dr Doolittle* was going to play when it opened in Minneapolis, elbowed his way to Zanuck's side. 'I want you to know, Dick, a year's run,' he said. 'A year minimum.'

'I thought the audience was a little quiet,' Zanuck repeated.

'Yes, it was, Dick,' Mann said. 'But it's the kids who are going to make this picture, and we didn't have many kids here tonight.' Mann seemed to search for the proper words. 'You've got to realise,' he said, 'that what we had here tonight was your typically sophisticated Friday night Minneapolis audience.'

Zanuck seemed not to hear. 'They weren't conditioned to it like *The Sound of Music*,' he said.

'That's my point, my point exactly,' Mann said.

The extract from *The Selling of the President* carries to an extreme this technique of verbatim dialogue weighted with unspoken irony. With great boldness, for this was his first chapter and, as Wolfe observes, the risk of boring his readers was considerable, McGinnis gives every word and gesture of Richard Nixon recording five takes respectively of two television political 'commercials' in the 1968 Presidential campaign. This is effective in two ways. The idea of a senior politician 'addressing the nation' is defamiliarised, and demystified, by showing in detail the cold, calculating, completely pragmatic approach of Nixon to his task. And by reading the text of each speech, with its variants, five times, we are compelled to recognise the hollowness and poverty of his language.

From these three examples, we can perhaps draw another conclusion concerning what the New Journalists have learnt about the use of dialogue in realistic fiction. Orthodox reporting, like orthodox historiography, tends to quote direct speech, if it can at all, that carries obviously important information ('Peace in our time') or that has memorable rhetorical force ('blood, sweat and tears') or both. What novelists have always known (and, of course, ballad writers and dramatists before them) is that, artfully presented, the most banal dialogue can be powerfully expressive of the attitudes and values implicit in a given situation. Michael Herr's vivid account of the 1968 siege of Khesanh, a Marine stronghold (or rather weakhold, for the Marines, it appears, were not very good at constructing defences) in the highlands of Vietnam, gains enormously from his ear for dialogue, an ear no doubt tuned by attentive reading of Hemingway and Mailer. Viewed objectively, the vocabulary of the 'Grunts' is pathetically limited, monotonously obscene, but out of their casual chaffing and grumbling Herr creates a convincing portrait of these bewildered, superstitious, unhappy

warriors, the interminable alternation in their speech of variants on
fuck and shit seeming an apt linguistic equivalent to the pointless
kill-or-be-killed of their situation.

Wolfe's third device – third-person point of view, what is called
'dramatised consciousness' in Jamesian criticism – is perhaps the main
foundation of the New Journalism's claim to be new. The other devices
are to be found in nonfiction writing long before the 1960s, but usually
'guaranteed' by a first-person narrator who is the reporter himself.
Orwell is an obvious example that comes to mind, though the status of
his 'I' is more ambiguous than may appear at first sight. Even the
third-person rendering of consciousness in free indirect speech is not
unknown in Romantic historiography and biography (e.g. Carlyle).
What seems to be new about the New Journalism is the extension of
this method to topical material, proposing to render the inner thought
processes of living people who are in a position to resent or repudiate
what is attributed to them in this way. It is another example of how the
New Journalism has thrived on the surrender of privacy in modern
society, and perhaps it has bloomed more spectacularly in America than
in England (Tomalin is the only British contributor in this collection)
because their libel laws are laxer than ours. Wolfe, significantly, sees a
future for the realistic novel only in 'certain areas of life that journalism still cannot move into easily, particularly for reasons of invasion of
privacy'.

The New Journalists defend the dramatised consciousness technique
as a more immediate and effective way of presenting hard facts obtained
by interviewing the persons concerned, or by other kinds of research.
It was by interviewing the murderers and other witnesses at great length
that Truman Capote re-created the events described in *In Cold Blood* as
experienced by the participants; and John Sack wrote *M* in the same
way. Tom Wolfe was accused of having invented the prelude to *Radical
Chic*, in which Leonard Bernstein imagines himself delivering an anti-
war speech from the stage of a packed concert hall and being interrupted by a Negro who rises out of a grand piano to make disconcerting remarks, but Wolfe states here with obvious satisfaction, that
'every detail of his "Negro by the piano" fantasy, including the Negro's
remarks, comes from Bernstein's own words as recorded in a book
called *The Private World of Leonard Bernstein* by his friend John
Gruen'.

Radical Chic shows how skilful Tom Wolfe can be in handling narrative viewpoint. After the vision of Bernstein described above, Wolfe
adopts the voice of what he calls 'the downstage narrator' to begin the
story proper:

Mmmmmmmmmmmmmmmm.   These are nice. Little Roquefort
cheese morsels rolled in crushed nuts. Very tasty. Very subtle. It's the

way the dry sackiness of the nuts tiptoes up against the dour savour of
the cheese that is so nice, so subtle. Wonder what the Black Panthers
eat here on the hors d'oeuvres trail? Do the Panthers like little Roquefort cheese morsels rolled in crushed nuts this way . . . For example,
does that huge Black Panther there in the hallway, the one shaking
hands with Felicia Bernstein herself, the one with the black leather
coat and the dark glasses and the absolutely unbelievable Afro, Fuzzy-
Wuzzy-scale, in fact – is he, a Black Panther, going on to pick up a
Roquefort cheese morsel rolled in crushed nuts from off the tray, from
a maid in uniform, and just pop it down the gullet without so much as
missing a beat of Felicia's perfect Mary Astor voice . . .

The narrator's voice is a subtle blend of Tom Wolfe himself and some
anonymous guest, of the reporter and the participant. The whole story
is narrated as though Tom Wolfe is eavesdropping on the thoughts of
the guests, articulating them and in the process imparting to them a
fine edge of parody and satire, which is turned both outwards against
what is seen and inwards upon what is felt:

what does one wear to these parties for the Panthers or the Young
Lords or the grape workers? What does a woman wear? Obviously one
does not want to wear something frivolously and pompously expensive,
such as a Gerard Pipart party dress. On the other hand one does not
want to arrive 'poor-mouthing it' in some outrageous turtle-neck and
West Eighth Street bell-jean combination, as if one is 'funky' and 'of
the people'. Frankly, Jean Vanden Heuvel – that's Jean there in the
hallway giving everyone her famous smile, in which her eyes narrow
down to f/16 – frankly, Jean tends too much toward the funky fallacy.
Jean, who is the daughter of Jules Stein, one of the wealthiest men in
the country, is wearing some sort of rust-red snap-around suede skirt,
the sort that English working girls pick up on Saturday afternoons in
those absolutely *berserk* London boutiques like Bus Stop or Biba,
where everything looks chic and yet skimpy and raw and vital.

The Roquefort cheese balls mentioned in the first quotation, and referred to at many subsequent points in the text, provide a good example of how a realistic detail can function as a symbol by highlighting
and repetition. As food the cheese balls are an index of an affluent
Park Avenue life-style. Their inappropriateness as food for Black Panthers symbolises the social contradictions implicit in the occasion, but
there is more to it than that. These contradictions constitute, in fact,
the special attraction of the occasion for the socialites: they are frater-
nising with their own social antitheses, enhancing their pleasure in their
own privileges by, as it were, putting them deliberately at risk.

God, what a flood of taboo thoughts runs through one's head at these
Radical Chic events . . . But it's delicious. It's as if one's nerve endings
were on red alert to the most intimate nuances of status. Deny it if you
want to! Nevertheless, it runs through every soul here. It is the matter
of the marvellous contradictions on all sides. It is like the delicious
shudder you get when you try to force the prongs of two horseshoe
magnets together . . . *them* and *us* . .

Delicious is one of the keywords of *Radical Chic*, recurring again and
again, and it sends us back to the delicious Roquefort cheese balls:
'it's the way the dry sackiness of the nuts tiptoes up against the dour
savour of the cheese that is so nice, so subtle'. The artificial juxtaposition of contrasting flavours and textures in the cheese balls, described
at the very outset of the narrative, thus corresponds to and anticipates
the juxtaposition of contrasting values and life-styles at the party.

The writing represented in *The New Journalism* straddles the line between literature and non-literature, and there are problems of dis-
crimination here which I have discussed at some length in *The Modes of
Modern Writing*. According to the theory propounded there, a piece of
reportage would deserve or acquire the status of literature if it responded satisfactorily to being read as if it were fictional. Wolfe's
claims for the New Journalism are diametrically opposed to this view.
He says it is

a form that is not merely *like a novel*. It consumes devices that happen
to have originated with the novel and mixes them with every other
device known to prose. And all the while, quite beyond matters of
technique, it enjoys an advantage so obvious, so built-in, one almost
forgets what a power it has: the simple fact that the reader knows
all this actually happened. The disclaimers have been erased. The
screen is gone. The writer is one step closer to the absolute involvement of the reader that Henry James and James Joyce dreamed of and
never achieved.

The claim that Mr Wolfe and his journalistic colleagues have succeeded where James and Joyce failed is sufficiently extravagant not to
need serious discussion. A more interesting question is how far one's
literary appreciation of this kind of writing depends upon believing that
it 'all actually happened'. When I read about Jean Vanden Heuvel
'giving everyone her famous smile, in which her eyes narrow down to
f/16' do I have to believe that this is a strictly or even approximately
truthful description in order to feel its comic force? Would the symbolic effectiveness of the Roquefort cheese balls in the text be affected
if I was assured by a reliable witness that they were never served at
the Bernstein's party? I think not. Of course, to the extent that we

do trust Wolfe's reliability as a reporter, *Radical Chic* has an interest and value on the level of information or gossip, and it would be
disingenuous to pretend that this is not an important part of the
pleasure we derive from it. But this is not *essential* to its literary value,
which I think is quite considerable, and analysable in precisely the same
way as one would analyse a successful piece of realistic fiction. The
point is that one could read *Radical Chic* as if it were a fictional text
without destroying its coherence or rendering any of its component
parts superfluous.

This is not to say that Tom Wolfe and his colleagues need not have
bothered to get their facts right. That is their discipline, the basic rule
of their chosen form, and without it they would be lost. It is entirely
understandable that Mr Wolfe should deeply resent the suggestion that
he and his fellow New Journalists have been inventing their stories
('that was precisely the reaction that countless journalists and literary
intellectuals would have . . . as the New Journalism picked up momen-
tum. *The bastards are making it all up!*'). But in a way this was the
highest compliment that could be paid to the New Journalists: an
implicit acknowledgment that their work (or some of it) belongs to the
sphere of literature.

15 Where It's At: The Poetry of Psychobabble

If you drive northwards out of San Francisco by the Golden Gate bridge you will find yourself entering an idyllic landscape known as Marin County. It has hills and valleys crammed with redwoods and eucalyptus, a spectacular Pacific coastline and, on its inner shore, looking across the Bay, sheltered coves, marinas and the picturesque Italianate harbor town of Sausalito. In this immensely desirable location live the affluent, progressive, trend-haunted and fad-obsessed Californians who are the object of Cyra McFadden's wickedly knowing satire, *The Serial: A Year in the Life of Marin County*.[1]

At the center of its story are the Holroyds, a not-so-young couple whose income and energies are severely strained by their efforts to keep up with the Marin County Joneses. As one of their friends says, 'Marin's this high-energy trip with all these happening people' and what these people are 'into' is 'the human potential movement' in all its ramifications (one character alone has tried, over the years, 'Gurdjieff, Silva Mind Control, actualism, analytical tracking, parapsychology, Human Life Styling, postural integration, the Fischer-Hoffman process, hatha and raja yoga, integral massage, orgonomy, palmistry, Neo-Reichian Body work and Feldenkrais functional integration'), physical fitness, ecology and the cultivation of everything ethnically exotic in dress, food and design. Kate Holroyd herself is heavily into women's liberation and macramé, while her husband Harvey, who works in a San Francisco bank and cycles home from the Sausalito ferry every evening on his ten-speed Motobecane, is all too susceptible to other liberated ladies in the area. In the course of the chronicled year the Holroyds have a trial separation, and experiment unsuccessfully with alternative partners and life-styles before, in the final chapter, renewing their marriage vows at a totally laid-back party where the Reverend Spike Thurston of the Radical Unitarian Church pronounces them conjoined persons and the guests shower them with brown rice.

The peculiar *frisson* enjoyed by a reader of *The Serial* derives from the narration of what is essentially a suburban soap opera in a style borrowed from the characters themselves, who are constantly asserting

188

their membership of a sophisticated, liberated, trend-setting elite. The book is therefore an invaluable guide to the dialect of the Bay Area, 'the consciousness-raising capital of the western world' as Cyra McFadden has justly called it, a golden treasury of the slang that is spoken there by the educated middle classes, and carried, by a kind of cultural gulf-stream, to every part of the world where English is spoken. The linguistic ingredients of this dialect are varied and sometimes difficult to discriminate. The Counter Culture of the 1960s, black ghetto slang, jazz and rock jargon, sporting terminology, are certainly key sources, and it tends to be adopted and disseminated around the world most readily by pop musicians, disc jockeys, top athletes and 'alternative' artists. But what this language is applied to by the cultured progressive middle classes is human relationships and states of mind. It is essentially a language of psychological description and negotiation.

For example, Kate's friend Martha feels that she has learned after five marriages that 'marriage was this dynamic process. You had to stay in touch with yourself if you were going to relate to the other person's feelings instead of just ego-tripping'; but she hesitates to get involved in counselling Kate because 'after all, she and Bill were still getting inside each other's heads, a high-energy trip that didn't leave a lot of space for outside interaction'. Kate herself puts off an intrusive acquaintance by saying, 'Harvey and I are going through this *dynamic* right now, and it's kinda where I'm at. I haven't got a lot of psychic energy left over for social interaction. So whatever it is, maybe you should just run it by me right here. Off the wall.'

All the published comment on *The Serial* that I have read has assumed that this idiom is self-evidently absurd and vicious, and that by merely exhibiting its intensive use in cold print Cyra McFadden has destroyed its potency and performed a valuable act of linguistic hygiene. The author herself has given considerable support to this view by her comments in interviews and articles. A former college teacher of 'bonehead English', she has presented her book as a polemic against sloppy and automatized speech, and has endorsed, as a generic term for the idiom her characters use, *psychobabble*, a word coined by R. D. Rosen in a critique of do-it-yourself ego-psychology entitled *Psychobabble: Fast Talk and Quick Cure in the Era of Feeling*, published in 1977, not long after *The Serial*. According to Rosen, psychobabble is

a set of repetitive verbal formalities that kills off the very spontaneity, candour and understanding it pretends to promote. It's an idiom that reduces psychological insight to a collection of standardized observations, that provides a frozen lexicon to deal with an infinite variety of problems.

Cyra McFadden agrees. Conversations conducted in psychobabble, she says, 'make any exchange of ideas impossible; block any attempt at true communication; substitute what Orwell called "prefabricated words and phrases" for thought.'[2] British commentators, always prone to fits of linguistic chauvinism, have eagerly concurred. In a long article in the *Guardian* heralding the British edition of *The Serial* and referring to Rosen's book, Christopher Reed declared that psychobabble is 'the Newspeak of our age – puerile pap, specious speech, yet a dangerously pretentious nonsense talk which one day could engulf us all.'[3]

I regard this consensus of opinion as simplistic and unduly alarmist, for several reasons.

1   Any language is necessarily a finite system applied with different degrees of creativity to an infinite variety of situations, and most of the words and phrases we use are 'prefabricated' in the sense that we do not coin new ones every time we speak. Spoken (as distinct from written) discourse is especially dependent upon verbal formulae because we cannot take in more than a certain density of information through the ear and because speech is not always primarily referential in function, but also phatic, affective, expressive, etc., and formulaic repetition may be useful for these purposes.

2   Slang (of which psychobabble is an example) is generated precisely to relieve the inevitable monotony and deadening familiarity of ordinary speech by providing an alternative lexicon which is both novel and yet easily acquired and widely applicable. It also serves to define membership of a particular social or cultural subgroup, and to this end may be made deliberately mystifying to the uninitiated (e.g. criminal argot), but most slang, and certainly psychobabble, is not deliberately exclusive in this way. Slang is the poetry of ordinary speech in a precise linguistic sense; it draws attention to itself *qua* language, by deviating from accepted linguistic norms, substituting figurative expressions for literal ones, and thus 'defamiliarizes' the concepts it signifies. Once slang becomes so common and familiar that it is no longer foregrounded in this way against the background of more orthodox usage, its days are numbered and it either disappears or is absorbed into the standard language.

3   The very success of psychobabble (for the sake of consistency I will adopt this heavily pejorative term) – the way it has spread across America and begun to penetrate English English[4] – suggests that it must answer some genuine linguistic need and possess some distinctive rhetorical appeal, which it would be worth trying to analyze and understand.

This brings me back to *The Serial*, which I found pleased and fascinated me to a degree that could not be accounted for solely in terms of satirical effect, or the author's stated intentions, but derived in large part from the purely aesthetic appeal of its dialect. Probably the English reader will react to this differently from an American – certainly from a Californian. What is no doubt familiar to the latter is still to a large extent novel to us, and its 'poetic' dimension consequently more perceptible. That is my justification for venturing a rhetorical analysis of psychobabble. I write in the spirit of an anthropologist who once did some field work in the area,[5] but is a little rusty and subject to correction by the natives. The general descriptive points I would make about psychobabble are these. It is a predominantly metaphorical type of discourse, and the metaphors are usually drawn from *the movement or oganization of matter in space*, though the vehicle[6] of a given metaphor is often extremely vague (this is what makes it both attractively flexible in application and vulnerable to criticism as lacking precision). Psychobabble is predominantly verbal rather than nominal in emphasis, and relies heavily upon the deviant use of adverbs and prepositions to give commonplace verbs a new, figurative force.

Now for examples from *The Serial*, beginning with some words and phrases that are already well established in English English.

For instance, *into*, as in the reference to 'an artist who was heavily into belt-buckle casting,' or the description of a former banking colleague of Harvey's who has 'dropped out' (itself a spatial-dynamic metaphor) and is 'into bonsai trees, meditation and Zen jogging.' In standard English, *into* is a preposition qualifying verbs of motion and investigation like *go, come, run, look*. As a qualifier of the verb *to be*, which expresses a steady state, it is anomalous, and it is only figuratively that *into* may be applied to activities which have no precise location in space, such as belt-buckle casting, the cultivation of bonsai trees, meditation and Zen jogging. Used in this way, *into* becomes a metaphorical substitute for participles like *interested in, absorbed by*.

Another deviant combination of the verb *to be* + preposition is the phrase *where* [pronoun] *is at*, as in 'Harvey and I are going through this dynamic right now, and it's kinda where I'm at.' This use of *at* is redundant in standard English, since the sense is adequately expressed by 'where I am.' However, by adding the tautological *at* in the emphatic position at the closure of the clause, the speaker implies that a position has been reached in a process of change which has been going on and is (by implication) likely to continue. Kate feels the need of a friend who knew 'where she was coming from and where she was at.' There is a kind of contradiction here, and in the previous example, in that Kate seems to see herself as both stationary and moving; and this illustrates one of Cyra McFadden's most effective devices for ridiculing psychobabble, namely to make its exponents mix their metaphors.

Where you're/I'm/he's/she's coming from is a metaphor of movement in space particularly favored by the Marin set, used to denote
the values or philosophy of life or personal experience that motivates
behavior and speech. 'I know where you're coming from' is roughly
translatable as 'I understand what you mean,' but additionally con-
notes that the addressee is undergoing a process of change and has in
some sense *moved* towards an encounter with the addresser. Another
popular phrase, again a metaphor of movement in space, is *get behind*,
meaning to accept, support, identify with. 'Weddings were much less
conformist now that people were getting behind marriage again,' Kate
reflects; and, told that one of her friends has become a Lesbian, ex-
claims, 'How does she *feel* about it? I mean, can she get *behind* it?'
When the two tropes are combined, the effect is comical. 'So you see,
Harvey,' says Kate in the course of one of their matrimonial rap-
sessions, 'I can't exactly get behind where you're coming from.'

Another, related, satirical device of Cyra McFadden's is abruptly to
expose the metaphorical nature of a psychobabble phrase by unexpec-
tedly bringing into play its literal meaning and application. Kate's
friend Martha insists on sending her husband's shirts to the laundry because she 'couldn't get behind ironing boards.' Harvey's daughter Joan
refuses to wash her father's socks because 'I'm not into that laundry
bag.' (*Bag* is, of course, another spatial metaphor in the same dialect,
meaning matrix of interests, concerns.) These are unintended collisions
of the metaphorical and the literal; but sometimes Harvey, who has a
thin core of resistance to psychobabble and the life-style it articulates,
will make conscious play with the same device. One evening he arrives
home from work to find his wife and mistress lying in wait for him with
a jury of feminist sisters. 'I know where you're coming from,' he
acknowledges as they accuse him of being a male chauvinist pig.

'So what are you going to do, Harvey? Where are *you* coming from?'
'I'm coming from the bank,' Harvey said. Nobody laughed.

Later, Kate refuses to tell him who she is meeting for a lunch date, on
the grounds that she is entitled to her privacy. 'Oh, sure,' says Harvey.
'Listen, I know where you're coming from. I just wondered where
you're going.'

As well as *coming from*, there is *coming down* (possibly a weather
metaphor deriving from the sea-fog that suddenly descends upon the
Bay area in summer), meaning 'happening' and usually applied to
something unpleasant or serious or worrying. 'Hey, look, what's coming
down here anyway?' Says Harvey, when he finds himself ambushed by
the women's libbers. And there is *come on*, meaning 'behave,' but
connoting movement again, as if the person to whom it is applied is

advancing upon the addresser with offensive intent. 'Stop coming on with all that incredible crap,' says Kate to Harvey at the beginning of the same scene, when he defensively addresses the women as 'Ladies.' Then there is, of course, *coming out*, which used to be done by debs and is now done by gays.

But the verb that is subject to the greatest variety of mutation in psychobabble is undoubtedly *get*. In addition to *get behind*, already mentioned, there is *get centered, get down, get it on, get* [noun or pronoun] *together, get off on* and *get to*. (I did not notice *get with it* in *The Serial*, so perhaps that is now out, as distinct from far out, like Kate's Danish Modern extendable dining table.)

Get centered is self-explanatory ('What did matter was being true to yourself, getting centered . . . '). *Get down* is more elusive, but seems to be a contraction of *get down to* (a task), as in 'That's why we're here [at a male–female consciousness-raising session] , you know. To really get down and relate.' But it can be applied to more hedonistic pursuits. For example, a party that is 'getting down' is evidently becoming mildly orgiastic.

Get it on with has a specifically sexual meaning and is equivalent to the English colloquialism 'have it off with,' though I am unable to unpack this particular metaphor. The Reverend Spike Thurston presides at Martha's fifth marriage wearing a purple Marvin Gaye teeshirt inscribed, 'Let's Get It On' – a witty play on literal and metaphorical meanings. *Get off on* is a double metaphorical expression, denoting the achievement of sexual excitement or climax of a masturbatory or fetishistic kind, but usually applied in *The Serial* to nonsexual gratifications. The following example brings out the distinction nicely:

It sent Kate really into the pits when she learned from her 'friend' Martha, who seemed to get off on laying bad trips on people, that Harvey was getting it on with Carol.

Note the other characteristic spatial-dynamic metaphors here – *into the pits* (= depression), *lay* (= inflict) and *trip* (= experience). Variants on *get it together* include *get my head together* and *get my act together*, all metaphors of assembling and integrating something fragmented and disorganized. *Get to* means to hurt, annoy or disturb. 'When the news of Kate's and Harvey's separation reached Martha . . . it really got to her' – a metaphor of penetration.

Another key verb in psychobabble is *hang*, meaning to act, behave, comport oneself. The injunction to 'hang loose' is familiar and expressive, conveying a quintessentially Californian state of relaxed readiness for new experience. *Hang in* seems to mean something like the English colloquialisms *hang on* and *hold on*, but without the connotations of strenuous effort those phrases have. 'Now listen, Harv,' his secretary counsels him when he is suffering from jealousy, 'you gotta stay loose, you know? Hang in there; go with it . . . ' And Kate tells Harvey later: 'So if you want me to hang in there any longer, you're gonna have to bring your energies to reconstituting this marriage entirely.' It has been plausibly suggested to me by two independent correspondents[7] that the metaphorical vehicle in this phrase derives from surfing. To 'hang ten' in surfing jargon is to cling to the front of the board with your ten toes while travelling at perilous speed down the face of a big wave. Presumably the preposition *in* originally evoked the concave shape of the cresting wave. *Hang in there* is, however, a phrase popular with all kinds of athletes – the 'in there' being readily applicable to stadia, arenas, etc.

Some other characteristic spatial-dynamic tropes of psychobabble: *To blow away* = to surprise, astonish, as in 'Martha's last wedding had just blown Kate away, so she was looking forward to this one too.' This seems to be a pastoral mutation of the 1960s' psychedelic idiom, *to blow one's mind*, with its connotations of electric overload.

To dump on (intransitive) = to inflict one's worries upon, as when Kate says to a psychiatrist friend, 'Leonard, I'm sorry to dump on you like this, but I'm on a really heavy trip right now.'

Flash on = notice, realize, think of, an image of an object suddenly illuminated, as in this fragment of gallery talk: 'symbolism's really heavy; did you flash on how all of her phalluses have these terrific mushroom clouds on top?'

Heavy = serious, grave, important, powerful, oppressive (see two preceding examples). The adverb *heavily* is frequently used as an emphatic of *into*, as in 'Julie had been the only other woman on the block who was heavily into macramé.'

Interface = relationship, as in 'she and Harry hadn't finalized the parameters of their own interface.' Sometimes used as a verb meaning to have a dialogue, as in 'we've got to interface about the menu.'

Off the wall = spontaneously, as in 'She had decided to play the whole scene off the wall, to just go with the flow' (Kate preparing to confront Harvey's girl friend for the first time). Presumably this is a sporting metaphor, an image of a ball bouncing. (There is an older, Eastern application of this phrase to mean 'mad, crazy, bizarre.')

Run [*it*] *by* = show, explain, as in ' "Martha," he said when she'd finished, "run that one by me again slowly, will you?" ' (Bill to Martha, when she proposes a mixed consciousness-raising group). An image of exhibiting a mobile object.

Swing with = accept, tolerate, as in 'minor annoyances Kate could have swung with had it not been for other, more oppressive problems.'

Upfront = honest, honestly, as in 'Harvey told everyone that living with Marlene was fantastic, but if he'd been really upfront, their relationship wasn't really a waterbed of roses.'

As I remarked earlier, adverbs and prepositions are particularly important in psychobabble, and the use of *out* illustrates this very clearly. It qualifies a great many words, both literal and metaphorical, usually connoting the breaking of some conventional limit or boundary, a dangerous but exhilarating excess, e.g. to *munch out* (to gorge oneself), to *mellow out* (relax as a result of taking dope), to *wig out* (to get very excited, a variant of the older 'flip one's wig'), to *freak out* (to get or cause to become very excited), to *gross out* (to disgust) and to *luck out*, which means not to run out of luck, but to find permanent good fortune. And, of course, anything admirably original or daring is *far out* or *outasight*.

Finally, I would note the metaphorical use of the word *space* itself, meaning, well, where a person's at. 'Kate wasn't really high on chest hair . . . but Leonard had a lot going for him otherwise, and Kate liked the space he was in.' 'I hear you, babe,' says Martha's husband, Bill, 'I just can't figure out what space you're in. Like, I'm just not in the same place, you know what I mean?' Used as a participle, *spaced out*, or adjective, *spacey*, the word refers to the slowing down of perception and loss of control of motor functions as a result of taking drugs.

This glossary is by no means exhaustive, but I hope it supports the generalizations I advanced earlier, that psychobabble is a predominantly verbal and metaphorical type of slang, which presents experience primarily in terms of the movement and organization of matter in space. It thus has a kind of systematic coherence which lends itself to 'poetic' patterning in a literary text like *The Serial*, and also expresses a definable ideology or world view, which might be summed up in Martha's words of counsel to Kate Holroyd: ' "Kate," said Martha soothingly, "it's all process, okay?" '

Human existence is seen as a process of incessant change, readjustment and discovery – no one's condition is static or fixed. This is ultimately a very optimistic world view of a characteristically American kind, since it banishes ennui and promises that no evil will be permanent. The rhetoric of psychobabble also tacitly allays the fear of death by avoiding metaphors drawn from organic life, in which change means eventual decay; its model of experience is drawn from physics, not biology – the individual is pictured in terms of energy and mass, moving about in a curiously timeless psychological space.

It is significant that psychobabble is verbal rather than nominal, abstract rather than concrete, in its emphasis, and hardly impinges at all on the world of material objects. Indeed, the characters in *The Serial* are almost obsessively literal in their allusions to concrete objects –

everything is very precisely ticketed according to its brand name or technical specification or place of origin, and the reason for this is not far to seek: these material objects, consumed and possessed, confer status and define identity in the subculture, and their indexical function in this respect would be blurred by 'poetic' language. Cyra McFadden's cataloguing of such objects is as observant as her ear for speech is finely tuned:

Harvey made a lot more money now . . . but they spent it on things they hadn't known existed ten years ago: Rossignol Startos and season lift tickets at Squaw; twin Motobecane ten-speeds; Kate's Cuisinart, which did *everything* but put the pâté in the oven; Stine graphics; Gumpoldskirchner and St. Émilion (Harvey had 'put down' a case in the vacuum cleaner closet); Klip speakers and the top-of-the-line Pioneer receiver; Brown Jordan patio furniture; Dansk stainless and Rosenthal china; long-stemmed strawberries and walnut oil from the Mill Valley Market; Birkenstock sandals and Adidas (Kate didn't actually jog yet, but she was reading *The Ultimate Athlete*) . . .

The basic structural irony of *The Serial* is indeed the spectacle of people allegedly dedicated to 'process,' spontaneity, freedom and liberation, in fact being trammelled and subjugated by static, finite objects and possessions. Still, there are worse human fates, and, just as I cannot agree with the wholesale condemnation of psychobabble, so I would not trust any middle-class, educated reader of *The Serial* who claimed not to feel even a twinge of envy for the life-style of its characters. As one of them says:

'Yeah, but who would live anywhere else? . . . Like, I went to this garage sale last weekend: live music, hot *hors d'oeuvres*, Parducci Vineyards Gamay Beaujolais. *Wow*, I said to myself, *only* in Marin. This is where it's at, you know?'

Notes

(Note: books cited were published in London unless otherwise indicated.)

2 Analysis and Interpretation of the Realist Text: Ernest Hemingway's 'Cat in the Rain'

1 See A. J. Greimas, *Sémantique structurale* (Paris, 1966), *Du Sens* (Paris, 1970), and *Maupassant. La sémiologie du texte: exercices pratiques* (Paris, 1976). I am particularly indebted to Ann Jefferson's long review of this last work in *Poetics and Theory of Literature*, II (1977), pp. 579–88.
2 Roland Barthes, 'Introduction to the Structural Analysis of Narratives' in *Image–Music–Text*, ed. and trans. Stephen Heath (1977; first published 1966), and *S/Z*, trans. Richard Miller (1975; first published 1970).
3 Tzvetan Todorov, *The Poetics of Prose*, trans. Richard Howard (1977; first published 1971), p. 47.
4 Jonathan Culler, 'Defining Narrative Units' in *Style and Structure in Literature*, ed. Roger Fowler (Oxford, 1975), p. 139.
5 Gérard Genette, 'Discours du récit' in *Figures III* (Paris, 1972). An English translation of this treatise, entitled *Narrative Discourse*, has been published by Basil Blackwell (Oxford, 1979). For the sake of simplicity I have not introduced the terms (*récit, discours, histoire, narration*) in which Genette and other contemporary French critics have, with bewildering inconsistency, developed the Russian Formalists' *fabula/sjuzet* distinction. These terms, and Genette's theory of narrative in particular, are very elegantly elucidated in Shlomith Rimmon's 'A Comprehensive Theory of Narrative: Genette's *Figures III* and the Structuralist Study of Fiction' in *Poetics and Theory of Literature*, I (1976), pp. 32–62.
6 Mark Shorer, 'Technique as Discovery', *Hudson Review*, I (1948), pp. 67–87, and 'Fiction and the Analogical Matrix', *Kenyon Review*, XI (1949), pp. 539–60.
7 See Leo Spitzer, *Linguistics and Literary History: Essays in Stylistics* (Princeton, NJ, 1948) and Eric Auerbach, *Mimesis* (Princeton, NJ, 1953).
8 Roman Jakobson, 'Closing Statement: Linguistics and Poetics' in *Style and Language*, ed. Thomas A. Sebeok (Cambridge, Mass., 1960), p. 358.
9 Joseph Frank, 'Spatial Form in Modern Literature', *Sewanee Review*, LIII (1945), pp. 221–40, 433–56, 643–53.
10 Roman Jakobson, 'Two Aspects of Language and Two Types of Linguistic Disturbances', in *Fundamentals of Language* by Jakobson and Morris Halle (The Hague, 1956).
11 This point was blurred in my discussion of Jakobson's theory in the first edition of *The Modes of Modern Writing*. It is clarified in a Prefatory Note to

the second impression of the book (a paperback edition published by Arnold in 1979).

12   Christine Brooke-Rose, 'The Squirm of the True', *Poetics and Theory of Literature*, I (1976), pp. 265–94 and 513–46, and II (1977), pp. 517–61.

13   The distinction is made at the beginning of *S/Z*, whose English translator renders these terms as 'readerly' and 'writerly'. The classic realistic novel is 'readerly': it is based on logical and temporal order, it communicates along an uninterrupted chain of sense, we consume it, passively, confident that all the questions it raises will be resolved. The modern text is in contrast 'writerly': it makes us not consumers but producers, because we write ourselves into it, we construct meanings for it as we read, and ideally these meanings are infinitely plural.

14   Carlos Baker, *Hemingway: The Writer as Artist* (Princeton, NJ, 1963), pp. 135–6.

15   John V. Hagopian, 'Symmetry in "Cat in the Rain" ', in *The Short Stories of Ernest Hemingway: Critical Essays*, ed. Jackson J. Benson (Durham, NC, 1975), p. 231.

16   *Ibid.*, p. 232.

17   My own effort was as follows: 'Bored young American staying with her husband at Italian hotel fails to rescue a cat seen sheltering from the rain but is provided with a cat by the attentive manager'.

18   Seymour Chatman, *Story and Discourse: Narrative Structure in Fiction and Film* (Ithaca, NY, 1978), p. 48.

19   It has been pointed out to me that tortoise-shell cats are usually female and that since feminine pronouns are applied to the 'kitty' in lines 26–7, this suggests that it and the tortoise-shell cat are one and the same. I am doubtful whether so specialised a piece of knowledge should be allowed to disambiguate the conclusion, and in any case it is not conclusive evidence. It seems clear that if Hemingway had wanted to establish that the two cats were one and the same, he would have described the kitty as 'tortoise-shell'.

20   Hagopian, *op. cit.*, p. 230.

21   *Ibid.*, p. 231.

22   Carlos Baker, *Ernest Hemingway* (Harmondsworth, Middx, 1972), pp. 159 and 161.

23   *Ibid.*, p. 165.

24   The hotel in Rapallo at which the Hemingways stayed in 1923 still stands (now called the Hotel Riviera) and its outlook corresponds closely to the description in the first paragraph of 'Cat in the Rain' – with one interesting difference. The 'war monument' is, in fact, a statue of Christopher Columbus, erected in 1914 by grateful local businessmen who had made their fortunes in America and returned to enjoy their affluence in the homeland. As it is inconceivable that Hemingway should have mistaken the nature of the monument, one may legitimately conclude that he converted it into a war memorial for his own symbolic purposes. These, it should be said, are much more obvious to the reader when the story is read in its original context, the collection of stories and fragments *In Our Time* (1925), many of which are directly concerned with the war, and the experience of pain and death.

3   How successful is *Hard Times*?

1   F. R. Leavis, *The Great Tradition* (Harmondsworth, Middx, 1962), p. 251.

2   John Holloway, '*Hard Times*, a History and a Criticism' in *Dickens and the Twentieth Century*, ed. John Gross and Gabriel Pearson (1962), p. 167.

3   David Craig, Introduction to *Hard Times* (Harmondsworth, Middx, 1969),
    p. 22.
4   *Ibid.*, p. 36.
5   'The Rhetoric of Hard Times' in *Language of Fiction* (1966).
6   F. R. Leavis, *op. cit.*, p. 249.
7   Robert Garis, *The Dickens Theatre* (1965).
8   Arguably it would have made a fitter conclusion to the novel if Bitzer's
    intervention had been successful. There is no natural or poetic justice in
    allowing Tom to escape, as Dickens seems to acknowledge by killing him off
    by fever in the epilogue; and all the 'good' characters, even Sissy, seem some-
    what compromised morally by their eagerness to save him from prison.
    Dickens no doubt wanted to bring the circus folk back into the story in a
    positive role, but the suspicion lingers that he thought it would be too black
    a conclusion to send a gentleman's son to prison.
9   John Ruskin, *Unto This Last*. Quoted by Robert Garis, *op. cit.*, p. 146.
10 In 'The Rhetoric of *Hard Times*', *op. cit.*, pp. 159-62.

5   Historicism and Literary History: Mapping the Modern Period

1   Ihab Hassan, 'POSTmodernISM: A Paracritical Bibliography', *New Literary
    History* 3 (Autumn 1971), p. 7.
2   Claude Lévi-Strauss, *The Scope of Anthropology* (London, 1967), p. 49.
3   Roland Barthes, 'Criticism as Language,' in *Twentieth Century Literary
    Criticism*, ed. David Lodge (London, 1972), p. 648.
4   See Hans Robert Jauss, 'Literary History as a Challenge to Literary Theory',
    New Literary History, 2 (Autumn 1980), pp. 7-37.
5   Karl Popper, *The Poverty of Historicism* (London, 1961), p. 3.
6   *Ibid.*, p. 10.
7   *Ibid.*, p. 41.
8   *Ibid.*, p. 54.
9   'One of the features of the age we are talking about is that it is remarkably
    historicist.' Malcolm Bradbury and James McFarlane, 'The Name and Nature
    of Modernism', in *Modernism*, ed. Bradbury and McFarlane (Harmonds-
    worth, 1976), p. 20.
10 Paul de Man, 'Literary History and Literary Modernity', *Daedalus*,
    99 (1970), p. 387. I am much indebted to this essay for the way it draws
    attention to the paradoxes in modernist attitudes to history.
11 Barthes, *Writing Degree Zero* (London, 1967), p. 9.
12 Barthes, *S/Z* (London, 1975), p. 4.
13 Popper, *op. cit.*, p. 152.
14 Quoted by Bradbury and McFarlane, *op. cit.*, p. 55.

6   *The Woodlanders*: A Darwinian Pastoral Elegy

1   Florence Emily Hardy, *The Life of Thomas Hardy 1840-1928* (1962),
    p. 185. Subsequently referred to as *Life*.
2   Cited by Carl J. Weber, *Hardy of Wessex*, rev. ed. (1965), p. 159.
3   *Athenaeum*, 26 March 1887. Reprinted in *Hardy: the Critical Heritage*, ed.
    R. G. Cox (1970), p. 141.
4   E. M. Forster, 'Woodlanders in Devi', in *New Statesman*, 6 May 1939, p. 680.
5   E.g. William H. Matchett, '*The Woodlanders*, or Realism in Sheep's clothing',
    in *Nineteenth Century Fiction*, IX (1955), pp. 241-61; and J. I. M. Stewart,
    Thomas Hardy, a Critical Biography (1971), pp. 132-3.

6 *Life*, p. 220.
7 Douglas Brown, *Thomas Hardy*, rev. ed. (1961), p. 30.
8 *Ibid.*, p. 78.
9 Quoted by Harvey Curtis Webster, *On a Darkling Plain* (1947), p. 41.
10 Jean R. Brooks, *Thomas Hardy: the Poetic Structure* (1971), pp. 228–9.
11 Northrop Frye, 'Literature as Context: Milton's *Lycidas*', in *Fables of Identity* (New York, 1963), pp. 119–20.
12 See Chapters 29–33 of the abridged edition of *The Golden Bough: a Study in Magic and Religion* (1922).
13 Anonymous, 'The Lament for Bion (After the Greek of Moschus)', *Macmillan's Magazine*, LV (1886), p. 183.
14 *Life*, p. 185.
15 *Life*, p. 203.

7   **Thomas Hardy as a Cinematic Novelist**

1   Leon Edel, 'Novel and Camera', in *The Theory of the Novel*, ed. John Halperin (New York, 1974), p. 177.
2   Roman Jakobson, 'Two Aspects of Language and Two Types of Linguistic Disturbances', in R. Jakobson and M. Halle, *Fundamentals of Language* (The Hague, 1956), p. 78. For a full discussion of the theory see my *The Modes of Modern Writing: Metaphor, Metonymy and the Typology of Modern Literature* (1977).
3   Roland Barthes, 'To Write: An Intransitive Verb?', in *The Structuralist Controversy*, ed. R. Macksey and E. Donato (Baltimore, 1972), p. 140.
4   *The Return of the Native*, V, 3; *The Woodlanders*, Chapter 18.
5   *Tess of the d'Urbervilles*, Chapter 16; *The Return of the Native*, IV, 3.
6   John Schlesinger's *Far from the Madding Crowd* (1967) made a good attempt in the early part of the film – particularly with a striking shot in which the camera moves rapidly and vertically away from Gabriel's flock until the sheep and the contours of the countryside become two-dimensional shapes in an abstract design – but gradually the melodrama of the story came to predominate.
7   J. Hillis Miller, *Thomas Hardy: Distance and Desire* (1970), p. 43.
8   Thomas Hardy, *An Indiscretion in the Life of an Heiress*, ed. with an introduction by Terry Coleman (1976).
9   This passage adapts a similar moment of speechless courtship in Stinsford church between Hardy's own parents, which he made the subject of a poem, 'A Church Romance: (Mellstock *circa* 1835)'.
10 In Florence Emily Hardy, *The Life of Thomas Hardy 1840–1928* (1962), p. 225.

8   **Pessimism and Fictional Form:** *Jude the Obscure*

1   Michael Millgate, *Thomas Hardy: His Career as a Novelist* (London: The Bodley Head; New York: Random House, 1971), p. 324.
2   Quoted by J. Hillis Miller in *Thomas Hardy: Distance and Desire* (London: Oxford University Press; Cambridge, Mass.: Harvard University Press, 1970), p. 206.
3   As the scene continues, there are several explicit references to this object in the text of the first edition (1895) which Hardy removed in revising the novel for the edition of 1903, and did not restore subsequently. This belated bowdlerisation of a scene which had caused great offence on the

novel's first publication (one reviewer described it as 'more brutal in depravity than anything which the darkest slums could bring forth') is rather to be regretted. See 'Note on the Text' in the New Wessex Edition of *Jude the Obscure*, ed. Terry Eagleton (Macmillan, 1975), p. 424 (p. 439 in paperback edition).

4   Miller, *op. cit.*, p. 158.
5   The railway, which is extending its steel tentacles into Wessex in *The Woodlanders* and *Tess of the d'Urbervilles*, seems to enclose completely the terrain of *Jude the Obscure*, and provides the typical mode of travel for its characters. Indeed, so much attention is given to the use of the railway, especially by Jude, to the problems, ironies, and frustrations of such travel – waiting for connections, missing trains, planning cross-country journeys – that it does not seem fanciful to interpret the railway (a 'closed system' which allows its users a strictly limited mobility) as a symbol for life in this novel.

9   Evelyn Waugh: Habits of a Lifetime

1   The appropriateness of this term to Waugh was first suggested to me by Martin Green, who developed the idea at length in his study of Evelyn Waugh's generation, *Children of the Sun* (1977).
2   Frances Donaldson, *Evelyn Waugh: Portrait of a Country Neighbour* (1967), pp. xiii–iv.
3   *Tablet*, 16 April 1966, p. 441.
4   Unpublished transcript of interview with Michael Nelson.
5   Harold Acton, *Memoirs of an Aesthete* (1948), p. 126.
6   *Ibid.*, p. 205.

10   The Fugitive Art of Letters

1   *A Little Learning*, p. 73.
2   'Mr Waugh Replies', *Spectator*, 3 July 1953.
3   In *A Little Learning* Evelyn Waugh states that, though placed in the third class of the History Schools, he did not take the degree because he was not prepared to fulfil the necessary residence qualifications. He appears as a graduate of Oxford, however, in the University's own reference books.
4   'My Father', *Sunday Telegraph*, 2 December 1962.
5   *One Man's Road*, p. 219.
6   *Evening Standard*, 22 January 1929.
7   *Life and Letters*, March 1929.
8   *Paris Review*, VIII (1963).
9   *Spectator*, 26 July 1935.
10   *Spectator*, 7 December 1934.
11   *Spectator*, 10 March 1939. The allusion is to Evelyn Waugh's *Robbery Under Law: The Mexican Object Lesson* (1939).
12   Born within a year of each other, they were educated at public schools and at Oxford, where they both read history. After several false starts, they both made literature their profession, publishing their first novels within a year of each other. Both were received into the Roman Catholic Church, Greene in 1926, Waugh in 1930. Both travelled widely and wrote travel books about Africa and Central America. Both reviewed regularly for the *Spectator*. Both have recorded that they made half-serious attempts at suicide in youth, and both have complained of *ennui* and expressed a yearning for extinction.

Mr Greene has described himself as manic-depressive and Evelyn Waugh manifested many similar symptoms. The two men were good enough friends for Waugh to have a joke at Greene's expense. Christopher Sykes recalled a meeting when Greene, describing his plans for *The Quiet American* exclaimed, ' "It will be a relief not to write about *God* for a change!" "Oh?" responded Evelyn with dangerous smoothness, "I wouldn't drop God, if I were you. Not at this stage anyway. It would be like P. G. Wodehouse dropping Jeeves halfway through the Wooster series." ' (*Sunday Times*, 17 April 1966)

13 *Spectator*, 6 November 1942.
14 *Commonweal*, 16 July 1948.
15 *Commonweal*, 17 August 1951; reprinted in *Month*, September 1951.
16 See: 'An Act of Homage and Reparation to P. G. Wodehouse', *Sunday Times*, 16 July 1961; 'Here's Richness' (review of Belloc's verse), *Spectator*, 21 May 1954 and 'Belloc Anadyomene', *Spectator*, 26 August 1955; 'Max Beerbohm: A Lesson in Manners', *Atlantic*, September 1956; 'Mgr Ronald Knox', *Horizon*, May 1948.
17 'Literary Style in England and America', *Books on Trial*, October 1955.
18 *Spectator*, 7 December 1934.
19 Review of *In a Valley of This Restless Mind*, *Spectator*, 27 May 1938.
20 *Spectator*, 24 March 1939.
21 *Tablet*, 5 May 1951.
22 *Life*, 17 November 1941.
23 *Life*, 8 April 1946.
24 *New Directions in Prose and Poetry*, 1948.
25 *Life*, 19 September 1949.
26 *The Road to Damascus*, ed. John A. O'Brien.
27 See: 'The Same Again Please: A Layman's Hopes of the Vatican Council', *Spectator*, 23 November 1962, and correspondence between Waugh and Abbot Butler in the *Tablet* between 31 August and 19 October 1963.
28 'A Literary Opinion', *Month*, July 1949.
29 'Youth at the Helm and Pleasure at the Prow', *London Magazine*, August 1953.
30 *Sunday Times*, 16 July 1961.
31 'The Death of Painting', *Playboy*, August 1956. (Reprint of a review originally published in *Time and Tide*.)
32 *Tablet*, 27 July 1946.
33 'Mr Waugh Replies', *Spectator*, 3 July 1953.
34 *Spectator*, 8 July 1955.
35 'Mr Wodehouse and Mr Wain', *Spectator*, 24 February 1956.
36 *Encounter*, December 1955.
37 *Sunday Times*, 7 January 1962.
38 *Sunday Telegraph*, 2 December 1962.
39 *One Man's Road*, pp. 373–4.

11 Ambiguously Ever After: Problematical Endings in English Fiction

1 Kate Millett, *Sexual Politics* (New York, 1970), p. 147.
2 Frank Kermode, *The Sense of an Ending* (1966), p. 18.
3 'Henry James: an Appreciation', in *Notes on Life and Letters*. Quoted by Alan Friedman in *The Turn of the Novel* (1966), pp. 76–7.
4 Interview in *Penthouse* (undated). My attention was first drawn to this case by Peter Handley.

5 A new Penguin edition of the novel, with the original ending restored, was published in 1979. In a letter to the *Times Literary Supplement* (11 January 1980), Anthony Burgess explained that he had 'only recently' discovered that the first Penguin edition omitted the final chapter which he had 'weakly agreed' to excise from the American edition. He also records that Stanley Kubrick was unaware of the existence of the original ending when he made his film of *A Clockwork Orange*.

6 Jonathan Culler, 'Some American Contributions to the Study of Narrative', forthcoming in *Poetics Today*. The analysis of the plot of *Daniel Deronda* is drawn from an article by Cynthia Chase: 'The Decomposition of the Elephants: Double-Reading *Daniel Deronda*', *PMLA*, 93 (1978), pp. 215–27.

7 So, perhaps, does my own novel *Changing Places* (1975), the last chapter of which teases the reader by examining every possible resolution of the four-cornered sexual plot but refuses to commit itself to any of them. This is perhaps an appropriate place to acknowledge that my reading of *The French Lieutenant's Woman* and *The Sense of an Ending* certainly influenced the writing of this chapter. And it may be some indication of the stubborn conservatism of the reading public that the only criticism of this novel which has been expressed with any regularity in reviews and private comment is a complaint about the radical inconclusiveness of the ending.

12 Turning Unhappiness into Money: Fiction and the Market

1 An Act of Parliament established PLR in principle in 1979, but at the time of this book's going to press its implementation is still being delayed by disputes between the various parties involved.

2 In 1979 these figures were revised upwards to 2 million and 600,000 respectively.

3 I.e. a 'loan-based' scheme, by which a writer's remuneration would be related to the number of times his book is borrowed from libraries, calculated by sampling. It was the Writers' Action Group's insistence on this principle that largely contributed to the 'procrastination' on PLR lamented by Dr Sutherland.

14 Tom Wolfe and the New Journalism

1 Reprinted in *The Novelist at the Crossroads and Other Essays on Fiction and Criticism* (1971).

2 Robert Scholes and Robert Kellogg, *The Nature of Narrative* (1966).

3 Robert Scholes, *The Fabulators* (1967).

4 *New Review*, I (1975), no. 12, p. 24.

15 Where It's At: The Poetry of Psychobabble

1 *The Serial* is published in Great Britain by Picador (1978) and in the United States by Knopf (1977).

2 Cyra McFadden, 'Psychobabble', *Harpers Queen*, February 1978.

3 Christopher Reed, 'The Psychobabble Enigma', *Guardian*, 14 January 1978.

4 I have had personal experience of the contagiousness of this idiom in the perhaps surprising situation of a university English department's examiners'

meeting. When a rather disappointing result was being discussed, I remarked (no doubt as a result of reading *The Serial* in bed the night before) that the candidate, though with a good record in course work, had not been able 'to get it together' in the final examinations. Within half an hour, two of my colleagues had used the same expression in similar contexts, though I had never heard it pass their lips before.

5   See my novel *Changing Places* (Secker & Warburg, 1975; Penguin, 1978).
6   I. A. Richards distinguished the two elements of a metaphor as the 'tenor' and the 'vehicle'. Thus in 'the ship ploughed the waves', the movement of the ship is the tenor and *ploughed* is the vehicle.
7   John Blackwell and Jocelyn Harris.

Index

(Note: page numbers in italics indicate substantial discussion.)